WESTMAR COLLEGE LIBRARY

P9-BAW-958

In the course of his climb, he has been a celebrity one day, an underprivileged citizen the next. In the evening, a sex idol, warmed by the excited glances of thousands of women. In the morning, just another Negro unable to rent the apartment he wants. On the edge of world-wide fame, he suddenly found that his personal conduct was being questioned by his own people.

It is difficult to realize that Belafonte's career is only ten years old. Having begun originally with a yearning to act—he turned to singing in desperation—he today stands on the threshold of a new career as a movie actor. This story of Belafonte is flashed on a wide screen, whose cast includes virtually all of the top Negro entertainers of our time. Biographer Shaw has devised an inter-chapter device, which he has intriguingly named Stereos, and through which he tells the harrowing stories of discrimination of a generation of Negro artists. Among these, Belafonte stands forth as "the artist par excellence of the American era of integration."

ABOUT THE AUTHOR

A frequent reviewer of books on jazz and popular music for the New York *Times* Book Review, Arnold Shaw has published numerous articles on music in *Harper's, Good Housekeeping, Saturday Review,* and *Esquire.* He is the editor of several definitive works on music, to be found on the shelves of music libraries all over the country. Associated with some of the big hits of the past decades, in his capacity as executive of various music publishing companies, he has himself composed a score of songs, classical and popular as well as in the folk music style. He has also been annotator of numerous jazz albums and one of his dramatic music stories was produced on network TV. Arnold Shaw first met Belafonte at an RCA Victor recording session in 1953 when Belafonte was cutting the now famous "Matilda, Matilda." His interviews with friends and relatives and associates of the singer have enabled him to write this fast-moving biography of a talented artist and fill it with anecdotes, incidents, and details of his personal life hitherto unknown.

Belafonte

Belafonte

AN UNAUTHORIZED BIOGRAPHY

ARNOLD SHAW

CHILTON COMPANY—BOOK DIVISION
Publishers
Philadelphia   New York

ML
420
.B14
S5

B4255

COPYRIGHT © 1960 BY
ARNOLD SHAW

FIRST EDITION

All Rights Reserved

Published in Philadelphia by Chilton Company,
and simultaneously in Toronto, Canada, by Ambassador Books, Ltd.

LIBRARY OF CONGRESS CATALOG CARD NUMBER: 60–9123

MANUFACTURED IN THE UNITED STATES OF AMERICA
BY QUINN & BODEN COMPANY, INC., RAHWAY, N. J.

45780

To my mother and father,
who tried to teach me to be
gentle, kind, and color blind . . .

Acknowledgment

I wish to express my indebtedness to a number of people who gave freely of their time and memories to help me enliven the book with personal anecdotes. In particular, I wish to acknowledge the contribution of Margurite Belafonte, Harry's first wife; Bill Attaway, novelist and TV writer, whose friendship with Harry dates back to the days of The Sage restaurant; Tony and Fran Scott, friends and associates, the former Harry's musical conductor for a year and the latter, his travelling secretary for the same period; Pete Kameron, music entrepreneur and artist manager, who has been a friend since Harry's first engagement in Las Vegas; and Edward O. Welker, RCA Victor recording executive, who supervised Harry's recording sessions for many years. All of these were kind enough to read the manuscript and to offer informative suggestions before it finally went from the typewriter to the typesetter.

I am grateful also to the following whose reading of the manuscript or galleys yielded helpful suggestions: Paul Ackerman, music editor of *Billboard;* Gene Cook, former music editor of *Life* and now a free lance photographer in the entertainment field; Abel Green, editor of *Variety;* John Hammond, veteran talent scout and now a member of the Artists and Repertoire department of Columbia Records; Leon Kellman of the William Morris agency; and Herbert E. Marks, president of Edward B. Marks Music Corporation.

To name all the other persons whom I have consulted or interviewed in the preparation of this biography would be impossible. But I would consider myself remiss if I did not acknowledge the assistance of the following: Osceola Archer,

Bob Bollard, Lord Burgess, Joseph R. Carlton, Dave Dexter, Herman Diaz, Syvilla Fort, Max Gordon, Bart Howard, Dave Kapp, Monte Kay, Eartha Kitt, Jimmy Komack, Bob Kotlowitz, Gary Kramer, Cal Lampley, Warren Ling, Norman Luboff, Buddy Phillips, Dick Pierce, Jack Pleis, Sidney Poitier, Henri Rene, Howard S. Richmond, Jack Rollins, Phil Rose, Herm Schoenfeld, Bill Smith, Harry Tobias, Paul Werth and Virginia Wicks. As recording executives, performers, publicists, editors, etc., they have all had direct contact with Belafonte and proved valuable sources of first-hand experiences and observations.

ARNOLD SHAW

The report on The Supreme Court desegregation decision appears courtesy *Time,* copyright Time Inc., 1954.

Quotations from *His Eye Is on the Sparrow* by Ethel Waters with Charles Samuels (Copyright 1950, 1951 by Ethel Waters and Charles Samuels), are printed by permission of Doubleday and Company, Inc.

Black, Brown and White Blues is copyright by the late William Broonzy.

Statements by Roy Eldridge, T-Bone Walker, W. C. Handy and other jazz musicians, as well as the Nat Hentoff review of Nov. 1953, which appeared originally in *Down Beat,* are reprinted by special permission of *Down Beat* magazine, Charles Suber, publisher.

The excerpt from Thomas Morgan's article *What Makes Sammy Run* is reprinted with permission from *Esquire,* October 1959, copyright 1959 by Esquire, Inc.

Lines from *God Bless the Child* by Arthur Herzog, Jr. and Billie Holiday (Copyright 1941) and from *Recognition* by Harry Belafonte (Copyright 1949) are used by permission of Edward B. Marks Music Corporation, copyright owners.

The quotation from *Thursday's Child* by Eartha Kitt (Copyright 1956) is used with the special permission of Duell, Sloan and Pearce, Inc.

Discography

Since the beginning of his career as a folk singer, Harry Belafonte has recorded for RCA Victor. Except for a few sides cut earlier for Roost, and Capitol, all of his single releases, EP's and LP's are to be found in the RCA Victor catalog.

1. "MARK TWAIN" and other folk favorites (1954) LPM-1022
   Mark Twain; Man Piaba; John Henry; Tol' My Captain; Kalenda Rock; The Drummer and the Cook; The Fox; Soldier, Soldier; The Next Big River; Delia; Mo Mary; Lord Randall

2. BELAFONTE (1956) LPM-1150
   Waterboy; Troubles; Suzanne (Every Night When the Sun Goes Down); Matilda; Take My Mother Home; Noah; Scarlet Ribbons (For Her Hair); In that Great Gettin' Up Mornin'; Unchained Melody; Jump Down, Spin Around; Sylvie

3. CALYPSO (1956) LPM-1248
   Day O; I Do Adore Her; Jamaica Farewell; Will His Love Be Like His Rum?; Dolly Dawn; Star O; The Jack-Ass Song; Hosanna; Come Back, Liza; Brown Skin Girl; Man Smart (Woman Smarter)

4. AN EVENING WITH BELAFONTE (1957) LPM-1402
   Merci Bon Dieu; Once Was; Hava Nageela; Danny Boy; The Drummer and the Cook (Cockney Air); Come, O My Love; Shenandoah; Mary's Boy Child; Cu Cu Ru Cu Cu Paloma; Eden Was Like This; When the Saints Go Marching In

5. BELAFONTE SINGS OF THE CARIBBEAN   LPM-1505
(1957)

>Scratch, Scratch; Lucy's Door; Cordelia Brown; Don't Ever Love Me; Love, Love Alone; Cocoanut Woman; Haiti Cherie; Judy Drownded; Island in the Sun; Angelique-O; Lead Man Holler

6. TO WISH YOU A MERRY CHRISTMAS (1958)   LPM-1887
LSP-1887

>A Star in the East; The Gifts They Gave; The Son of Mary; The Twelve Days of Christmas; O Little Town of Bethlehem; Deck the Halls; The First Noël; Mary, Mary; Jehovah the Lord Will Provide; Silent Night; Christmas Is Coming; Medley: We Wish You a Merry Christmas, God Rest Ye Merry Gentlemen, O Come All Ye Faithful, Joy to the World, I Heard the Bells on Christmas Day

7. BELAFONTE SINGS THE BLUES (1958)   LOP-1006
LSO-1006

>A Fool for You; Losing Hand; One for My Baby; In the Evenin', Mama; Hallelujah I Love Her So; The Way That I Feel; Cotton Fields; God Bless the Child; Mary Ann; Sinner's Prayer; Fare Thee Well

8. LOVE IS A GENTLE THING (1959)   LPM-1927
LSP-1927

>Fifteen (Theme of "The World, the Flesh and the Devil"); I Never Will Marry; I'm Goin' Away; Small One; Bella Rosa; All My Trials; Green Grow the Lilacs; Times Are Gettin' Hard; Turn Around; Go 'Way from My Window; Delia's Gone; Walkin' on the Green Grass

9. PORGY AND BESS (1959): Harry Belafonte   LOP-1507
and Lena Horne   LSO-1507

>A Woman Is a Sometime Thing; Summertime; Oh, I Got Plenty of Nothin'; I Wants to Stay Here; Bess, You Is My Woman; It Ain't Necessarily So; Street Calls: Strawberry Woman, The Honey Man, Crab Man; My Man's Gone Now; Bess, Oh Where's My Bess?; There's a Boat That's Leavin' Soon for New York

10. BELAFONTE AT CARNEGIE HALL (1959)   LOC-6006
                                             LSO-6006

Darlin' Cora; Sylvie; Cotton Fields; John Henry;
Take My Mother Home; The Marching Saints;
Day O; Jamaica Farewell; Man Piaba; All My
Trials; Mama Look a Boo Boo; Come Back,
Liza; Man Smart (Woman Smarter); Hava
Nageela; Danny Boy; Merci Bon Dieu; Cu Cu
Ru Cu Cu Paloma; Shenandoah; Matilda

11. MY LORD WHAT A MORNIN' (1960)   LPM-2022
                                          LSP-2022

Wake Up, Jacob; My Lord What a Mornin';
Ezekiel; Buked and Scorned; Stars Shinin' (By
'n' By); Oh Freedom; Were You There When
They Crucified My Lord; Oh Let Me Fly; Swing
Low; March Down to Jordan; Steal Away

Stereos

Contents

Act III: JULIE

Curtain Raiser

Ceiling chandeliers are dimmed and blink out. Table lights are turned off. Conversation thins and dies.

In seconds, the glittering Empire Room, a scene of opulent revelry, becomes a cavernous shelter, dark, silent, and expectant.

In the darkness, all eyes sweep toward one spot with anticipation. Suddenly, a single beam cuts a long cone of pink light. At the end of it, a face appears.

It is a handsome face, clean-cut, boyish, the black hair, close-cropped, the dark eyes, large and intense, the lips, full and sensuously expressive.

A husky resonant voice rises out of the breathless quiet like a fountain of silk and velvet.

In the soft shadows, avid female eyes search out the white of his shirt, open at the neck in a seductive V that seems to plunge almost to his navel. Dreamily, they contemplate the attractive figure, sheathed in black, form-fitting slacks, cinchbelted with two oversized curtain rings. Magnetically, they are held by his tight, catlike movements, and the feeling he communicates of coiled tension and erotic power.

Harry Belafonte, the first Negro matinee idol, is on.

Harry Belafonte, the balladeer who crashed his way out of a Negro slum and clambered to the topmost heights of the entertainment world, is on.

Harry Belafonte, who made exciting theatre of the folk ballad and became the first folk singer in entertainment history to command giant audiences, is on.

Harry Belafonte, restless, moody, charming, high-strung, and unpredictable, is on.

[1]

Harry Belafonte, who grew up with a burning hostility toward whites and found his own people hostile when he divorced a Negro to marry a white, is on.

Harry Belafonte, driven by a violent urge to success, battered by the cutting indignities of discrimination, tormented by the hurt he has inflicted on people who have helped him, is on.

Harry Belafonte, bursting with inexhaustible energy, an obsessive passion for perfection, and a need to be loved, is on.

Harry Belafonte, the golden-voiced million record seller, who can mesmerize a crowd with his songs, and make them laugh and cry and sing, is on.

And a captivated audience sits enchanted—and applauds and stamps and whistles and shouts and begs for more and more . . .

Of Harry Belafonte, pretty, doll-like singer Diahann Carroll has said: "From the top of his head right down the white shirt, he's the most beautiful man I ever set eyes on."

In a Southern air terminal, Belafonte stooped for a drink of water. As he pressed the faucet, he felt a tap on his shoulder. Glancing up, he saw an attendant pointing to a fountain a few feet away. Belafonte looked at the wall over his spigot. It had the word "White." Over the fountain to which the attendant was directing him was the word "Colored."

A sixty-year-old matron wrote to Harry: "When you visit St. Louis, I shall come to hear you sing every night of the week. I asked permission from my husband—and he says it's all right. Is it all right if he comes too?"

One evening after a concert Harry sat all through the night in a Southern airport waiting for a plane. It had been impossible to find a place for him to sleep. In the morning he went to the ticket counter to inquire about the arrival time of his plane. The white agent glanced up at him and, with hatred narrowing his eyes, announced it would be along "when it was damned good and ready."

These are the violent contrasts that infuse Belafonte's career

[2]

and life with a complex and disturbing mélange of emotions. Today he is a celebrity. Tomorrow he is a second-class citizen. Here he is applauded, besieged, hailed. There he is suddenly hounded from a men's room. In the evening he is a love god, warmed by the adoring glances of thousands of women. In the morning he may be just another colored man, unable to rent an apartment he wants.

Today Harry is a man of wealth and world-wide fame. Yet he has a continuing fight, not only to remain on top as an entertainer, but to be accorded the amenities and cordialities taken for granted by almost any white man. As a writer recently wrote of Sammy Davis, Jr.: "In the spotlight, he and his audience are colorless. In the real world, he is a colored man who has made it and yet can never make it all the way."

This is the story of a sensitive man's struggle to attain maturity. An underprivileged childhood, a broken home, uneven competition with a favored brother, color discrimination in his own immediate family, prejudice and hostility in the world outside his home—all these conspired to create an insecure and mixed-up human being. The exterior of the man was marked by defiance, belligerence, and almost undirected hostility while the inner core was tender, gentle, and desperately in need of love and acceptance. Wedded to these motivations, perhaps, as a result of them, there was a relentless drive for success. Somehow, Harry overcame early limitations of personality and background.

But as time went on, he began to distort personal and business relationships in an unconscious attempt to gratify blocked emotional needs. As he became conscious of the fictions he was creating, he was driven to acts that overwhelmed him with feelings of guilt. The whole process of growing up was made even more complicated because, as a friend of Harry's, Bill Attaway, has said: "He had the difficult job of maturing under the tremendous weight and pressure of success. Most of us do this in some dark and quiet corner, and it's not an easy process then. To do it in the limelight as a celebrity is really rough. Harry had no chance to make a private error."

Tremendous success did not bring relief from great inner turmoil nor did it bring maturity. In his first marriage, dissolved after eight years, he was the artist, the bohemian intellectual struggling against engulfing middle-class mores, with his wife—a woman of charm and intelligence—frowning on his friends, his wild and seemingly unattainable yearnings and his show business type of life. But the conflict ran deeper in that Margurite possessed the relaxed, worldly outlook of a Negro that had grown up in a segregated community while Harry was torn by the hostilities and the tensions of a Negro who had grown up in a discriminatory, integrated society. In this boil of turbulent emotions, Harry searched for his own identity and sought to achieve this without stifling his creative urges or sacrificing his identity with his own people. Maturity came more slowly to him as a person than as an artist.

This is the story of a man who has been a storm center of controversy almost from the start of his career. Today there is still no unanimity about Harry Belafonte, except for his power and talents as a performer. Folk purists continue to cry fake, even though Harry asserts that his approach to folk material always was highly personalized. Friends accuse him of lacking gratitude and of shunning his early associates and helpmates. But Harry still has his first guitar accompanist with him. Some critics assail him for being pretentious, pompous, and theatrical. Others assert that his high seriousness is precisely what sets him apart—and entitles him to the calling of artist rather than entertainer. Among those who work for him, there are some who fear him and find him demanding, overbearing, and completely self-centered. Others admire his unquenchable energy and envy his relentless drive for perfection. Some reject his constant pronouncements on Negro problems as lip service while others single him out as one of the few performers with a dedicated social conscience and a broad cultural outlook. Whites regard him as arrogant, smug,

[4]

and belligerent, while Negroes condemn him for having passed into the white world.

Of Little Rock, Harry has said: "If there were no Little Rock today, it would mean that the status quo still prevailed." If there were no controversy about Harry Belafonte, it would mean that he was just another successful entertainer. No one believes that.

Harry's struggle to make it and the large dimension he has attained is a matter of historical significance, for his personality, his psychology, and his material are a vivid expression of the yearnings of the Negro people in our society. Harry may not wish to be a spokesman of his people, but he cannot help being the foremost symbol in the entertainment world of their frustrations and hopes.

This is the story of a man whose amazing career is not only a great personal triumph but central to one of the major issues of our time.

A world of difference separates Belafonte from another Negro singer of folk ballads and blues—a poor, itinerant, turn-of-the-century laborer who was twice convicted of murder and who twice literally sang his way out of state penitentiaries. The self-styled "King of the Twelve String Guitar Players of the World," as Huddie Ledbetter called himself, and the inspired writer of *Good Night, Irene* and other folk ballads, never achieved the adulation, the acclaim, or the wealth of Belafonte.

Before Harry, there were other successful Negro artists— folk singers like Leadbelly, Blind Lemon Jefferson, Blind Sonny Terry, and Josh White; blues singers like Ma Rainey, Bessie Smith, Ethel Waters, Big Bill Broonzy, and Billie Holiday; comedians and dancers like Bert Williams and Bill Robinson; pop singers like Billy Eckstine, Ella Fitzgerald, Sarah Vaughan, Billy Daniels, and Nat (King) Cole; jazzmen like King Oliver, Satchmo, Fletcher Henderson, Duke Ellington, Dizzy Gillespie, Charlie (Bird) Parker, and others too numerous to mention.

[5]

Like that of the predecessors who have influenced him, Harry Belafonte's unique art is the product of his own creative personality. But the acceptance of that art is determined by forces outside himself. That Harry's eminence and wealth outstrip what most of his forerunners were able to achieve is in part a testimonial to him. But the gap that separates him from each owes its existence to the struggles and suffering of all—and the people of which they are but an expressive segment—for independence and equality.

For all its astronomical achievements, Harry's career is only ten years old. Yet in that brief span he has been able to achieve a stature far beyond the dreams and practical attainments of his precursors. To do this an artist needs the remarkable combination of talents that are Harry's—superb showmanship, striking visual appeal, dramatic power as a singer, sensitivity as an actor, tremendous personal magnetism, and courage in facing public issues. But great stature tends to come with great social currents—and Harry's standing rose to unanticipated heights with the great upsurge of feeling that accompanied the historic decision of the U.S. Supreme Court outlawing segregation of schools.

Harry may be the King of Calypso and the first Negro matinee idol, but he is also the expressive embodiment of the movement for racial equality and the artist par excellence of the American era of integration.

No man is an island and no man's career develops in a vacuum. To give the reader a sense of the relationship of Harry's struggles as a Negro artist to those of other Negro artists, I have created an interchapter device, which I call "Stereos." Their purpose is to project the story of Belafonte's life and career on the wider screen, and with the extra dimension, afforded by the related experiences of his show business predecessors and contemporaries. No attempt has been made to arrange the "Stereos" in chronological order, since they correlate with Harry's experiences, not in terms of time but of the anguish they caused the participants. The reader will sense that progress has been made in the elimination of prejudice—also that much yet remains to be done.

Today, at the beginning of his second decade as an entertainer, Harry figures on the American show business scene in four capacities: as a million-dollar performer; as a militant and successful image of his race; as a matinee idol with an appeal to women of many races; and as an entertainment entrepreneur whose enterprises have grown steadily from publishing music to making pictures to producing plays, with the end nowhere in sight. Firmly established as the leading folk singer of our time, he is now embarked on a full-fledged career as a movie actor. Unlike the challenge of his first decade, when he was struggling for acceptance and success, the problem of his second decade is how to use that success—for he is now what Emily Coleman of *Newsweek* aptly termed "a corporate enterprise."

"Art is a mirror of life," Harry told a radio audience recently. "But the important thing is to reflect that life so as to make it better."

And a close friend said recently: "Despite his tremendous success, he hasn't stopped caring. He still wants to be a good human being as well as a successful one. If he feels his maturity, and his life has become more serene and better integrated, there is no indication that he has lost his concern about people, or the things he needed and wanted when he was struggling to find himself."

Growth has always been a magical concept to Harry. Years ago, at the height of the calypso craze, he told an interviewer that he refused to stay put, that he refused to be typed or to stand still. "I've got to grow," he said. "Anyone who tries to stop me with nonsense about what is or isn't commercial is in for a fight."

The fight goes on, if one is to judge by a very recent statement of Harry's. "The great grosses, the great attendance records," he observed, "they are no end in themselves. What I now want to do is put my best foot forward as an artist. I've not really begun to go where I really want to go. . . . Now I want to ally myself with those individuals and those situations which make for exciting artistic statements."

This is the story of how Harry Belafonte grew—and may yet grow. It is not an authorized story. But it is as accurate and as authentic as dedicated work can make it. I have had the cooperation of scores of people—people close to Harry as well as observers of the show business scene—but not of Harry Belafonte himself.

Act I

MELVINE

Oh, what will you leave your mother, my son?
What will you leave her, my handsome young one?
My love to keep you, mother,
My love to keep you, mother.

Oh, make my bed soon
For I'm sick to the heart
And fain would lie down.

—*Lord Randall*

1. The Lily White Beaches of Miami

The manager of the Miami club listened to the applause with pleasure. Business was good. It had been good all week. He watched the lanky, thin, good-looking young singer try to beg off. But the girls in the audience wanted more. They liked the boy. There was something awkward about him. And there were times when you could feel the tension under his relaxed pose. But they liked him. It was a physical thing. They responded to the mere sound of his voice, the features of his face, the way he moved. His voice caressed them, played with them, provoked them. They reached out to touch him when he passed.

The applause mounted. The manager tried to catch the singer's attention. Originally, he had warned the boy not to go for more than one. "Leave 'em begging." Night after night, the girls asked for more. Night after night, the manager had extended the boy's program. It made the other acts angry. They complained that after young Belafonte it was hard to reach the crowd. It was like trying to talk to people whose love had just soared to a peak. The listeners were spent, relaxed, uninterested.

The manager waved to the singer. "Give them another!" But the boy was not looking toward him. The manager trotted toward the door leading off the small oval stage of his club. It was The Five O'Clock on Miami's Collins Avenue at 20th. Owner: tunnel-mouthed comedienne Martha Raye. The manager had to intercept Belafonte before the singer left the stage for good. The applause became louder.

The manager was out of breath when he reached backstage. Suddenly, he was amazed at what he saw. On-stage Belafonte

smiled brightly, graciously, attractively, looking tall and ath-
letic. Off-stage the smile vanished, the figure sagged. In an
instant the young singer looked troubled, tense, exhausted.
The manager was mystified. Harry was not a drinker, nor did
he keep late hours.

"Go on, Harry!" the manager shouted. "Give 'em more!"

Harry studied the manager's face for a moment, his own
a strange mixture of doubt and, almost, distaste.

"You were the greatest tonight, Harry!" The manager was
unable to fathom the expression on Belafonte's face. Harry
nodded without pleasure. "You can't leave them now, Harry!
Go, man! And see me after the show. Good news!"

Harry nodded again and stepped back on-stage. The applause swelled, like the chords of a giant organ, then subsided
as Belafonte turned to the small combo backing him.

"Farewell to Arms," Harry whispered to the bandleader.
The year was 1950—and America had not yet said farewell
to Korean arms. Before the year was out The King, as Al
Jolson was known inside show biz, was to die suddenly in a
hotel room after exhausting himself entertaining troops on
the Korean front. At midcentury, show biz generally was suffering the TV jitters. Movieland's moguls were daily checking
inroads of The Monster and nightly watching their TV screens
with amused horror. Live radio, retreating in the face of TV's
onward march, was banking on "dahling" Tallulah Bankhead
and her 1½ hour Big Show, designed by NBC to "knock off
Benny on CBS." The battle of the speeds (78 rpm vs. 45 rpm
vs. 33⅓ rpm and the big hole vs. the little hole) was causing
havoc in the record industry. Tin Pan Alley was also being
disturbed by a wave of hillbilly hits, written and recorded
out of Nashville, Tennessee. Irving Berlin, dean of Broadway
tunesmiths, felt obliged to warn: "Any song the public ac-
cepts is a good song."

The public accepted *Tennessee Waltz,* a million copy seller
for Patti Page, and *Chattanooga Shoe Shine Boy,* a smash for
Red Foley. Also a new, lusty, folk-singing group The Weavers
whose sound is today echoed in The Kingston Trio, and who

had the country warbling Leadbelly's *Good Night, Irene* and hand-clapping to an Israeli song *Tzena, Tzena*. A tall, Irish blonde, Rosemary Clooney, achieved vocal stardom with an Armenian novelty *Come on-a My House,* written by William Saroyan and his cousin, Ross Bagdasarian, later to endear himself to the country's teen-agers with *Witch Doctor* and *The Chipmunk Song.* Big names in the nitery circuit, drawing top money from some of those considering young Belafonte for bookings, were Billy Eckstine, Billy Daniels, Nat (King) Cole, Tony Martin. Also Frankie Laine, who had just driven a *Mule Train,* abetted on the hit recording by the whipcracking of bearded oboist Mitch Miller.

The year was 1950. Young Harry Belafonte, sporting a pencil-line mustache, sat perched soulfully on a high stool. *Show Biz, from Vaude to Video,* written by *Variety* editor Abel Green and comedian Joe Laurie, Jr., appeared the following year. It did not contain a single mention of Harry—an indication of how fantastic was to be his rise to stardom.

When the audience at Martha Raye's Five O'Clock Club heard the opening chords of *Farewell to Arms,* a song Harry had recorded the previous year, a murmur of excited anticipation swept through it. The manager of the club waited in the wings as Harry warbled the lovely melody. It was Christmas week, and the crowd was high and pleasure-bound. But they hung on Harry's every note as if he had put a spell over them.

Applause shattered the silence with the suddenness of a summer storm. The manager himself came to as if he had been in a trance.

"Harry! You're a magician!" he exclaimed, as Belafonte came off-stage. He embraced the young singer and patted his back fervently. "There's no stopping you!"

Harry's off-stage look had neither magic nor satisfaction in it.

"Say, what's wrong! You don't look right, Harry. And you oughta be happy."

"Why?" Harry demanded.

"Because we want you for another week."

There was no pleasure in Belafonte's handsome face. "No can do," he said.

"What!" the manager exclaimed. "What's that mean?"

Harry drew himself up to his 6 feet 2 inches. "It means I'm not available."

"What are you handing me?" the manager demanded. "Your agent tried to sell you for an extra week. Singers are a dime a dozen."

"Thanks," Belafonte said.

"You want a little more money? You got it!" the manager shouted.

"It's nothing like that," Harry said.

The manager hesitated. "Say, what's eatin' you anyway, Harry?"

Harry bit his lip. "I just can't take it any more."

"You what?" the manager snorted. "How long have you been singing anyway? There are guys who been knockin' their brains out for years. You! Why, you're not singing for two years! And three and a half bills a week ain't hay, either!"

"It's not the money," Harry said. "Financially, I'm doing great. Why, only a year ago I was looking for a job around New York's garment district. My wife was expecting a baby. I didn't know where the next dollar was coming from."

"Then what's griping you? You're gonna be a big star, Harry. What's the big Mr. B. got that you haven't?"

"He's on top," Harry said glumly.

"What! Am I to blame for that?" the manager demanded. "Because Billy Eckstine's on top!"

Friends of the period say that Harry had a knack for making others, particularly white people, feel responsible for all his problems.

"Maybe, Mr. Belafonte, you're in too much of a hurry," the manager added.

"I'm just sick of the grind," Harry said. "It's so meaningless, crooning about moon and June. And I'm fed up on that 'good-looking-boy-that-girls-go-for' routine."

"You're outa your mind. Or you're kiddin'! What *do* you want?"

[14]

Harry narrowed his eyes. He knew. But he replied: "I know what I don't want."

"You mean that you're not staying?"

Harry drew his shoulders back. "That's right. I just wasn't made to be a pop singer."

"What's wrong with being a pop singer? And havin' the chicks eat outa your hand. And pulling down the loot you're making!" The manager shook his head in disbelief.

"It's just not for me," Harry said. "It's phony and insincere—like most song lyrics."

The manager was exasperated. "I hope you know what you're doing."

Harry walked a few steps and turned. "What I do know is that I can't go on doing what I'm doing now . . ." He shrugged his shoulders and gritted his teeth. "Maybe I'll never be an actor. But I sure-as-taxes am not going to be just another singer."

"An actor!" The manager furrowed his brows and looked at Harry through a squint. "Isn't it tough enough considering—" He did not have to complete his thought about Negro discrimination. "But an actor!" He smiled sympathetically. "I wish you luck, Harry, but you sure-as-taxes are buying yourself a truckload of grief."

Harry's glance froze. There was pride and anger in it. Both "Don't you think I know that? I went into singing because Broadway only had Uncle Tom parts for me." Harry sniffed disdainfully. "But I'd rather act than be the greatest singer in the world."

Some years later Harry said: "In those days Miami had curfews for Negroes. I had to have special transportation after hours, special accommodations, special bathrooms, special everything. To cross from the colored section of town to the white, I had to show a pass. I began to think. Why should I be giving up my rights and dignity for this kind of thing, for something I didn't like anyway."

Harry turned from the manager of the Five O'Clock and walked slowly toward his dressing room. The manager followed Harry with his eyes, admiring his decision, wondering

[15]

at his courage, and feeling deep down that he was a flip. To throw up a job paying three and a half bills a week and a chance at the bigtime!

When Harry returned to New York from his Miami walkout, he did a strange thing. Friends were amazed and amused. Agents, bookers, people in the entertainment world thought he had gone loco. With two acquaintances, Harry went into the restaurant business in New York's Greenwich Village. The one-arm hamburger joint was called The Sage. Here Harry was to find himself, and Belafonte the ballad singer was born . . .

So, in 1950, the high-strung man who yearned to be an actor and who soon afterward became the most celebrated folk singer in the world, gave up his career as a pop singer.

In the fall of '51 *Variety* wrote of Harry's departure from the ranks of pop singers: "Some years ago Harry Belafonte bowed as a pop singer, but attempted to make headway in an era in which he had to compete with singers such as Billy Eckstine. He reached the standard act status but apparently front-line coin and prestige eluded him—consequently a changeover in style to that of a folk balladeer."

In 1953 *Down Beat's* interpretation: "Briefly he reached as high as $650 a week at a club in Florida. But his records didn't sell and the demand waned as fast as it had waxed. By the end of 1950 Harry was fed up with being a popular singer who wasn't popular."

In 1957 a writer for *Coronet* reported: "In Miami when he finished a night club engagement, the manager asked him to stay another week. 'I suddenly flipped,' Belafonte recalls. Not only did he refuse to extend the engagement, but he stridently announced he was through with this type of singing. His friends thought he was mad."

As recently as March 2, 1959, *Time* Magazine wrote: "One night when he was playing the Five O'Clock club in Miami at $300 a week, he chucked pop singing 'like a thief in the night.' Says he: 'What I was singing was junk.'"

In May 1959 the Miami incident was described as follows

in *American Weekly:* "Harry's indifference to his singing engagements and his chip-on-the-shoulder attitude brought about his downfall even more quickly than he had risen. After he displayed his incompetence and impertinence for all to see at Martha Raye's Five O'Clock Club in Miami, Miss Raye fired him."

Which magazine do you read?

STEREO

THE SUPREME COURT, MAY 17, 1954

"It was 12:52 P.M., May 17, 1954. At the long mahogany table sat the nine Justices of the U.S. Supreme Court.* From the red velour hangings behind the bench to the great doors at the back of the room, every seat was filled. Earl Warren, Chief Justice of the United States, picked up a printed document from his desk and began to read in a firm clear voice.

"There was an awesome quiet in the high-ceilinged, marble-columned courtroom. The eight Associate Justices gave Warren rapt attention. In the press section, reporters strained forward to catch every word. Departing from custom, the court had not given newsmen advance copies of the opinion. Shortly after the Chief Justice began reading, the first bulletin clacked out over the Associated Press wires: 'Chief Justice Warren today began reading the Supreme Court's decision on the public school segregation cases. The court's ruling could not be determined immediately.' At 1:12 the AP sent a second message to editors all over the world, who had been awaiting the momentous decision. Warren was attacking segregation in schools, but 'the Chief Justice had not read far enough in the court's opinion for newsmen to say that segregation was being struck down as unconstitutional.'

"When Warren finished reading at 1:20 the ruling was crystal clear: the U.S. Supreme Court held that racial segregation in the public schools violates the Constitution. The decision was unanimous.

"In its 164 years the court had erected many a landmark of U.S. history. None of them except the Dred Scott case (reversed by the Civil War) was more important than the school segregation issue. None of them directly and intimately affected so many American families. The lives and values of some 12 million schoolchildren in 21 states will be altered, and with them eventually the whole social pattern of the South. The international effect may be scarcely less important. In many countries, where U.S. prestige and leadership have been damaged by the fact of U.S. segregation, it will come as a timely reassertion of the basic American principle that 'all men are created equal.' "

—*Time*, May 24, 1954

* Associate Justice Robert Jackson, recovering from a heart attack, had left the hospital that morning so all nine Justices could be present when the great decision was read.

[18]

2. "Frenchy"

Harry Belafonte "sang" his first note in a hospital delivery room in the days when the jazz age lay dying and Coolidge "prosperity" was zooming to its dizziest heights. But he grew up in the years when lengthening bread lines and street-corner apple sellers spread across the land.

In 1927 Babe Ruth slammed sixty home runs. Tunney licked Dempsey. A young comedian, who had not yet acquired a middle initial to distinguish himself from heavyweight boxer Joe Louis, was left for dead in a Chicago hotel room by the hired killers of a club he no longer wanted to work.

In 1927 a young flyer returned from the first solo flight across the Atlantic to the most spectacular welcome ever given an American citizen. Tin Pan Alley celebrated with *Lucky Lindy*, a song whose sales never approached Gene Austin's Victor recording of *My Blue Heaven*. Saccharine ballads like *Girl of My Dreams* and *Among My Souvenirs* swamped the air waves. *Ol' Man River* came out of the hit score of *Show Boat* to be added to the limited repertoire of the baritone voice. A tune called *Shake That Thing* brought record fame to singer Ethel Waters.

Like his friend-to-be, actor Sidney Poitier, Belafonte was born in 1927, according to his own statements.* In fact the two birthdays are scarcely a week apart—Sidney's on February 20 and Harry's on March 1. Because he became known as the King of Calypso, many have assumed that Harry hails from the Caribbean. This is only partly true. Harry did spend much

---

* Our time places such stress on being lean and young that the exact age of most celebrities and business executives is subject to correction from time to time.

of his youth in Jamaica. Here again, there is a parallel with Sidney Poitier, who grew up on Cat Island in the Bahamas although he was born in Miami.

Harry, too, was born in the United States—in The Lying-In Hospital on East 70th Street, New York City. Baptized Harold George Belafonte, Jr., in the Roman-Catholic faith, he grew up in an area famous for jazz and notorious for overcrowding and poverty—Harlem. Both his parents came from the West Indies. His mother, Melvine Love, was from Jamaica (B.W.I.) and his father, from Martinique (F.W.I.). During World War I, while serving as a cook in the Royal Navy, his father gave up his French citizenship to become a British subject. Each of his parents was the product of a mixed marriage, his paternal grandfather and his maternal grandmother both being white.

"On both sides of my family," Harry has said, "my aunts and uncles intermarried. If you could see my whole family congregated together, you would see every tonality of color, from the darkest black, like my Uncle Hyne, to the ruddiest white, like my Uncle Eric, a Scotsman."

Harry was raised mainly by his mother, of whom he has said with appreciation: "The determination to keep my head in the face of hardships and misfortune was the gift my mother gave to me . . . She taught me by her own example the meaning of struggle and how to live with hardships and keep alive the flame of hope for something better."

Melvine Belafonte was at times a domestic servant and, when opportunities appeared, a dressmaker. People who know her describe her as a sharp, rather touchy woman with a pronounced West Indian accent, who always looked—and does so even today—more like Harry's sister than his mother. Without being hostile, she was wary of white people. If Harry walked with pride and dignity from his earliest days, the credit is hers. She was, and is today, an extremely proud woman. In fact, when a New York newspaper ran a rags-to-riches profile of Harry and stressed how poor he was in his youth, she was quite upset and displeased. Despite the privations and difficulties of her own life, she never gave up the fight to make a better one for her children.

Whatever personality problems Harry may have even today stem from his relationship, or rather nonrelationship, with his father. A vagabond with a love for the sea, Harry George Belafonte, Sr., frequently shipped out as a chef on British merchant boats. When he was in port his treatment of Harry's mother did little to lessen his son's inner tensions. These took a somewhat traumatic turn when Senior sailed off for good with another woman. Just as the woman who superseded Harry's first wife in his affections was to be white, so the female who broke up his childhood home before he was six was white.

Even before this, Harry's feelings about "white" had begun to assume a hostile hue as the result of another situation. Belafonte senior, being West Indian, had strong caste ideas. So-called "white" characteristics were regarded as superior to Negro. Blue eyes were preferred over brown or black. Soft hair was preferable to wiry, kinky hair. And, of course, the whiter the skin, the better. In all these respects, Harry's younger brother was "more white" than Harry, with the result that Belafonte senior showed an unmistakable preference for Dennis. That this worked havoc with Harry is hardly surprising. Harry has never been able to forget. Reminiscences of his boyhood seldom omit references to the painful and uneven competition he faced within his own family because of color.

Parenthetically, it may be added that while Harry may have had a problem in identifying with his people, as some writers have claimed, the more serious "color" problem was created for him by obstacles hindering identification within his own immediate family.

Actress-blues singer Ethel Waters faced a similar color problem in her own family. As she tells it in her autobiography *His Eye Is on the Sparrow,* she was born out of wedlock when her mother was raped at the age of twelve. Her paternal grandmother, who was virtually white, blocked the marriage of her son (John Waters) to the girl he had raped.

"I didn't like white people," Ethel writes, "or even Negroes

[21]

with light skin. Mom [her maternal grandmother and the woman who actually brought her up] had never stopped drumming into me how badly my other grandmother had treated us.

"Whenever I lived with Louise [her mother], I made life a nightmare for my stepsister Genevieve, who was lighter in color than I and was treated much better by my mother.

"*Yaller dog* and *yaller puppy* were my favorite names for Genevieve. But I'd warn her, 'I'll kill you if you ever say I'm dark. Don't you ever dare say I'm blacker than you!'"

In short, Harry—not unlike Ethel Waters—was sensitized to the color problem as a youngster, not only by what white people did to Negroes but by the way white color prejudices were echoed among his own people

Considering his father's preference, it may seem surprising that Harry still remembers those brief periods when Senior was at home as the happiest. This, despite the quarreling that went on at such times between his parents. But this memory is itself an indication of how much young Harry needed a father. The lack was never to be filled, although Harry was to try again and again, down the years, to find a substitute father in older men with whom he became associated. In Harry's admiration of the sheer strength of certain folk singers and in his gravitation toward strong, mature women, there are also intimations of an insecurity that the absence of an affectionate and protective father early helped develop.

Unlike his contacts with his father, Harry's contact with poverty was apparently not fleeting. When his father was not shipping out as a chef, he depended for work on the WPA. At times the family was on home relief, living in one room of a dark, six-room, cold-water flat, shared with four other families.

"We were too poor to own a radio," Harry told a New York reporter, working on a profile. "We went hungry frequently. We didn't even have our own hand-me-downs for clothes. My father's things were mostly the work clothes of a sailor. I was too thin for such castoffs as there were, and my brother Dennis [four years younger] was too small. My mother's meager earnings went for food and coal. Winters were horrible."

To the pinch of growing up with an itinerant father and the privations of poverty were soon added the tensions of Negro-white relationships. Trouble mushroomed as soon as Harry was registered in school—P.S. 186 at the top of a hill on 145th Street and Amsterdam Avenue. He had to walk through blocks that were preponderantly white. There were always the taunters and the bullies. Classes were mixed.

"I grew up fighting," Harry has said. "I fought about children's nursery rhymes, about 'Eeny, meeny, miny, mo, Catch a N . . . by the toe.' I fought about being bumped in the hall."

At times he joined hands with street gangs and fought with more formidable objects like rocks, bottles and trash cans.

As a pupil, Harry was something of a disciplinary problem. He had a good mind, perhaps, too good in comparison with his classmates. Being bored, he was obstreperous. In later years Harry's mother—by then Mrs. Wright—would quip that she was summoned to school so often that when Harry's teachers called the roll of pupils in the morning, they would call her name right after Harry's.

When Harry was nine, his mother packed him, his brother Dennis, and herself off to Jamaica. It was Harry's second journey to the Caribbean. For the two youngsters, this was not just a visit. Harry was to remain until he was about thirteen, his brother Dennis, for a shorter period. At one point Mrs. Wright returned for a visit and took Dennis back with her, leaving Harry by himself.

Figuring in the decision to have Harry complete his schooling in Kingston instead of New York were a number of factors. Item 1: Harry as a disciplinary problem. Item 2: The hazards of bringing youngsters up in the tough, increasingly delinquent environs of Harlem. Item 3: The possible desire of Harry's mother to create a new life for herself in view of the permanent defection of Belafonte, Sr.

What probably provoked the action by Harry's mother were two accidents in which he was involved. In one, Harry injured an eye when he fell on a pair of scissors. The eyeball was pierced and he was left with a defect that in later years was to threaten his vision. Not long after the eye injury, Harry chased a ball into the street and was struck by a car. The concussion cleared up quickly, but a broken left leg kept him in a cast up to his hip for many months. Thereafter, Melvine Love decided that the streets of Harlem posed too many hazards for her sons, particularly restless and high-strung Harry.

Kingston was not without its problems for Harry. During the winters he was boarded at various private schools. As an American attending schools with a British tradition, he found himself something of a misfit. He wore knickers and black stockings, whereas most of the native youngsters dressed in shorts. He was a baseball fan. His classmates favored cricket, which impressed him as a sissy game. When he told them so, there were heated arguments and fist fights. Eventually, the headmaster learned of these and decreed a public caning for Harry.

This was the British equivalent of the ruler on the palms of the hand. A boy had a choice of taking the punishment standing up or via "the stretch." If he chose the latter, four boys held him face down above the ground, legs and arms spread akimbo, while the caning was administered on the buttocks. A boy could thus hide his tears and shame from his classmates.

Harry elected to take his caning standing up. As the repeated blows of the cane brought pain and swelling, his assembled classmates watched for him to flinch or cry. When Harry did neither, the door was opened to his being accepted by them. Acceptance came slowly. But the sense of being an outsider never completely disappeared.

When he was not at boarding school, Harry lived with various relatives. This did not lessen his feeling of being a misfit. In the 1930's the Negro community of Jamaica, not unlike Haiti today and other islands in the West Indies, was sharply stratified, with caste distinctions arising from color. Harry's position in the color spectrum was such as to prompt a resurgence of the inferiority feelings his father had stirred in him. He had the misfortune to be on the darker side of the family.

"The darker family members," a friend of Harry's explained, "would not have to eat with the servants. But they were not generally permitted to sit at the same table with the light-skinned. The dark-skinned would not have to walk if they went somewhere. But they could not ride in the same carriage as their light-skinned relatives."

Harry was a lonely boy and troubled. And the more troubled he became, the more belligerent. Frequently he sat in class without hearing a word his teachers said. His mind was filled with unresolved and painful questions, and he tried to think of something remarkable he could do or become to break down all barriers. For a time he spent every free moment around the stables at the race track, dreaming of a day when he would become Kingston's leading jockey—and be accepted by everybody. But after a while it became apparent that he was growing too tall to be a jockey. He tried smoking rope and fasting to stunt his growth. It was useless. Then he began casting about for other careers that would make him famous and powerful and beloved.

Years later, Harry was to call Billie Holiday's song *God Bless the Child*—with its celebration of childhood independence and self-reliance—"the greatest song in the world." It is not difficult to see why.

And yet Harry's memories of Kingston are not entirely unhappy. As against the cold, dirty streets of Harlem, his playground was miles and miles of sun-drenched beaches, made exciting by the unceasing roar of the surf and the ebb and flow of the blue-green Caribbean. Exotically scented flowers and tropical fruits grew in profusion, filling a growing youngster's eyes and mouth with easily accessible delights. There was a sense of freedom and lonely peacefulness in wandering along the white sandy beaches and over the endless winding roads. In Kingston's crowded streets, Harry's ears became attuned to the sound of calypso singers whose lilting and crazily accented songs later figured so prominently in his career.

[25]

Of his years in Jamaica, Harry has said: "I still have the impression of an environment that sang. Nature sang and the people sang, too. The streets of Kingston constantly rang with the songs of piping peddlers or politicians drumming up votes in the lilting singsong of the island. I loved it. I loved also night gazing. I used to climb up a mango tree and lie back and munch mangoes and gaze through the leaves at the star-filled sky."

Harry's singing art is a fusion of great extremes. The gentle and the tender constantly vie with the tense and the violent. The sweet and the lovely alternate rapidly with the brutal and the cruel. Laughter quickly succeeds anger. Warm and sunny Jamaica, perhaps, accounts for the one strain, as cold, dirty, tough Harlem may be responsible for the other.

When Harry was thirteen, his mother sent for him. Doubtless she felt that opportunities for education, for growth, and for work were too limited on the island. Back in the States, Harry found himself in a white neighborhood in Harlem where he faced racial prejudice anew in some of its subtlest and meanest forms.

Sidney Poitier was sixteen when he returned from the Bahamas to his birthplace. Miami was for Sidney what Harlem was to Harry. Not unaware of the existence of racial prejudice, Sidney had had little to do with the white community in Nassau. For all its semitropical similarity to Cat Island, Miami was to strike Sidney the first full blows of rejection he ever suffered.

"I couldn't understand it," he said. "Every sign in Miami. 'White' and 'Colored,' every rebuff, was like saying to me, 'You're not a human being.'"

Harry's mother had managed to secure an apartment in a low rental area at 130th Street and Amsterdam Avenue. She was within walking distance of employment. But the population around them was preponderantly white, composed mainly of Irish and an ever-increasing number of Spanish.

To a newspaper feature writer, Harry is reported to have said: "It played a lot of havoc with us. Here we were two

Negro kids in a white neighborhood. The desire to belong was there. My brother was a bit darker than me. He used to say he was Greek or Spanish. I said I was from Martinique. The kids nicknamed me 'Frenchy.'"

Since Harry's brother was lighter, not darker, than himself, this statement is in part either a feature writer's or a Freudian slip. There is no question, however, that both youngsters tried to pass.

But then they would have to listen to the white kids telling anti-Negro stories and jokes. They would have to act as if it did not matter at all, as if they were disinterested. But it did matter. Harry was possessed then, as he is now, of a fierce racial pride. The temptation to pass was terrific, as it has been for some light-skinned Negroes. He cannot recall what story, joke, or incident aroused his fury. There was a violent fight and the deception was dropped. Thereafter, life was a series of never-ending fights.

Harry hated them. But there was no way in which he could avoid them. It was like the air he had to breathe. There were bullies among his own people, whom he had to take on. There were white bullies whom he had to beat. Harry learned how to fight—with his wits, with his fists. Surrounded by a world of the hostile, he became a "touchy" youngster who lashed out at the drop of a syllable he didn't like. There was one point beyond which he would not go. He would have nothing to do with switch blade knives or zip guns—treacherous weapons fabricated out of wood and heavy rubber bands, but capable of killing.

"Don't ask me why I refused to carry such a weapon," he has said. "Maybe it was my mother's influence. How she kept my brother and me out of jail those years, I will never understand. It was her greatest victory."

Harry added: "I still have the scars of street combat. But the emotional scars were worse. I was good at most sports. When they chose up sides, they always chose me first. I was acceptable then. It never carried over. Sitting on my stoop on a Saturday, I'd see the guys going by all dressed up. They were on their way to a party. They never invited me.

"This was not only violently painful but something I could not reason out. It sort of shut me up inside myself."

Harry's is an explosive personality. Lying just beneath the surface of the gentle face, the slim, trim figure, and the soft, well-modulated voice is an angry man who can erupt in an instant. The sense of pent-up energy, of contained anger, of explosive power, give electricity to his appearance on a night club floor. They add interest and excitement to his movements on a movie screen.

The storm raging within Harry has not yet completely subsided. A TV director who attempted to define Harry's dramatic power came up with one word: *Hostility!* "Within him," said Don Medford, "is a hard core of hostility. Like Brando, like Jimmy Dean, like Rod Steiger, Belafonte is charged with it. This is the quality that has given a demon drive to his career and overpowering conviction to his art."

STEREO

BESSIE SMITH

Of pioneer blues singer Bessie Smith, jazz critic George Hoefer has written: "Her blues could be funny and boisterous and gentle and angry and bleak, but underneath all of them ran the raw bitterness of being a human being who had to think twice about which toilet she could use. You can't hear Bessie without realizing why Martin Luther King doesn't want to wait any more."

3. The White Poinsettia

Harry met Frances Margurite Byrd, the girl who became his first wife, in the fall of 1944. The scene was the pretty campus of Hampton Institute at Newport News, Virginia. He was a sailor training to be a Navy storekeeper, and she was a senior studying to be a child psychologist. Worlds apart in background, point of view, and temperament, he told her at their first meeting—hardly a meeting and certainly not a date—that he was going to marry her.

Situated strategically in the mouth of the James River, Hampton Institute was playing host to an Auto Mechanics group and a Navy unit of approximately 2,000 sailors. The military and the Navy were stationed at one end of the campus while the women's dorms were at the other. Social privileges were exchanged. The girls were permitted to invite the gobs to their dances while the boys could invite the coeds to their movies.

However, there was a large group of students who felt that the presence of the Armed Forces on their campus detracted from the college atmosphere. Of this group, Margurite Byrd was one of the most vocal—to the point of leading a delegation to the President's office. Their cry was *Give the Gobs the Go-By*. Had Margurite and her cohorts been successful, she and Harry might never have met.

Despite her leadership in the student fight, Margurite had been appointed senior adviser to the freshman women, a signal honor. In September 1944 she had returned to Hampton before the opening of the semester to participate in the weeklong pre-semester indoctrination program. Among the activities at which she officiated was a freshman garden party on the lawn of the President's home.

Shortly before the party, a group of sailors had marched across the campus, much to the annoyance of Margurite and other upperclassmen. As the academic hen party got under way, the sailors—who were not invited to the student affair— lined up on the outside of the fence surrounding the President's home and lawn. There they proceeded to enjoy the proceedings, not without spirited remarks. Margurite drew most of the comment since she was "the high-heeled one," "the one with the stockin's," and "you with the nose in the air." Serving tea and cookies, she passed rather close to the fence at one point. The good-natured heckling rose to a crescendo.

"May we have some tea? No sugar, sugar!" a voice taunted.

"Pass the cookies, please, cookie!"

"You take the tea, man! I'll take the doll!"

Margurite pretended not to hear and kept her head turned away from the gobs on the fence.

"How stuck up can one doll get?" someone called.

Without meaning to, Margurite turned on the heckler. She tried hard to freeze him with a sharp look. It brought a ripple of laughter. As she tried to stare the whole gang down, the laughter became wilder. It annoyed her no end. But most annoying was one laugh that somehow stood out of the whole chortling group. It was not so much a laugh as a hoot—a derisive snort that seemed to mock all authority and sham. It took all the will power she could summon not to make a comeback. Irritated, she swung around and retreated. But young Harry Belafonte, tall, thin and bony-faced, had achieved what he wanted. Margurite had noticed him, or so he thought.

When the party was over and Margurite was walking back to her dorm, she suddenly became aware that a sailor was tagging along behind her. She tried not to pay any attention. But the gob kept trotting behind her, filling the distance between them with provocative little taunts. At the same time, he kept asking for a date. Rather, he kept telling her that she couldn't find a better date than him. After a while, Margurite stopped, turned, and informed her taunter that she didn't care for the sailors on the campus as a group and that she wasn't making dates with any sailor. As she spoke her piece, she

[30]

realized that her pursuer was the gob with the hooting laugh.

"And certainly not with you!" she exclaimed. "Not if you were the last sailor on the sea!"

Before Harry could say anything, she pirouetted on her toes and was off at a fast walking clip.

Like a dog looking for a home, Harry was at her heels in a flash.

"You better be nice to me," he warned.

"Why?" she snapped, and continued walking.

"Because one of these days," he purred, "I'm going to end up being your husband!"

Margurite pulled up short, looked Harry over as if he were loco, and broke into derisive laughter. She was provoked, amused, and intrigued—all at once.

When she reached her dorm, she went in without turning her head.

Harry had proposed, as it were. And on their first "meeting." It was some time before he was able to make even a date with his unsuspecting bride-to-be.

At the time of the freshman garden party on the President's lawn, Harry was a hurt and an angry young man. He had enlisted in the Navy in the middle of his second year in high school, walking out of meaningless classes at George Washington High in the Bronx.

Harry had chosen this school because of a neighborhood girl whom he liked. Neither his feeling for her nor hers for him were strong enough to overcome the impact of the things he hated. What he was asked to learn seemed useless. It contributed nothing to help solve his immediate problems. He hated life in the slums of Harlem. He hated the daily reminders of the humiliating status to which his skin color reduced him. And he hated having to fight constantly to assert his simplest rights as a human being.

Mingling with the hatred, there was in him, too, a destructive feeling of loneliness. Devoid of a sense of identity or direction, he felt helplessly small in a vast, unconcerned universe. Closely knit families sometimes alleviate such young

[31]

torment. But Harry had no real home, despite a devoted mother, and no protecting family. For much of his youth he had lived on distant shores, a second-class citizen among his own relatives. Poverty may help build strength. It never gives it. Add discrimination, perhaps the most destructive force, and you have the makings of a disturbed personality.

Painfully unhappy, Harry was suddenly caught up in the feeling of patriotism sweeping the country. People were doing things together. They seemed to have a united purpose. Little people everywhere were rising to fight dictatorship and race hatred. To Harry, the Navy looked like a great way to escape his own misery.

Scoring high in the IQ test, he was enabled, after boot training, to attend the Navy's Storekeeper School at Hampton. His initial experiences were upsetting. Virginia was a segregated state. Wherever he turned, discrimination was an accepted thing. Second-class citizenship for Negroes was an accepted thing. Harlem gang wars almost seemed better.

Among the sailors, there were long, heated discussions. Inevitably, the recruits split on issues along the so-called Mason-Dixon line. Southern Negroes had one point of view. Those who came from the North had another. About the only thing the Northerners and the Southerners could agree on was that the Civil War was good and necessary, even if it was costly. Beyond that, the Southerners took the position that the Northerners had run away from the Negro problem and left them to face it alone.

"I didn't think so then," Harry said recently, "but now I think they had the right slant. Not that Negroes don't have problems in the North. But they're different and there's no comparison. Regardless of how the position of the Negro improves in the North—the Negro problem will continue to exist so long as it exists in the South."

There were personal incidents of discrimination, which Harry would like to forget. At one moment, during his 28-month hitch in the Navy, a call went out for blood donors for a critically ill hospital patient. Harry volunteered, along with other men, and was chosen for the needed transfusion.

There are two versions of what happened on Harry's return to the base. One has it that Harry felt dizzy and asked to be relieved of guard duty for the night. In considering his request, Harry's C.O. allegedly discovered that he had given blood to a white patient. Thereupon, instead of guard duty, Harry was assigned to scrubbing "the head," recruit lingo for toilet. Angered, Harry went temporarily AWOL. Net result of his gesture: a turn in the brig.

The other version of this story leads to the same ending: a turn in the brig. But according to this account, Harry could not have given blood to a white patient. Not in Virginia anyway. Wartime or not. Instead, the tale runs that Harry returned to the base, after the transfusion, tired and slightly dizzy. Instead of asking to be relieved, he went on guard duty —and proceeded to fall asleep. The brig sentence seemed unfair, and the unfairness itself implied discrimination.

There were other problem situations—inevitable considering that this was the first time Negroes had been permitted to enlist in the Navy. But the experiences of Negroes in the Army —among them, those of Sidney Poitier—were frequently no less disturbing. Poitier also joined the war effort to escape an oppressive situation. Lying about his age, he was in uniform a year and eleven days, "a period so distressing," according to a friend, "that he still finds it hard to talk about it."

Assigned to an all-Negro company stationed at Northport, L. I., Poitier found himself "even more of an alien" than he had been in civilian life. His youth, naïveté, and musical West Indian accent made him "the butt of the barracks." Driven to the verge of a breakdown, he was sent to Mason General Hospital, where it was decided that his difficulty was "utter bewilderment."

"The world," Sidney explains, "was just too big for me—I was a kid, I was lost, and they decided that I had to go home."

Disturbing though they might have been in some ways, Harry's Navy days were without traumatic incident. And after he met Margurite, his being stationed at Newport News had its pleasant, also instructive, side. In fact, Harry looks back to the Navy as the place "where he discovered there were other things besides poverty and loneliness and the struggle for survival."

"It was like taking a deep breath," he has said. "There was fellowship and literature and folklore and history and discussion and debate and there was the culture of my people. There were the important questions of knowing who you were and why you were and what you were, and where you had come from and where you were going. And I began to discover that there was Harry Belafonte, an individual who was *somebody* and who belonged."

At the time of her first meeting with Harry—"encounter" would, perhaps, be more accurate—Frances Margurite Byrd had identity, position, and direction. The daughter of a Washington, D.C., real estate man, she was the second youngest of five children. They called her "Frankie." Her father was not wealthy, but he created a comfortable and stable, middle-class home at 501 "T" Street. All the Byrd children were put through college. All became teachers. One brother is an instructor at Virginia College. The other teaches Structural Engineering and is a member of the State Education Board in the Capital. Her eldest sister is a Home Economics teacher while the other is a music instructor. Margurite herself was to become a teacher after getting her Master's degree at New York University. She was also to earn a Ph.D. in psychology after postgraduate study abroad at the Sorbonne in France and the University of Heidelberg in Germany.

Unlike Harry, Margurite had grown up in a segregated community. She had gone to segregated schools and attended segregated theatres. Whatever the limitations, it was a self-contained community and without the kind of tension characteristic of mixed communities. Harry's burning indignation and hostility were to be new experiences to her.

"I was comfortable enough," she said recently, "so that I didn't feel that I was being denied something by not associating with white people. I went to school. I made my marks. My mother had three hot meals on the table each day. She kept me clean. My father bought the clothes I needed. I went to Sunday school. I saw the movies that my parents recommended. As a family, we went to the zoo, on picnics, to baseball games.

"We had no worries and we didn't know or care about anything outside. It was our world and a good one. I'm not saying that this kind of isolation is healthy. But you're not touched by external tensions until you get outside. Then, you look back and say: 'Well, I don't want this cramped type of cosmos for my children. They're being denied a world-wide experience. It's a handicap and I don't want it.'

"But until I moved out, I wasn't dependent on white people in any way. I didn't need them. My father and mother took care of me. It was different from people who have been brought up in a place like New York where you have a bit of acceptance in the white world, a bit, or a lot, of rejection, but inevitably dependence."

So, here was Harry, tense, insecure, quick-tempered and belligerent. And here was Margurite, relaxed, soft-spoken and calm. And it was the fall of 1944, and multicolored leaves were beginning to drift dreamily from the stately trees onto the green lawns at Hampton.

Defeated in his attempt to date Margurite after the lawn party, Harry returned to his barrack wondering whether she was a teacher or a student. She had acted so supercilious. And she had been hostess at the student tea. Perhaps she was an instructor. Harry wasn't fazed. He began making inquiries. After a time he learned her name. Then he began calling her. Since his unit arose at six A.M., he thought nothing of phoning her each morning at that unseemly hour. It was annoying but provocative. After classes she would return to her dorm to find Harry hanging around. Despite the morning phone calls, he would pay no attention to her. She ignored him.

Margurite has a habit of balancing her shoe on the toe of her foot and letting it swing loose. Even these days when she appears on lecture platforms for the NAACP, she unconsciously allows one shoe to dangle on her toe. It was to be her downfall. One day, as she and several roommates were chatting in front of the dorm—and Harry and several sailors were nonchalantly chatting nearby—he approached her, bent down suddenly, and snatched the loose shoe off her foot. Then, like a playful puppy, he retreated to a safe distance. If he expected Margurite to plead for her shoe, he was in for a surprise. She turned swiftly on her remaining heel, and to the amusement of the other gobs and to Harry's amazement, limped into the dorm on one shoe and one stockinged foot.

"Hey! Don't go!" Harry shouted, and started to chase into the dorm after her. The dorm was, of course, out of bounds to sailors and all males. As the other sailors intervened to stop him, a new thought flashed across his mind. He walked away, laughing to himself and tossing the shoe playfully in the air as if it were a ball.

Thereafter, Harry's six A.M. phone calls to Margurite became a game. She wanted to know when he was returning her shoe. It was wartime, and shoes were not easy to come by. Harry wanted to know when he was getting a date. For three days, it was a stalemate. Then Margurite gave in, and they went to their first movie together.

There were many movies after that and many walks along the leaf-strewn lanes of the campus. But there was no amour. Most of all, there were endless discussions. "Our entire courtship," Margurite has said, "was one long argument about racial issues."

Quickly she became aware of the storms raging inside Harry—the search for a direction, the uncertainty about his future, the hurt and the resentment, and the pent-up anger over his second-class citizenship. Well reasoned and well read, she sought to give Harry perspective on the changing position of the Negro in American society and in the world. Partly under her prompting, he began reading books on the history, the art, and the culture of the Negro. There is no indication that these substantially reduced the tensions within Harry.

He and Margurite argued constantly—clashes that had their origins in Harry's explosive hostility to the world around him and in Margurite's comfortable acceptance of it. But Harry

[36]

admired her, and he felt that she liked him. And she did, despite the arguments and the distance at which she kept him.

Christmas 1944 was a turning point. Harry had completed his Storekeeper's course and was being sent off to the West Coast for possible active duty in the Pacific. The parting was tender. Margurite was returning home to Washington for the holidays, and Harry was going off, perhaps to war. Without knowing what the future would bring, and certainly without feeling that Harry was to be her future husband, Margurite accepted a signet ring and a gold locket from him. What intrigued her even more than both of these gifts was a four-foot plant that Harry gave her. She had known red poinsettias, but Harry's plant was the first white poinsettia she had ever seen.

As Margurite boarded a crowded Christmas coach for Washington, she carried the plant in her arms, treasuring it as if it were a newborn baby. Holiday trains are always crowded. But this was wartime. There wasn't an unoccupied inch of space. All the way from Newport News to Washington, an excited Margurite struggled to protect her plant. It was not easy, and she did not escape a certain amount of ribbing. But when the train pulled into the station at Washington and she stepped down into the waiting arms of her mother and father, it was a matter of personal triumph that the four blossoms on Harry's plant remained intact.

As her father reached out to embrace her, he was startled to hear Margurite's breathless cry: "Please, Daddy, it's a white poinsettia! * It's so rare. Oh, do watch out for the blossoms!"

What Harry would have done with his gift had he known that it was named after a white Southern planter, I will not presume to guess . . .

* Anxious to describe a white poinsettia accurately, I checked Webster's Collegiate Dictionary for any insight it might offer. Here is the vivid word picture drawn in this lexicon: "*poinsettia:* n. [NL., after Joel R. Poinsett (1779–1851), of South Carolina.] *Bot.* Any of a genus (*Poinsettia*) of chiefly tropical euphorbiaceous American herbs or woody plants having alternate leaves, and cymose inconspicuous green flowers, subtended by bright-colored involucral leaves."

STEREO

ETHEL WATERS

At the beginning of the twenties, Ethel Waters was one of the top acts on the T.O.B.A. circuit (Theatre Owners Booking Association), a circuit of independent Negro theatres. Despite attractive offers and her popularity as a blues singer, she was afraid to accept bookings in white theatres with white audiences. Not that working for Southern theatre owners before Negro audiences and in Negro theatres was without its dangers, physical as well as emotional. An instance of the hazards then facing a Negro entertainer occurred at a theatre in Atlanta.

Before her first show, Ethel's pianist—Pearl Wright—discovered that the stage piano was not properly tuned. As Ethel reports the incident in her autobiography *His Eye Is on the Sparrow,* she went to the theatre and tried to explain to the owner, Charles P. Bailey, that the piano had to be retuned.

Bailey wanted her accompanist to use the piano in the pit. Ethel explained that this was not possible because at one point in her act, her dancer had to talk with her accompanist, something she could not do if her pianist was down in the pit, half under the stage. Although Ethel offered to have the piano tuned at her expense, Bailey refused.

"No Yankee nigger bitch is telling me how to run my theatre," he announced.

"And no Georgia cracker is telling me how to run my act," Ethel responded.

"I'm Bailey," he said, "I'm standing on my grounds as the owner of this theatre. And if you don't do what I say, I'll kick your ass out of here."

"I'm Ethel Waters," she replied, "and I'm standing on my grounds. And you or no other cracker sonofabitch can tell me what to do."

After that, Ethel, who was a woman of strength and determination, just sat out two shows. Before the beginning of the third show, a new piano arrived and Ethel went on. But this was only the beginning of her problems. Ethel knew that, on another occasion, another great blues singer, Bessie Smith, had had an argument with Bailey—and the theatre owner had beaten her up and had her thrown into jail.

[38]

Two days after the argument, Ethel was cautiously approached by a backstage Negro worker, who warned her that the theatre owner was planning "something bad." Bailey's plan, as he suspected, was not to pay her on Saturday night so that she would make a fuss. "That will give him an excuse for beatin' you up and maybe puttin' you in jail." She would know that this was Bailey's scheme if she did not receive her half week's pay in the middle of the week along with other acts.

Sure enough, when midweek payments were made, Ethel was omitted. Then she knew that she had to leave Atlanta fast.

When she tried to buy tickets at the railway station, she discovered to her dismay that the ticket agent had received orders not to sell her any. On her return to her hotel, she found that two policemen stood posted in front, one was stationed at the rear, and all were under orders not to let her leave, except to go to the theatre.

Her only chance out of Atlanta was through a suburban railway station where the agent had not been intimidated by Bailey. All through a terrible, sleepless night, Ethel, her accompanist, and her dancer secretly watched the policemen, praying that they would let up their vigilance.

At 5:30 A.M., the cops did. They went for coffee. In a flash, the three entertainers slipped out of the rear door. Now that they were out, they wondered how they would get to the station. By accident, an old man came by driving a horse and buggy. They stopped him. Knowing how her people love funerals, Ethel explained that they had just received news of the passing of a dearly beloved relative and that they had to catch a train immediately. For five dollars, the old man agreed to drive them to an out-of-the-way station. A train on its way to Nashville, Tennessee, was flagged down by the stationmaster.

When they arrived in Nashville, Ethel Waters, who is a deeply religious woman—a fact that is evident even in the title of her autobiography—went directly to the Western Union office and sent a telegram to Charles P. Bailey, of Atlanta. It read:

"WHO GOT EFFED THIS TIME?"

4. A Dream Deferred

The night that Harry saw his first play was the night that he discovered his future direction. It was in December 1945. Honorably discharged from the Navy earlier that year without seeing overseas duty, Harry was working as a maintenance man's helper. Boss-man was his stepfather, who took care of a group of buildings in Harlem. Moving from apartment to apartment, repairing broken windows, jammed locks, stuffed drains, etc., Harry was presented with a pair of theatre tickets by a pleased tenant. An inveterate movie-goer, he had never seen a legitimate play. His first inclination was to throw the ducats away. But he had little spending money, and here was a chance to take a girl out "on the cuff."

The play was a two-acter *Home Is the Hunter* by Samuel M. Kootz. The cast was composed of unknowns. The theatre was a Harlem playhouse on West 126th Street. The production was by the experimental American Negro Theatre. The play ran for one night. But it did not matter. It might have been a stirring and long-lived *Hamlet* as done by a distinguished company of actors headed by Sir Laurence Olivier.

That winter night in December 1945, a spark was ignited in Harry which, in one evening, became a raging fire. Harry left the ANT playhouse so excited that he wandered about the cold Harlem streets for hours. When he finally returned home, it was to retire to a sleepless bed. All night he lay in a kind of daze, his mind aflame with images that made his breath catch and set his heart palpitating. They were images of Harry Belafonte as an actor. Imaginary applause rang in his ears. Imagined audiences roared and cheered. And there in the limelight stood Harry Belafonte, smiling and bowing. It was a dream that was never to leave Harry after that night. In one cold evening, and through a production that was a turkey, Harry became stagestruck. When he arose after a restless night, it was with the determination, intense and unyielding, to become a successful actor.

The next three years were, for Harry, years of hopeful preparation, of hard study and, at the end, of heartbreaking frustration.

Harry had no clear idea of how one became an actor. He did the most obvious thing. Between his chores as a handyman, he wandered down to the American Negro Theatre playhouse. He was too shy, too introverted, to step forward and ask questions. He just hung around, hoping he knew not for what. During a rehearsal, he drifted backstage. No one challenged him. He gazed about enthralled. It was a new world. He had never in his life been on a stage and the backstage world of scenic props, colored lights, curtains, pulleys, flats, was a newly discovered never-never land.

As Harry stood there, bug-eyed and bewildered, someone shoved a piece of scenery into his hand. A voice told him to move it. He did. After that, he helped shift some props. For several hours, he performed one stagehand task after another. It was exciting. What stirred him even more was the camaraderie of the group, the earnest desire of all its members to make the theatre work and their pleasure in working together. Here, one was not alone. One was part of something. The ANT needed volunteer help. Harry began coming around regularly. Before long, he was a regular stagehand.

Although it provided no income, stagehanding was a dream come true. It gave Harry contact with people, with the new and magical world of the theatre. After painting scenery, moving stage props, stringing cables, the next step was acting. Harry was much thinner then. His face was on the bony side. But the good looks were there. Underneath the apparent uncertainty and confusion, Osceola Archer, director of ANT, sensed a natural dramatic flair. After a time, she offered him a small part in Frank Gabrielson's *Days of Our Youth*.

At first Harry tried to pass it up. He was uneasy about his

[41]

lack of experience. And suddenly he was troubled by the whole idea of being an actor. He wanted adulation and the limelight. But with his schooling on the tough streets of Harlem, he felt that there was something exhibitionistic about acting. He tried to say no. Members of the cast went to work on him. They overcame his shyness and fears. Soon he took his first hesitant, but happy, steps across the boards of a stage. His second acting assignment was a more challenging part. Miss Archer picked Harry for the juvenile lead in a comedy about Harlem social climbers, *On Striver's Row.*

"I did not know until later," Miss Archer said recently, "that a photographer made a movie of *Striver's Row* on his own initiative. One night, quite by accident, he ran it for me. The production was not bad for an off-Broadway repertory group. But what was startling was Harry Belafonte's contribution. The screen just lit up the moment he stepped on-stage. It was an amazing thing to see because he was just a boy, inexperienced and untutored. Nevertheless, he exuded something that was as inescapable as it was inexplicable.

"The only thing you can call it is personal magnetism. Harry Belafonte had it when he was just starting. It was not something that came with success. On-stage, the electricity and the tremendous appeal came through even then."

After his second role, Harry knew that acting was much more than exhibitionism. He determined to learn all the things he had to know in order to become an outstanding actor. He had to excel. As in anything he was to do, he could not be satisfied unless he was better than his competition. He had to prove that he could run faster, stay up later, beat the drums harder, draw larger crowds, or act better.

Questions elicited the information that there was a Dramatic Workshop, run by a famous German director, Erwin Piscator. Associated with the New School for Social Research on 12th Street in Manhattan, it accepted students under the GI Bill of Rights. As a Navy vet, Harry was eligible. He enrolled. He also left his mother's home—his family disapproved of his desire to act—and moved down to Greenwich Village. With

[42]

three other Workshop students, he shared a flat in Bleecker Street that cost each of them $9.50 a month.

For more than two years Harry was a dedicated student. For more than two years Harry explored, not merely the exciting world of the theatre, but the provocative world of books, of music, of culture.

"The Drama Workshop days," a friend has said, "were the days of the Great Awakening for Harry. What he had scorned as a high-school student now became of the greatest moment to him. Education had once been a meaningless word. Now it became an exciting adventure into the unknown and a voyage of vital consequence to him. These were hopeful and happy days for Harry, just as his school years were unhappy and disturbing. The theatre educated him as school had not, and uncovered in him deep cultural and social drives."

Four of Harry's classmates at the Drama Workshop were Tony Curtis, Marlon Brando, Elaine Stritch, and Sidney Poitier. With Marlon Brando in his training group, it is hardly surprising that Harry was not regarded as a standout performer.

"There was no question about Marlon," Dr. Saul Colin, one of the Workshop teachers, said recently. "But I doubt that any of us expected Harry to become so successful as he did in just a few years. We watched him grow as an actor during those years, and he showed promise. But that's about it—promise."

And Dr. Colin added: "Harry was a shy young man—almost as shy as he was handsome. But he was earnest and serious-minded. Perhaps, his most noticeable traits were his insatiable curiosity and eagerness to learn. If he was not standout, he was, after all, in a large group, most of whom had background, training, and experience that Harry lacked.

"I remember Harry in those days as being extremely well behaved. Despite his shyness, he was always friendly to everyone. He wasn't as social-minded then as he is now. But that was because he was so preoccupied with his own development."

Harry drove himself as hard as any of the students in the Workshop. He went to classes diligently, rehearsed constantly, and practiced all the skills an actor must master. It was at this time that he first learned the dramatic use of hands, body, and face which later made him so expressive a singer, literally a singing actor. He became an avid reader, straying from books on the theatre to volumes on the most abstruse subjects. He participated in Workshop projects, displaying a special interest in Shakespeare. Among the roles he assayed were small parts in *Taming of the Shrew* and *Romeo and Juliet*. He appeared also in several Workshop musicals.

One of these, presented at the Rooftop Theatre on Houston Street, was seen by a young producer. Monte Kay later was to play a pivotal role in launching Harry on a singing career. But when he saw Harry at the Rooftop, he was an aspiring producer as Belafonte was an aspiring actor. In short, he too was out of work. Harry did two numbers in the production: *Recognition,* a song for which he wrote both words and music, and *Lean On Me,* one of whose writers was Alan Greene, a friend who conducted his record dates in '54 and again in '58. Since Harry had not previously sung in public, he half-spoke the lyrics.

Monte was so impressed by Harry's unaccompanied rendition that he went up to compliment him after the show. Harry was pleased but not excited. He wanted to act, not sing. But Kay told him that when he got a job as a producer, he would find a spot for him. He did—not too long afterward.

In the audience at the Rooftop, and not too impressed by the whole production, was a teacher at the Bethany Day Nursery in New York. Margurite Byrd's reaction might have been the result, not of what she saw or heard but of how she felt about one of its principals. She was fond of Harry—quite fond —but not of his friends, the bohemian kind of life he was leading, or the way he thought about certain things. He was practically the only guy she was dating, and he kept telling her— he didn't ask—that they were going to get married. She was uneasy and confused.

After their poinsettia parting in '44, she had not seen him for almost two years. They had corresponded while he was on the coast in the Navy and while she did graduate work and taught at Hampton. But it was casual. Then, around Labor Day of '46, as she was readying herself to leave Washington, Harry had come ringing her doorbell. He was in the Capital with a youth protest group marching on the White House with a petition. She was overjoyed to see him. About to leave for New York to take up her first teaching job, she was happy to have a friend in the big city. But in line with the admonition of the Dean of Women at Hampton "to generalize and not to specialize," she was depending on Harry to introduce her to other men. She hoped that she had made her intentions clear by returning the gold signet ring he had given her at Hampton.

Nevertheless, once she was in New York taking graduate courses at N.Y.U., Margurite began dating Harry. The endless arguments that had gone on at Hampton started all over again. Once again, Harry's attitude toward the racial question became an issue. Only now they clashed over something quite specific.

Riding the subways of New York, Harry would scrawl comments on advertising posters that provoked or annoyed him. A car card for a cosmetic lotion promising straphangers that it would preserve the soft white beauty of their hands, elicited the penciled demand: "But what about Negro hands?" A placard urging tolerance would acquire a handwritten postscript: "There is prejudice in America!" Across an advertisement for a soap that promised to handle your skin gently, Harry would scribble derisively: "What if your skin is yellow or black?"

Margurite regarded this behavior as immature and infantile. She would remonstrate with him, reprimand him. She would argue that his marking up signs achieved nothing. It did not change anything, and he would only get into trouble if he was caught. Somebody has to speak out, Harry would counter.

[45]

"You're not speaking out," Margurite would say. "You're just letting off steam. The thing to do is grow within yourself and make yourself important enough to be heard."

"How does a Negro become important," Harry would demand, "when he can't even get a decent role as an actor?"

Here was another source of tension between them, rather than friction. Having grown up in a stable middle-class household, where her mother was always home and her father came home each day at exactly the same hour, acting seemed to offer only a hazardous and irregular kind of livelihood. It was no future for anybody and certainly not for a Negro. Margurite thought that Harry should be preparing himself for one of the professions.

Her middle-class mores were also shocked by what went on at the Village parties to which Harry took her. "I had not experienced romantic love up until then," she has said, "and I doubt that I would even have recognized it. My family had surrounded me with a certain kind of protection and instilled in me the highest moral code. A woman did not give herself to a man until she married him.

"Then, to be thrown into contact with that Village crowd. They weren't called beatniks then. Bohemians, I guess. Or just theatrical personalities among whom I constantly heard the expression, 'No inhibitions!' Why, when I had first come to New York, I was quite shocked to see men and women embrace and kiss each other when they met on the street."

Despite the conflict of outlook and her own, perhaps unexpressed, feeling that marriage was not for them, Margurite continued to see Harry—and to try gently to change him.

"I was very fond of him," she admits. "But I think my fondness was that of trying to protect him. He reminded me of a big kid that was about to get into trouble if somebody didn't watch and help him. I had to keep him from becoming a delinquent. And as I saw it, he was on the verge, with this scrawling on subway signs and lashing out at people. It wasn't like the juvenile delinquency of today when knives and guns are used. But it was still an attack on people. I felt that I had to protect him from people as well as from himself."

And how did Harry feel? Harry was drawn to Margurite by the very things that prevented her from accepting him. She was a rock, a solid rock, in a heaving sea of uncertainty. She knew what she wanted, and she knew where she was going. Middle-class values, against which he rebelled as an artist, made her attractive to him. And so he kept telling her they were going to get married. He never asked for her affirmation. He stated it as an unquestioned fact.

Margurite did not regard it as one until late in May 1948. Their courtship had been traveling a rocky up-and-down road when Harry suddenly made himself scarce for several weeks. He was rehearsing in an off-Broadway production *Sojourner Truth,* a play based on the remarkable exploits of the famous Negro woman abolitionist who fought slavery in the days of the underground railway. The director was Osceola Archer, with whom Harry had worked in his first roles at ANT. As the days wore on, Margurite tried to act as if the absence of her "delinquent" did not matter. But deep down, she knew that it did.

Harry did not invite her to the opening on Thursday night. He waited until he saw the reviews. Then he phoned her. It was Friday, May 21, 1948. The mere sound of his voice made Margurite aware that she had missed him more than she had thought she could miss anybody. She did not care that it was just hours before curtain time. She did not care that he had not thought enough of her even to call her once in several weeks. All that mattered was that Harry was calling her and that he wanted her to come. She dressed faster than she had ever dressed in her life and, with the help of a cab driver who broke every city ordinance, arrived at the 92nd Street Y.M.H.A. in time for the play.

That evening she was impressed by Harry's histrionics, even overwhelmed. His role was that of the nineteen-year-old son of Sojourner Truth, played by the well-known actress, Muriel Smith. Margurite was aware of no one on-stage except Harry, and she saw even him, not in his stage role, but as the delinquent subway scrawler and striving actor whom she had been missing terribly for weeks. When the play was over and people were backstage congratulating Harry on his performance, Margurite came to add her own. As she stood listening to others voice their praise, suddenly she felt very possessive of the talent and the personality that were Harry Belafonte. Secretly, she hoped that he would "ask" for her hand again.

Before he took her home that evening, Harry did. His approach was rather novel and one that Margurite could not easily rebuff, even if she had had a mind to do so. The setting was a romantic one: the East River Drive with the arch of the Tri-Borough Bridge outlined in a graceful curve of spaced lights against the night sky. As they walked along in the spring night, listening to the tugboats on the river and gazing out over the dark expanse of water, Harry pulled his coup. He maneuvered Margurite close to the low parapet lining the walk. Then, without warning, he swung her out over the edge and dangled her precariously over the black, viscous waters of the river. Since Margurite could not swim, the experience was not without its terror, even though Harry's purpose was to elicit a "yes" to his oft-repeated proposals of marriage.

"I was thrilled to get the proposal," Margurite has said. "But I cannot forget how shocking it was to me that nobody at all came to my assistance. There were many strollers on the Drive. How did they know that Harry was not some madman determined to drown me in the cold waters of the East River? I knew he was cutting up. But still I was frightened, since I can't swim. There must have been quite a frantic note in my pleading that he put me back onto solid ground. Nevertheless, no one paid the least attention to my plight. People passed us by without more than a curious glance at a girl being dangled threateningly over the water. It was then that I realized how alone one can be in a city like New York and how cold and unconcerned New Yorkers can be—and were about me. Of course, it was really a very happy moment for me."

Joyfully, Margurite accepted Harry's proposal. The following day they went down to City Hall to get their marriage license. They returned empty-handed. It was Saturday, and the Marriage License Bureau was closed. Harry was particularly unhappy. He was afraid that Margurite would change her mind by Monday morning. She spent the weekend reassuring him that the "yes," which was so slow in coming, would not become a "no." The following Monday, Harry picked her up at the Bethany School and, during her lunch hour, they rushed down to City Hall and took out their wedding license.

They were married on Friday, June 18, 1948. Margurite taught school that day until noon. Then, most of the teachers, including Mrs. Dorothy Beers, the director, and Dr. Samuel Berenberg, the school physician, accompanied her to City Hall. Although Margurite had become a Catholic earlier that year—she was baptized around Easter—they did not have a church wedding. Her only relative at the civil ceremony was an aunt from Jersey City, who came to represent her parents. Margurite had called her mother the preceding evening to announce the happy tidings. Her parents were not pleased that they did not know the groom. They did not remember Harry from the one brief visit he had paid to their home. Nor were they satisfied with Margurite's vague answers as to what he did for a living. Neither journeyed north for the ceremony. Harry's best man was a close friend of the time, Milt Otts.

Since Margurite was teaching, their honeymoon had to be telescoped into a blissful weekend. Harry had to spend part of that weekend working, since he was on the entertainment staff of a summer camp—and Beaver Lodge in Pennsylvania became the scene of the honeymoon. Came Monday, and Margurite was back in her classroom in Manhattan. All that summer, while Harry worked at the Lodge, Margurite taught school in the city. Weekends, she traveled to Pennsylvania so that Harry and she could be together.

Act II

MARGURITE

In thy dark eyes' splendor
  Where the warm light loves to dwell,
Weary looks, yet tender
  Speak their fond farewell.
Nita! Juanita! Ask thy soul if we should part!
— *Juanita*

5. "Recognition"

Not until almost twelve months after their marriage did Margurite and Harry Belafonte have an apartment of their own. It was an extremely trying time, with Harry floundering in his efforts to launch himself as an actor and to achieve some degree of financial independence.

When Harry returned to New York after the "honeymoon summer" at Beaver Lodge, Margurite continued to live at the Teachers' Dormitory of the Bethany Nursery. Although the dorm was for single teachers and those female, Harry managed to stay with her. The other teachers knew he was in the dormitory when he was there. But somehow his presence remained a well-kept secret, and no issue was ever raised by the school administration.

Margurite was earning 75 dollars a week while Harry earned nothing as an actor in search of a job. He visited producers' offices, registered with as many agents as he could, hunted plays in rehearsal, read for the few roles available to a Negro actor. It was a grueling and fruitless grind.

Broadway had seen plays with Negro actors almost from the turn of the century when vaudevillian Bert Williams had "smiled his way into people's hearts" and been accepted in the legitimate theatre. Before World War I there had been a few serious problem plays about Negroes. But it was the twenties that brought such impressive opportunities for Negro actors, as Eugene O'Neill's *The Emperor Jones* and Paul Green's *In Abraham's Bosom*, a Pulitzer prize play. During the thirties, an increasing number of plays, among them Marc Connelly's Pulitzer prize-winning *The Green Pastures*, DuBose Heyward's *Brass Ankle*, Langston Hughes's *Mulatto*, John

[53]

Wexley's *They Shall Not Die*—provided fine dramatic roles for the talented Negro actor.

Harry's decade—the forties—saw a continuing flow of plays with Negro characters, among them vital vehicles like Philip Yordan's *Anna Lucasta* and Lillian Smith's *Strange Fruit*. But, as Sterling Brown has noted, "serious drama of Negro life was rare and the Negro playwrights noticeably absent." For a young, aspiring, and unknown actor like Harry Belafonte, the opportunities for finding a place or a role on the Broadway stage were, of necessity, so rare as to be nonexistent. As he continued his lonely and frustrating search, the truth slowly burned its way into Harry's unhappy consciousness.

"It was just impossible," he has said, "for me to get work in the theatre. The closest I ever got to the Broadway stage was when I got an Equity card for a Theatre Guild tryout in Westport, Connecticut. The show ran for three weeks but never got to Broadway."

The approach of Christmas found Margurite entering her fifth month of pregnancy. There were discussions about Harry's taking a regular job, any job. Basically, this was what Margurite would have wanted, even if the Broadway theatre were more receptive than it was. Basically, this was what Harry did not want even though he could not find an acting job. Tensions mounted. It was decided that Margurite would return to her parents' home in Washington for the remaining months of her pregnancy and the birth of her baby. Harry remained in New York, lonely, detached, and disturbed. Something of his state of mind may be gathered from the way he spent some nights at his mother's apartment on Amsterdam Avenue, some at an uncle's on West 156th Street, and others at the home of a friend, Alan Greene, who was to serve as his musical conductor in later years.

As he wandered about looking for an acting job, the worst part of the day was dusk, when the big electric signs began to light up along Broadway. It was as if the footlights came up in a giant theatre—and the house lights dimmed and an expectant hush fell over the audience. A mood of deep depression settled over him. But he could not tear himself away from the theatrical district. Night after night, instead of returning to one of his various lodgings, he would roam around Broadway peering at the brightly lit marquees with an overwhelming sense of longing, pain, and unfulfillment.

That fall, Broadway theatregoers were viewing *Harvey, Mister Roberts, Edward My Son,* and *A Streetcar Named Desire,* which brought stardom to Marlon Brando, one of Harry's Workshop buddies. Audiences were enjoying such musicals as *High Button Shoes, Look, Ma, I'm Dancing,* and *Where's Charley?*

But for Belafonte, the question was, "Where's Harry?" And the anguished answer was nowhere, nowhere. Time and time again, he wondered if he would ever have the thrill of seeing his own name on a Broadway theatre marquee. He could not persuade himself—he just could not believe—that it would not come to him. And yet, here the world of the theatre flowed by him as if he did not exist.

One day, in confused desperation, he decided to take a regular job. As an expectant father, he could not do less for Margurite and the baby. After all, his friend, Sidney Poitier, who also wanted to act, worked as a delivery boy in the garment district. Sidney trundled dresses about in a hand truck through the congestion and traffic of the area around Seventh Avenue and 37th Street, just below the theatre district. So why shouldn't he?

Stories have appeared in many publications, including *Time, Current Biography,* and RCA Victor Records' Press Information, stating that Harry abandoned his theatrical quest late in 1948 and took a job in the garment district. In another publication, details are given as to how he worked, first, as a wrapper and delivery boy at 45 dollars a week and, then, was promoted to an inside job as a dyer of swatches at slightly better pay.

An interesting chapter in the history of American press-agentry and journalism could be written on how stories like these start, grow, and are perpetuated. The simple fact is that, while Harry may have done odd jobs in the garment district, and did take a regular job, he never actually went to work at it. At the zero hour, a happy accident intervened and launched Harry on a career as a jazz singer, which moved John S. Wilson, then of *Down Beat* and now of *The New York Times,* to nickname him "The Cinderella Gentleman."

Down Beat, incidentally, has the right story on what happened with Harry's garment district job. "The night before he was to start this new 'career'—pushing a hand truck around the garment center," *Down Beat* reported on March 11, 1949, "he walked into the Royal Roost . . ."

There, as *Down Beat* headlined its story, "Unknown, Belafonte Just Sang Self Into Roost Job."

Located between 47th and 48th Streets on the west side of Broadway, The Roost was one of two midtown clubs sponsoring the new type of esoteric jazz then being brewed in Harlem. The other cellar club, importing the new jazz from Minton's, the 118th Street hangout of the bop crowd, was pointedly known as Bop City. Situated on Broadway and 49th, the entrance to Bop City was between the Brill Building, housing over one hundred Tin Pan Alley publishers, and the Turf, a restaurant where the Alley's songwriters went for "coffee an'" when they were too lazy to cross Broadway to the Old Lindy's, now defunct.

It was at The Roost that the Cinderella slipper was tried on Harry's tired foot on a rainy evening in January '49. Almost the first person Harry saw after he descended the flight of marble steps to The Royal Roost was Monte Kay, the bespectacled, intellectual-looking and soft-spoken producer whom he had met at a Theatre Workshop presentation. Without suspecting it at the moment, this rainy evening in January 1949 was to be the beginning of a two-year cycle in Harry's career during which he functioned first as a jazz singer, then as a pop singer, and found fulfillment in neither role.

The Roost was then pursuing an advanced jazz policy, booking such exponents of the flatted fifth as the late Charlie (Bird) Parker, saxist Charlie Ventura, eighty-eighter Tadd Dameron, and trumpeter Miles Davis. Also trumpeter Dizzy Gillespie with the beret, the goatee, and the heavy black glasses, soon to become cult appurtenances of the bop crowd.

To Harry's pleased surprise, Monte Kay turned out to be one of the club's managers.

"How would you like to do a number tonight?" Kay asked in his casual way.

Harry laughed. "You're putting me on."

It had been a spontaneous thought. Now, Kay considered it. "No," he said. "It might be an idea. How about it?"

"Dressed this way?" Harry asked.

"What do you think the boys on the stand are wearing?"

"I have no music," Harry fenced. "What about accompaniment?"

"Do it the way you did it that night on The Rooftop. You had no accompaniment—as I recall it."

"It was *a capella*," Harry affirmed. As time went on, Harry was to develop a passion for polysyllabic words and recondite phrases, and to use them on every possible occasion.

"Then it's settled."

Harry hesitated.

"I'll call on you when the club's better filled."

Kay went off to attend to his chores as co-manager of The Roost with Harry's eyes following him uneasily. Harry was tempted to run after him and ask for a rain check. But the temptation to go on was even greater. Whether Harry knew that each Monday night at The Roost was Cinderella Night for amateurs and had come for that reason is not clear.

He took a seat in the bull pen, an area where customers paid just an admission charge. First introduced on Broadway by The Roost, the bull pen had no tables. Customers could just sit and listen to the music without eating or drinking, or worrying about a minimum or cover. When Harry sat down, the long benches were well filled with young people, some of them still in Army or Navy uniform, while the table section of the club was rather empty. The music played by the bop jazz group was loud, fast-tempoed and raucous with crazy, offbeat accents and shrill, earsplitting harmonies. Harry did not hear a thing. He sat there numb, half hoping that Monte Kay was kidding, half dreaming that this was his big chance.

When Monte finally called on him, he remained in his seat,

unaware that his name had been announced. It was after Monte began motioning and the youngsters around him all turned toward Harry that he realized he was on. His knees felt like sponge cake. He did not know whether he could make the stage. When he turned at the microphone toward the audience, his mouth was so dry that no sound came out at first. His upper lip stuck to his teeth, and he had to use his fingers to pry it away.

Finally, he sang *Lean On Me* and *Recognition*. The latter, his own first published song, was an expression of the frustration he felt as a Negro at being deprived of recognition as a man. Two of the embittered lines: "They won't let me forget I'm dark" and "My color's put a veil on me." But the chorus of the song spoke triumphantly of his determination to put his "shoulder to the wheel of freedom and help it roll along." It was a moving number, and one into which Harry poured all the painful feelings and emotions of frustration pent up within him for years. Thereafter, he sang the only pop songs he knew: *Blue Moon* and *Stardust*. He was nervous and awkward. Skinnier than he should have been, he did not move gracefully, and he did not know what to do with his hands.

"But there was something about him," Monte reports, "that the audience liked. I had the feeling that, despite his inexperience and lack of showmanship, he had real appeal. He was not a smash. But there was promise in him. Let me put it this way. I was impressed enough to offer him a job."

Harry could not believe it. "You're joking." He laughed nervously. "Man, this is not something to kid about," he cried. "This is too important to me."

"I'm not joking," Monte said, in his quiet way.

Harry glanced around the club, not believing his ears.

"It won't pay much," Monte said, "just scale. And it'll be for one week. When can you start?"

"Tonight," Harry said. Then he thought quickly. He had no repertoire to speak of. He had no clothes. "When would you like me to start?" he asked.

"Monday is off night," Monte said. "Let's make it next Tuesday. Okay?"

"Okay." That gave him some time to prepare. Harry shook Monte's hand and turned to leave the club. He had to phone the good news to Margurite, in Washington. Would she be surprised! He started racing at a fast clip. After a few steps, he halted headlong. He swung around to Monte.

"How much is scale?" he asked.

"Seventy a week," Monte said.

To sing in a Broadway night club and to make seventy simoleons a week! It did not seem possible. Riding home in the subway that night, Harry could not keep from breaking into song. He felt good. He did not really want to be a singer. He wanted to act. But as an expectant father, at least he was not without a job. That was important to him.

The initial one-week engagement at The Royal Roost was extended to two weeks, then to four weeks, and then it kept being renewed so that Harry remained at the bop jazz club for a total of twenty weeks.

Guesting for columnist Dorothy Kilgallen in the *Journal-American,* one of the owners of The Royal Roost, Ralph Watkins, wrote in July 1958: "To find new talent for The Roost, I devised a contest called Cinderella Night. It was held on Monday, the off night, and young hopefuls would come in to try for a chance at a week's booking. One night a lad came in who'd been doing odd jobs in the garment center, and he won a stanza. After the first week, he had his own following, so I decided to abandon the contest and keep Harry Belafonte on."

While he was still at The Roost, Harry made his first appearance at Carnegie Hall, almost ten years to a day before he gave several SRO one-man benefit shows at the home of New York's Philharmonic Symphony Society. Margurite came up for the occasion from Washington, uncertain about what Harry was doing at the show place of the longhairs.

To her surprise, what she attended was a jazz concert, then much more of a novelty than it is today. With amazement, she saw Harry, whose whole existence had seemed to hinge on his fulfillment as an actor, receive a plaque from the Negro newspaper *The Pittsburgh Courier* as "the vocal find of the year." Before she returned to Washington, Margurite paid her first visit to a New York night club, The Royal Roost, to hear her husband perform his nightly vocal stint. She was quite amused by Harry's apparent assurance as a performer and both overwhelmed and shocked by the circus atmosphere of the club. Afterward, she returned to Washington while Harry continued his nomadic existence in New York, sleeping occasionally at his mother's, at times at an uncle's, or at some friend's house. For Harry, it was a time of hope—confused hope—even if he was not doing exactly what he wanted to do and his wife lived in one city and he in another.

"His personality is appealing," *Down Beat* reported, "and his stage presence superior to many better established singers. Belafonte is a slim lad with a style similar to, but not an imitation of, Billy Eckstine's."

(In this comment, dated March 11, 1949, *Down Beat* stated that Harry was twenty-four years old. This would make his birthday two years earlier than that given in most official accounts.)

Before The Roost engagement was over, Monte Kay became Harry's first personal manager. He was joined in this enterprise by a tall, pretty, blonde publicist, Virginia Wicks. Together, Kay and Wicks sought to create an image of Harry as a jazz singer and, after a time, to enter him in the pop singing sweepstakes in which the handsome Mr. B. (Billy Eckstine) was then the lead horse.

While he was still at The Roost, Harry cut his first commercial record date. It was supervised by Kay and released on a Roost label. *Recognition* was on one side; *Lean On Me* was on the other. They were the two songs that Monte had first heard Harry "sing," that Harry had used at his audition at The Roost, and that were to be the mainstay of Harry's act for some time to come. Harry never was in a hurry to add new songs to his repertoire.

The Roost label was the worry of three partners. One was Monte. The second was Ralph Watkins, an owner of the club. Teddy Reig, currently a producer of jazz records for the Roulette label, was the third man.

A local New York disk jockey, Symphony Sid, played Harry's first record as if it were *The Star-Spangled Banner*. Almost 10,000 copies were reportedly sold in the New York area alone.

"Since New York is only about ten percent of the national record market," Monte has said, "we had a potential million copy seller on our hands. We just didn't know it. Harry didn't think the record was that good. Perhaps we didn't either."

In a recent interview over KRHM of Los Angeles, Harry discussed the significance of his engagement at The Roost, more specifically, the value of his singing to the accompaniment of a combo consisting of Miles Davis on trumpet, Bud Powell on piano, Tommy Potter on bass, Max Roach on drums, and Charlie (Bird) Parker on alto—in 1949, the pioneering elite of modern jazz.

"So powerful was the influence of the music they were playing," Harry told interviewer Paul Werth, "that I felt driven to a certain experimentation in that field. Only a small segment of the public was ready for it.

"Moreover, I became so subservient, tonally and musically, to what these cats were playing, there was very little room for concentration on lyrics or story. Rather than think of lyrics, I had to think exclusively in terms of the vocal gymnastics necessary to compete with the instruments. It was a valuable experiment but before long I knew that this was not my style."

As The Roost engagement drew to its inevitable close, Harry was on the prowl for an apartment in which to settle his wife and expected child. Adrienne Michele Belafonte was born on May 27, 1949 at Adams' Private Hospital in the city where Margurite had been born and raised. Baptized at the Holy Redeemer Catholic Church in Washington, D.C., she had as godparents publicist Virginia Wicks and Margurite's brother David. Adrienne remained in Washington with her grandparents even after her mother returned to New York in June to help Harry ready a place for her.

It was not easy to rent an apartment in Manhattan at this time—and even more difficult for a Negro family. Eventually Harry found a place in a block of old-line, five-story railroad

[61]

tenements on 156th Street, a few doors west of Amsterdam Avenue. It was an apartment in which he had stayed occasionally while Margurite awaited the arrival of their child in Washington. He took it over from one of his uncles, buying the secondhand furniture along with "the lease." Until Christmas 1953, when Harry purchased a two-story attached house in Elmhurst, not far from La Guardia Airport, the fourth-floor walk-up at 501 West 156th Street was to be home to him.

From June to September, when Adrienne was moved to New York, Harry and Margurite were busily occupied trying to make old furniture look new. Day after day they would take the old, chipped, and stained finish off chairs and tables, sandpaper down to the natural grain, then shellac and varnish and sandpaper and lacquer and paint. It took the summer, but together they redid the entire apartment. Came September, and the Belafonte family, including Adrienne, was together for the first time since Margurite and Harry's marriage more than a year earlier.

Margurite's mother, who brought their four-month-old child up from Washington, moved in with the couple, remaining with them until they moved to their own home in Elmhurst. Without someone to take care of Adrienne, Margurite could not return to her teaching job—and Margurite was to continue teaching for six years of their married life. Although Harry's finishing salary at The Royal Roost was almost three times his starting salary, there was no indication when he would secure another booking or for how long. The life of the new singer seemed to offer no more security than that of the actor.

STEREO

LUCKY MILLINDER

Because of the wartime shortage of musicians, Negro bandleader Lucky Millinder added white instrumentalists to his band.

"At one point," he said, "I had nine white and eight colored musicians. Of course, everybody in the band understood that we were out to make money, not trying to make history. In Southern towns, the white musicians would avoid walking around with their instruments in case the question came up whose band they were with, which could have led to trouble.

"We never had a major incident, though we came pretty close a couple of times—and we played many Southern towns where mixed performances were forbidden by law. In some towns, I knew the Chief of Police, which helped. Often the musicians would have to pass for Puerto Ricans.

"I remember one night, when I had a drummer who looked unmistakably Jewish, the cop kept asking questions while the band was playing. After the set, he walked up and looked the drummer straight in the eye for quite a while.

"Then he said, 'Yeh, he's a nigger all right,' and walked away satisfied."

6. The Cinderella Gentleman

The two-year period between Harry's debut at The Royal Roost and his walkout from The Five O'Clock Club of Miami represented a series of false starts that, in the end, brought him to a blank wall.

First, there was the contract with a major record company. Partly on the strength of the showing made by the Roost recording, Monte and Virginia were able to interest Capitol Records in Harry. Not as a jazz singer. Not as a folk singer. But simply as a pop vocalist. Capitol was then not so big or strong as it is now—but it boasted such hitmakers as Nat (King) Cole, Peggy Lee, Kay Starr, Les Paul and Mary Ford, and others. To young Harry Belafonte, it looked like an important and exciting step upward to be included in this company roster on a one-year contract.

Harry actually cut his first Capitol date on July 19, 1949, while Margurite and he were busily preparing their new apartment for Adrienne. Included in the date were a movie theme song *How Green Was My Valley*, a song called *Deep As the River*, and two standards: *They Didn't Believe Me* and *Close Your Eyes*.

His style was imitative of early Sinatra in the slowness of the tempi and of Billy Eckstine in the heaviness of the vibrato, particularly on low notes. Clearly, Harry was trying to find himself and, occasionally, some of the notes. None of the sides attracted very much attention—and deservedly so.

Six months later, on December 20, Capitol recorded four more selections with Harry. In addition to three pop standards *Farewell to Arms*, *Whispering*, and *I Still Feel a Thrill*, the date included one spiritual: *Sometimes I Feel Like a Mother-*

less Child. As with the previous four sides, however, neither the disk jockeys nor the public showed much enthusiasm. When Harry's contract came up for renewal, Capitol failed to exercise its option.

What might have been a fast ascent into the starry realm of the entertainment world was, thus, like a rocket that never left the ground.

Just about the time that Harry was cutting his second date for Capitol, Monte Kay was asked to produce a show for a new jazz spot. Irving Levy, the concessionaire at The Roost, had taken over the lease of a defunct night club, The Clique, at 52nd and Broadway, and renamed it in honor of the alto saxophonist destined to become the most influential figure of modern jazz, Charlie (Bird) Parker. In addition to inspiring the widely recorded jazz ballad *Lullaby of Birdland* by pianist George Shearing, Birdland went on to become the mecca of jazz fans the world over. Irving Levy, incidentally, was stabbed to death on its premises only recently.

The first show presented at the new Birdland was a two-hour Cavalcade of Jazz produced by Monte Kay. Employing a local disk jockey, William B. Williams, as narrator, Kay tried to tell the story of the growth of jazz from New Orleans Dixieland to New York bop. Different combos appeared to exemplify the different stages and types of jazz. Oran (Hot Lips) Page played original New Orleans style. Trumpeter Max Kaminsky offered samples of Chicago Dixieland. The late saxophonist Lester Young, nicknamed Pres by Billie Holiday because of his pre-eminence in the field, played his own original brand of cool tenor. Bop was brilliantly represented by Bird himself. Blind Lennie Tristano and his piano were on hand to display the most far-out type of cerebral jazz.

As part of the cavalcade, Harry Belafonte sang a number of standards. *Variety's* laconic comment: "On vocals Belafonte is okay, if not particularly standout on a brace of romantic ballads."

Indicative of Harry's inner gyrations—also of a direction that he later was to take—was a curious incident that occurred during the Birdland booking. One evening he asked Pee Wee

Marquette, the em cee, if he could sing a folk tune as an encore.

Pee Wee said "No." "The cash customers," he announced in his strident, high-pitched voice, "shell out bucks for bop *Pennies from Heaven.*"

The following evening two friends of Harry's came unannounced to the cellar club. One was Bill Attaway, a novelist with whose sister Ruth, Harry had studied acting. The other was a guitarist, Craig Work, with whom Harry occasionally ran over folk songs. Craig carried his guitar hidden under his coat while Bill Attaway ran interference and prevented the cashier, headwaiter, and others from spotting the concealed instrument. After Harry finished the last number of his set program, he signaled Craig, who moved up to the edge of the stage and began playing *A Rovin'.* (Harry was to record this folk ballad on his first RCA Victor date two years later.) As if he was reacting spontaneously, Harry joined in and sang the tune to Craig's accompaniment. The jazz audience was surprised, interested, but hardly overwhelmed.

During the following year, Kay and Wicks succeeded in booking Harry at a few New York clubs and a few out-of-town places. He was not spectacularly successful. Among the more extended appearances was a five-week stint at Café Society Downtown, located in New York's Greenwich Village. By this time, as is clear from a *Variety* review in May 1950, Harry's singing style had become more pop and less jazzy. *Variety* displayed somewhat more enthusiasm than it had in connection with the Birdland date. It praised Harry's "great sensitivity" in the handling of ballads, questioned his use of "wide variations" in rhythm numbers, and concluded that he was "still a vocalist of promise."

Jazz critic Barry Ulanov, author of the readable and colorful *History of Jazz in the United States,* was better impressed. "Harry greets his audience," he wrote in *Metronome,* "with a bolder stance and a more vigorous voice to go with it." He noted that Harry had changed his repertory, giving up the fight for recognition in favor of "a handsome selection of standards, *Skylark, Lover, Stardust, The Nearness of You.*" He ticketed Harry's taste, technique, and voice "in the groove known as cool," approved his languorous phrasing, and praised "some excellently managed *a capella* moments." But he found deficiencies in "some uncertain intonation and a tendency to hunch over the microphone."

In short, Harry's appearance at Café Society Downtown, successful though it was, did not make Billy Eckstine's vibrato catch in his throat.

Harry's unspectacular invasion of the entertainment world did not make things easy at home. It made no sense to Margurite that he earned 200 dollars a week for one month and then was unemployed for two. She did not like it that she had to spend her days watching over other people's children while her own child was being raised by someone else, even if it was her mother. With her family background and upbringing, she felt strongly that it was the man's responsibility to provide economic stability for the home and the woman's to be home to bring up the children.

Harry's attitude toward Negro-white relationships, which had caused so many arguments between him and Margurite, had not changed very much. A friend of these days, painter Matthew Feinman, recalls that when he played chess with Harry and arranged the chessmen at the beginning of the game, Harry would invariably say: "I'm taking the black— because they're better than the white. They're the best, man!"

During their courtship, arguments between Harry and Margurite over his hostility to whites had been lengthy discussions, in a sense, "abstract" discussions, sometimes with more heat, sometimes with less. Now, however, when the question arose of Harry's finding some more regular form of employment and providing a more stable domestic economy, their discussions took the shape of disagreements. Disagreements as to what made a home. Disagreements as to what a man did with his dreams. These disagreements were seldom even as heated as the arguments over his racial hostility. But the issues haunted the Belafonte household, particularly when Harry was not working, like the ghosts of Negro discrimination.

[67]

Nor did the presence of Margurite's mother in the Belafonte household ease the situation. Mrs. Byrd was not the type of woman who interfered. On the other hand, there was no question as to how she felt. Harry's friends of the period say that when they visited his fourth-floor walk-up in upper Harlem, Mrs. Byrd gave them only the most perfunctory recognition. She did not approve of Harry or his friends, and there was no mistaking her attitude toward either. For his part, it is reported that, in all the time she lived with them, Harry could never get himself to call her "Ma," "Mom," or "Mother." It was always "Mrs. Byrd." Since the divorce from Margurite, Harry refers to her as "Nanna," because that's what Adrienne and Shari call their maternal grandmother.

Mrs. Byrd's rejection of her son-in-law, and his inability to accept her, was an unfortunate thing. Harry had a tremendous need to be accepted, to be loved, not only at this time but for many, many years to come. At one point in his life, he was to call his psychiatrist, a woman, "Mom," and her manager-husband "Dad" just as, more recently, he was drawn to the girl who became his second wife partly because of the warmth with which he was received by her parents. Mrs. Byrd's failure to accept her son-in-law deprived his first marriage of a vital cement.

A basic source of tension between Mrs. Byrd and her son-in-law was, of course, his lack of a college education. This is not too difficult to understand. Harry was an uneducated man —he had not completed high school—married to a very educated woman, while all Mrs. Byrd's children held respected positions in the academic world. Even if Harry had been immediately successful as an actor or as a singer and even if he had been able to provide for his family, Mrs. Byrd would not have regarded his achievement too happily. This outlook was not unique with Harry's mother-in-law. It is characteristic of the feeling that Negroes have even today about members of their race who become teachers or enter any profession requiring college training. The truth is that when Harry later wanted to divorce Margurite, he found it more difficult to explain his action to his people precisely because she is a teacher.

[68]

Harry himself had long been sensitive about his lack of college education. Mrs. Byrd's attitude—and the fact that all his brothers-in-law and sisters-in-law held college degrees—only intensified this sensitivity. For years afterward, while on a night club floor, he would find some moment to say: "I am reminded at this time of something one of my profs at Hampton told me . . ." It was a long time before he could drop this pretense.

A close friend of these troubled days was Sidney Poitier, whose early life paralleled Harry's in so many ways. The two had met for the first time at the American Negro Theatre, where Sidney had come in response to an "Actors Wanted" ad that appeared in *The Amsterdam News*. Up to that time, as was the case with Harry, Poitier had never seen a play. Less schooled even than Harry, he could read only haltingly. Moreover, he had a pronounced West Indian accent, which seemed to emphasize his other limitations. Rejected by the directors of ANT, Poitier went into a self-training period directed mainly at increasing his fluency and eliminating the accent. By day, he pushed a dress dolly in the garment district, as Harry almost did at a later date. Evenings, Poitier glued his ears to a cheap radio and sat for hours repeating words, phrases, sentences.

Accepted on his second trial, Poitier provided janitorial services to ANT in the Harlem high school where the group's acting classes were held. When the student group was casting *Days of Our Youth*, Poitier requested the understudy role assigned to a fellow student—Harry Belafonte. Poitier knew that Harry would have to miss some rehearsals because of an outside job.

Between jobs, Harry and Sidney, who had become close friends, leaned heavily on each other. "We'd split unemployment checks and theatre tickets," Harry recalls. "Sometimes, when we could only wangle one theatre ticket, we'd take turns. One of us would see the first act, come out with the stub and a synopsis. The other would go in for the second act, and so on."

While Harry was struggling, with the help of Kay and

Wicks, to "make it" as a pop singer, Poitier came up with the idea of their joining forces. It was to be "Belafonte and Poitier" in a night club routine emphasizing comedy, fast repartee, and buffoonery.

"We worked out every day on the roof of my building on 156th Street," Harry reports. "We'd try out things. Lose our tempers when they wouldn't work. Start over again with a fresh idea and then have it blow up in our faces. After a frustrating period of rehearsals, we decided that friends we would always be. But our talents really didn't lie in the comedy direction. We were both out of our element."

Apparently the decision was a sound one for both as the future was to prove for each. During this period, Poitier's imagination also took a very practical turn. Having discovered the insecurities of the acting trade, Sidney kept coming up with schemes designed to provide solvency during jobless stretches. At one time he came to Harry with a scheme for going into business in the West Indies.

"The idea," Harry explained, "was to harvest a certain kind of conch—a big shellfish—and to extract all the proteins and calories and bottle the juice to sell as a body-builder. It sounded fine. But what with the bottling costs, the Federal food laws, this, that and the other, it could not be worked profitably."

This turn of thought would suggest that Harry was not unconcerned or untroubled by the imbalance between Margurite and himself over his employment situation. It perhaps indicates why—lark that The Sage venture was to be for Harry—he considered going into the restaurant business at all after the Miami fiasco.

Altogether, Harry's association with Kay and Wicks endured for the better part of two years. All through the period, neither of Harry's co-managers had the feeling that Harry had found himself or that he was committed to what he was doing.

"He functioned as a jazz singer of the day's pop songs," Monte told me recently, "because he felt that that role might eventually bring him to what he really wanted deep down to do—act. The truth is Harry did not consider himself a singer. More important: his singing lacked the passion and the dramatic intensity that he later contributed to folk singing.

"That's the strange thing about Belafonte. He had the stamp of the true artist even then. He had to believe what he was singing. Otherwise, his work as an interpreter suffered. The fact is that the lyrics of most pop songs bothered him. He thought they were saccharine and insipid, and that they exploited the feelings of immature women.

"His concern with the lyrics of songs made him a kind of odd ball among music people. The jazz set was concerned mainly with melody and with melodic variation—breaking notes, manipulating rhythms, adding intriguing licks and countermelodies. They just accepted the lyrics of songs as something that was there. Pop singers, too, did not make too much of a fuss about the words.

"Not Harry! He was lyric conscious. He was intent about what the words said. Whether they said something with sincerity and with truth. Because most pop songs impressed him as phony in sentiment and cliché in expression, he could not give of himself—completely, intensely, dramatically—as he later did with folk ballads.

"Incidentally, he talked occasionally even then about the directness and truth of such folk ballads as he knew. I don't think he knew too many. Nor did he have any idea that he was going to turn to folk singing. He was just marking time, as I see it, until he reached his true goal—acting.

"Truthfully, neither Virginia nor I were surprised at what happened in Miami. Sure he was doing well. Making a comfortable three to four bills a week. And the women fans were going for him in a big way. But we both thought it was just a matter of time when he would throw his hands in the air and say 'I'm through!' "

Today the public image of Belafonte is of an extremely emotional singer—a man whose voice is charged with explosive feelings, who gestures dramatically, and who projects with tremendous power. That's Belafonte the folk singer.

In the years in which he sang pop songs, the Gob with a

Throb—as his billing read—wore a mustache, a tuxedo, a soulful expression, and sometimes sat on a high stool. His voice was rather high-pitched and somewhat thin.

"But he had a sound even then," Monte Kay has said. "He had the mark of an up-and-coming singing star. Identity! Identity of sound! It was just a matter of developing other qualities. Study and experience would do that."

In retrospect, Harry has described his pop singing days as follows: "I stood stiff with my hands folded over my abdomen, so to speak. I sang to the ladies—one mushy love song after another. I couldn't get worked up over any of it, except how unreal the lyrics were. I'd sing my four or five little pop ditties, take my little bow, and run off backstage and—ha!—look in the mirror and ask who was I kidding. My most notable achievement was that I cut my first record of the first song I ever wrote—and it sounded like Rin-Tin-Tin with a head cold . . ."

"Harry was a nothing singer then," a close friend has said. "He had no style, no delivery, no nothing. His idea was to sit on a stool, with his hands folded in his lap, his Christopher medal hanging down in front, and try to look moody and soulful or something."

Another associate of this period offers the following picture of Harry: "He was always late for bookings or rehearsals, but he'd always have some excuse. It was like dealing with a child, one who was bright, charming, but undependable.

"The minute he'd get his hands on some money, it would just disappear. He'd then show up in an expensive overcoat or a cashmere sweater. He just didn't know how to handle money and there were constant hang-ups.

"Once he told a reporter he was on his way to Hollywood to test for a picture . . . Of course, there was no picture and he had to be taken off the hook. Harry could win you over with a big 'I've been a bad boy' smile and you'd think to yourself, 'Oh, the big kid,' shrug your shoulders, and forget whatever he had pulled."

Harry looks back on this period without any satisfaction. "In 1948 I switched to singing," he has said, "and accepted a two hundred-dollar-a-week engagement in the now defunct

Royal Roost on Broadway. A salary like two hundred dollars looked big to me then, and probably sounds like a lot of money to many people today, but it didn't do much for me and my family then. Between paying for managers, a press agent, I found myself in debt constantly. There were times when I thought I couldn't keep going. There were other times, under critical prodding, I contemplated quitting show business and finding steady security in the form of an eight-to-five job."

Martha Raye's Five O'Clock Club in Miami proved the breaking point. It was Christmas 1950, and Harry took off the tuxedo in which he sang jazz and pop songs for good. Returning to New York, he was elated that he had given up what he regarded as a phony role. But—*Where to now? And to what?*

STEREO

MILT HINTON

For many years, Milt Hinton, bassist from Vicksburg, Mississippi, toured with the Cab Calloway band. At Fort Lauderdale, Florida, band members ran into some Northern people on vacation and some Northern musicians who knew them from the Cotton Club in Harlem.

"Both the people who used to know us from the Cotton Club," Hinton reports, "and those Northern white musicians would talk to us between sets. But the Southern people would resent it. Sometimes it would be so bad at intermission we couldn't get off the stand for a drink of water unless we had a police escort. I remember it. There were two police in front and two behind, and we had to walk through the dance hall that way just to get a drink of water. And you know they would poke at us through the police! So you can see we didn't feel like playing much. After intermission we always had a tough time because the drinking had started and the insults got worse."

[73]

7. The Sage

The year was 1950. The place was Greenwich Village, that maze of Manhattan streets west of Fourth Avenue and east of Ninth, south of 14th Street and north of Houston, where striving, young, penniless artists and writers still gravitate and where, as in any Bohemia, life is wilder, morals are freer, clothes are crazier—in short, people live creatively (read crazily) while they wait for their creative talents to be recognized.

Three young men stood talking on a street corner. To be precise, it was the corner where Seventh Avenue South meets four other vagrant streets, among them Fourth, Grove, and Christopher. The three had just emerged from a cafeteria where the coffee cups are brushed by more and different kinds of hirsute adornments than one might have found in a nineteenth-century beerstube. The three were clean-shaven. They were all broke. They had met by chance. They had had coffee. And now they were talking about a vacant store just off the corner on the east and south side of the intersection.

As hungry (for food) and hungering (after fame) young men will do, they were speculating about what would happen if the three of them joined forces and opened a restaurant. At least they could all eat! That appealed to them and handed them a laugh. Then they decided that, with the problem of subsistence solved, each could be more selective about what he really wanted to do—Bill Attaway, a Negro novelist, about his writing; Ferman Phillips, a developing Negro actor, about his acting; and Harry Belafonte, a reluctant singer who wanted to act, about his acting.

That's how a hamburger-hash joint called The Sage came

[74]

to open its doors in Greenwich Village one morning around Christmas of 1950. The original proprietors were Attaway and Phillips. On his return to New York after the Miami fiasco Harry joined the two.

At the Sage, over short orders, crazy talk and much horseplay, Belafonte the ballad singer was born.

Of the three proprietors, Harry was in 1951 the least advanced in his chosen career. Bill Attaway already had three published novels to his credit—including *Let Me Breathe Thunder* and *Blood on the Forge*. Eight years later (in 1959) Ferman Phillips, who had already gained some acceptance as an actor, was to serve as Harry's stand-in in his independently produced film *The World, The Flesh and The Devil* and to play a minor character in Harry's second independent film *Odds Against Tomorrow.*

Few things about The Sage were not accidental. Even the name was an accident. When the original proprietors went to a sign maker to get the cheapest sign he could devise, they found that he had four letters remaining from a previous job. Attaway and Phillips had their choice of EGAS, GASE, AGES, or SAGE. They picked the last-mentioned, although history was to prove that none of them was—when it came to running a restaurant.

The Sage was a hole in the wall, "a little greasy spoon joint." Counter stools and a few tables accommodated a total of a dozen customers at one sitting. Ferman, the actor, took care of the décor. Attaway, the writer, composed the menus.

"I," says Harry, "why I just sort of charmed the customers when the hamburgers came out burned."

Each of the partners worked an overlapping twelve-hour shift so that The Sage remained open close to twenty-four hours a day. As in most one-arm joints, the cooking was done directly in front of the window. Writer Attaway slung the hash more frequently than singer Belafonte, who did more of the waiting. The clientele consisted of a select group of indigent Village-ites, jazz musicians, dope addicts, theatre people, alcoholics, folk singers, and hoods.

During Harry's Birdland days, he had hung out at a short-order restaurant known as the Bird-in-Hand. Located on the west side of Broadway between 51st and 52nd, it was a kind of auxiliary to the uptown Lindy's on the corner opposite the Capitol Theatre. Bird-in-Hand catered to the hopefuls of the entertainment world as Lindy's played host to the successfuls.

When the uptown crowd learned of Harry's restaurant, they began coming down to the Village. A group would line up on the stools, order as little as they could, and proceed to ride him. There would be complaints about the food, sneers about the service, and gibes at the waiter.

"Hey! You, with the beady eyes!"

"Wanna pick up your feet, man, along with that cup of coffee?"

After a few brushes with the invaders, Harry and his partners devised a counteroffensive. No matter what the provocation, Harry would take each gibe and every complaint with a complete dead pan. In turn, the uptown crowd tried harder and harder to get a rise out of him. The net result of the horseplay, as the partners hoped, was increased business for The Sage.

Harry's only comment on the part he had to play: "Once you're in show business, you just can't get out! This is my biggest role to date."

Harry was not averse to turning the tables on his own partners occasionally. One evening Tony Scott, the jazz clarinetist, who had gotten to know Harry rather well during his Roost booking, came into The Sage. Since he was playing at Café Society, just around the corner, Scott was dressed in a tux. Bill Attaway, who was at the griddle, took one look at the swell and did an instantaneous burn.

Scott had already had his dinner, so he proceeded to order a cup of coffee. It came up lukewarm. Tony was surprised, not that it was, but that The Sage proprietors had learned so quickly. (Give a customer a cup of hot coffee and he sits there warming a needed seat. A cool cup promotes turnover.)

He called to Harry, who had delivered the cup. Harry came over. But before Scott could complain, Harry was off to another customer. For the next half hour, Scott sat nursing the one cup while he ostensibly tried to gain Harry's attention.

[76]

Every time Harry passed, he passed some crack. Harry ignored them and him. But Attaway, who had had his eye on the seat that Scott was monopolizing, kept growing hotter.

Harry fed the flame. "He's not bothering me too much," he would say to Bill.

The next time Harry passed Scott, the clarinetist raised his voice so that Attaway could hear the gibe. Bill dropped his spatula on the hot griddle and made for Scott. He was reaching for Tony to toss him out of the shop when Harry intervened.

"Throw the bum out," Harry laughed. "But don't hurt his hands. That's the best jazz clarinetist in the country."

Only then did Attaway realize that Harry had been working with Tony to provoke him.

Weekdays The Sage closed its doors at two o'clock in the morning. For several hours thereafter, it became a rehearsal hall, whose cramped confines echoed with the improvised songs of a male chorus. Soloist and conductor of the chorus was Harry. Basic personnel: the waiters, who sometimes had to wait for their weekly pay from The Sage and some of whom are now part of the Belafonte Singers. Many a Villager returning home in the early hours of the morning must have done a double-take to see all the counter stools of The Sage occupied and a tall, handsome Negro leading the occupants in song. Sometimes, a late passer-by, thirsting for a cup of java, would rap at the door.

"Can you sing bass?" Harry would ask the surprised customer—depending on whether the chorus of that night needed basses or tenors.

If the passer-by had the right voice, he got the java and a chance to sing. Otherwise, he was told that The Sage was closed for the night—and Harry went back to his chorus.

Greenwich Village has always had a strong folk tradition. As a haven for indigent artists and writers, and as a Bohemia that prizes freedom of expression and behavior, the Village has always emphasized values that are characteristically folk in nature. Even today, you can wander down to Washington Square Park on a Sunday—and there clustered around a circular wading pool are hundreds of youngsters raucously chanting folk tunes. Mixed in among the singers are guitar pickers, bass players, and sometimes musicians with improvised instruments, all of whom provide spontaneous accompaniment.

The Village, as well as the characters who stopped at The Sage for "yeats," helped to deepen Harry's developing interest in folklore. Harry occupied himself buying every folk record he could find. Weekends he would hop down to Washington and dig through the archives of the Library of Congress.

"When Harry came back from those trips," Bill Attaway reports, "we would spend two or three days at the place working out arrangements. I'd help rewrite the words. Millard, or his pupil Craig Work, would tinker with the melody. During these periods, we'd get darn little sleep.

"Audiences are good for a performer. But there are times when a man needs the relaxed atmosphere when no audience is breathing down his throat. Then he has a chance to experiment and learn. Harry tried out lots of things for the first time at The Sage. And he sure did a lot of learning and experimenting. We all did."

One of the things they learned was that Harry was not only handsome, but that he had tremendous appeal to the ladies. It happened one evening when there was no choral singing and Harry and Bill were cleaning up the place after they had closed the door. Harry had the jukebox playing, and he was improvising some dance steps, using a mop handle as his partner.

Two girls came by and tapped on the window. Harry went to the door and explained that the place was closed. Both girls could hardly stand. They pleaded for black coffee. Harry relented. Sitting at the counter and savoring their coffee, they half watched Harry as he danced with his mop. After a while, Harry motioned to one of the girls. She slid off her counter stool and did a few turns with him. Harry returned her to her perch and resumed mopping.

Suddenly, the other girl began sobbing. Within seconds, the sobs lengthened into unmistakable wails. The other girl patted her friend's back and tried to calm her. But the tears rolled.

"Why won't he dance with me?" the girl cried.

[78]

Not until Harry took the girl into his arms for a few wobbly turns around the cramped floor did she quiet down.

Perhaps the most obvious thing that The Sage proprietors learned was that you can't run a business without proper financing. It was a discovery that was quick in coming. Since the three partners had started with virtually no capital, they were unable to buy many of their staples from wholesale houses. Fantastic as it may sound, it was the neighborhood A & P that furnished much of their supplies. In that way, they could purchase as money came into the till. The fact that they were turning over their meager profits to the A & P was something in the nature of higher mathematics to them.

Before long, it was the first customer of the day who supplied the capital—on a short-term loan—that kept the place going. Soon they were writing checks, which friendly cashiers were asked to hold.

"Some of them," Bill Attaway has said, "just kept holding them and holding them. Why, for several years after The Sage folded, Harry or I would run into somebody with an uncashed check. We paid on every one."

Week by week it became harder to meet their small payroll. One Monday the waiters and certain other creditors were so far behind that Harry had to go back to the bank and draw out every cent he had in a savings account.

"I think it was his last money," Bill Attaway mused. "Man, he was sure a nervy guy. He just didn't know where or when he'd ever see the dough again. But he did it. And he didn't complain either."

In the midst of all their difficulties, a friend of Harry's, Morty Freeman, decided that he had to make a trip to Israel. According to Bill Attaway, Morty, who is a cantor in the Jewish faith, is the man who acquainted Harry with *Hava Nageela*, and other Israeli folk songs. Freeman, who had a good voice, also had a far-ranging familiarity with the folk music of many countries, and he was a mainstay of The Sage chorale.

When Harry learned that Morty Freeman did not have enough money to make his trip, he and Attaway cooked up a party. The well-fixed proprietors of The Sage contributed six hams gratis.

"We cut the stuff so thin, you could see through it," Bill laughed. "We charged seventy-five cents a sandwich. At the end of a long night, we had close to seven hundred dollars. Even though The Sage could have paid a lot of back bills with the money, Harry insisted that we give it all to Morty. So he had his trip abroad. Incidentally, we tried to run several parties to save The Sage. Practically nobody showed up."

The partners were more successful in raising rent money by playing poker. It was not difficult to locate one of the city's many floating card games. Harry and Bill would enter the game on Saturday afternoon. Their figure was that, by then, some of the players who had begun with the game on Friday night would be tired. Easy marks for Attaway and Belafonte who were fresh! It worked some weekends. Playing through Saturday night into Sunday, the two managed to win enough to keep The Sage going. There were weekends when Harry went directly from poker to the baseball game in which he always played on Sunday morning.

When poker failed them, a girl named Ann Mayrson, who ate breakfast at The Sage, came to their rescue. Ann had worked for *Time* Magazine for years. She was on the verge of quitting to open a store in the Village. Her severance pay was to provide the capital for what became known as The Basket Bazaar, which is still to be found on West Third Street. Part of the severance pay, however, went to The Sage at one of its more critical moments in a life of continuing crises.

In the sixth month of The Sage's existence, it was the Consolidated Edison Company that brought matters to a head. Suddenly, the owners of The Sage were faced with a demand for a five-hundred-dollar deposit. Consolidated claimed that they were using more gas than the Waldorf—hotel, not cafeteria. Then they were hit with a bill for back unemployment insurance taxes, which they had neglected to deduct and pay.

For the next two months, while they struggled to keep the place going, Attaway and Belafonte hunted for a buyer. They did not know from day to day whether they could open the following morning. This was the period when the first diner in was out of luck if he had any cash on him. Between Attaway's formidable arguments and Belafonte's charm, it was a

[80]

hard-hearted customer, indeed, who avoided paying for his morning cup of coffee with a loan. In the meantime, the search for a buyer continued. What with running the restaurant and hunting an out, Attaway and Belafonte went with little sleep for months. By then, the third owner of The Sage had left the place to them.

When they finally found somebody who would pay enough for the key to cover Ann Mayrson's loan plus some other debts, Attaway and Belafonte signed the bill of sale. They themselves received nothing and left with nothing. They simply handed the key over to the new owner, who was to rename the place Simple Simon, and, knowing that Ann Mayrson would get her money, walked off whistling. Eight months after the hopeful beginning in December 1950, the crazy experiment was over. It cost Harry 2,000 dollars, a large amount considering the state of his finances, but a small one considering what his newly found interest in folk singing was to bring him.

"I remember Harry," Bill Attaway has said, in reminiscing about The Sage, "as a guy of tremendous fortitude. During all those months when we were loaded down with debts and the ultimate crash seemed inevitable, Harry never once asked out. He could have—you know. It was Ferman Phillips and I that started the place. And after Phillips left, Harry could have done likewise. But he stayed to the end, working around the clock and without any bellyaching. The one thing that bugged him was Ann Mayrson's loan. Once we had a buyer who was willing to cover that, Harry was willing to let go.

"Well, maybe not willing. You see, the restaurant made a lot of sense to Margurite. I think that Harry went into it in part to please her. She hoped that eventually he would return to his studies and take up some profession. But even running a restaurant made more sense to her than being a struggling actor or singer. I believe that Harry wanted to prove that he could do it, that he could be a successful businessman.

"I don't think that he anticipated that The Sage would become a folk song laboratory for him—as it did. And I'm not even sure that Margurite had any inkling of what went on at night after we closed the doors."

Margurite Belafonte admits that she visited The Sage only

two or three times during Harry's eight months' proprietorship. And she stayed only a few moments, just to pick up Harry when they were going out or home.

"I had the feeling that he did not want me there," she says. "He didn't think it was the right kind of environment for me. That was how I interpreted it."

Of The Sage, Harry has said: "It was a tremendous experience. It was an informal place, and people—characters—would drop in just to sit and talk. The atmosphere was like Saroyan's saloon in *The Time of Your Life*. Maybe the food wasn't too good. But the talk was. And there was warmth. There was excitement. There was confusion. But there was hope."

The Sage was, in short, the kind of place where a man could vegetate or find himself. Harry did the latter—with the help of the many characters who dropped in; under the stimulus of the nightly song fests; through his research in the folk song field; but most of all, as a result of the friendship and collaboration of a man who dropped in for a cup of coffee and stayed to become Harry's second manager.

STEREO

BILL ROBINSON

At a benefit one night, Bill Robinson was introduced as "one of the great Negro dancers of all time." Everyone applauded vigorously, except comedian Joe E. Lewis.

"Why do you call Bill one of the great *Negro* dancers?" Joe later asked the master of ceremonies. "Would you introduce Fred Astaire as one of the great white dancers of all time? I don't know whether Bill's black or white. All I know is that he's great!"

BELAFONTE

Two Recent Studies by Photographer
Eugene Cook

Above: During filming of "Odds Against
Tomorrow"

ght: During a performance

Harry shortly after the war

A Youthful Sailor—Harry before his first marriage (about 1944)

THE YOUNG UNKNOWN

Harry and Margurite Belafonte on their wedding day, June 18, 1948

(Photos on these two pag

HARRY BELAFONTE

Summer, 1948—
Honeymoon days at
Beaver Lodge, Pennsylvania,
where Harry worked on the
entertainment staff

courtesy of Margurite Belafonte)

Meeting of first Harry Belafonte Fan Club. Harry holds baby Adrienne. (Photo courtesy of Margurite Belafonte)

Left: Harry proudly displays to two-year-old son David his 5-lb. bass caught in Lake Mead, during a singing engagement at the Hotel Riviera, Las Vegas, Nev. (Courtesy, United Press International, Inc.)

Proud young father with first born daughter Adrienne. (Photo courtesy of Margurite Belafonte)

BELAFONTE—
FAMILY MAN

Below: Harry, baby Shari, Margurite and Adrienne in their East Elmhurst home (N. Y. Daily News Photo)

ALWAYS THE LOVING FATHER

Above: Harry greets baby Shari during rehearsal break at Riviera Hotel, Las Vegas, Nev. (Photos on this page by D. C. Gunn, Las Vegas)

Below: Frolicking with his look-so-much-alike daughter Adrienne, Hotel Riviera, Las Vegas, Nev.

Above: Shari and Adrienne with Harry in the Nevada sunshine during a singing engagement at the Hotel Riviera. (Photo by D. C. Gunn, Las Vegas)

Right: Little Shari and Adrienne about the time Belafonte's marriage to Margurite came to its end. Adrienne was a very unhappy child during that period. (Photo by Wm. Bowles, courtesy of Margurite Belafonte)

Right: Photographer Archie Lieberman took this charming picture of Harry and Adrienne (Courtesy, Black Star)

Julie and Harry Belafonte pay a visit to Shelley Winters on a movie set. (Photo, courtesy Culver Service)

Above: Jan. 31, 1957—Merle Oberon, Joan Collins and James Mason congratulate Harry after his Cocoanut Grove opening in Hollywood

Left: Jan., 1957—Harry shows his Annual Brotherhood Award of the National Conference of Christians and Jews (the first Negro so honored) to producer Jack Warner, who received his award for distinguished civic service from the Conference

(Photos on this page courtesy of Wide World Photos, Inc.)

A recent publicity picture of beautiful Margurite Belafonte. She devotes much time to the organization of benefits and lecturing for the NAACP

A family songfest. (Photo by Martha Holmes)

BELAFONTE,
MOTION
PICTURE
ACTOR

Above: 1954, scene from "Carmen Jones" with Dorothy Dandridge, 20th Century-Fox film

Left: 1957, with Joan Fontaine in "Island in the Sun," 20th Century-Fox film

THE ACTOR-PRODUCER

Clowning with young fans on location for film "Odds Against Tomorrow" which Harry produced

A scene from "Odds Against Tomorrow" with actors Ed Begley and Robert Ryan

(Eugene Cook Photos)

THE DEDICATED
RECORDING
ARTIST

(Photos courtesy
of RCA Victor)

L. Below: With pianist Bob Haring, Jr.

R. Below: With Bob Corman, musical director.

BELAFONTE
AT EASE

(Wide World Photos,

Above: April, 1958—Harry with wife Julie at a press conference, Hotel Plaza-Athenee, Paris (Wide World Photos, Inc.)

Above: Sept. 11, 1958—Harry and Julie celebrate at Maxim's in Paris after his first French performance (Wide World Photos, Inc.)

Right; Aug., 1958—Harry, Julie and baby David on arrival at Nice for a brief vacation (Courtesy, United Press International, Inc.)

BELAFONTE,
ENCHANTING
WEAVER
OF SONGS

(Photographer Eugene
Cook took these action
shots)

8. Like Brothers

Jack Rollins was an assistant to Max Gordon, the theatrical producer, when he decided to dedicate himself to Harry's career. Jack was the most influential person to emerge out of the Sage period, but he was nevertheless only one of many who contributed to Harry's development as an artist and, more specifically, to his evolution as a folk singer.

In addition to Bill Attaway, who became Harry's collaborator on many folk adaptations, wrote scripts and record album liners for him, and who remains a devoted friend even to the present, there was Morty Freeman, the Jewish cantor, guitarist Millard Thomas, who became Harry's permanent accompanist, and jazz clarinetist Tony Scott, who later became Harry's musical arranger and conductor.

During the Sage days, Scott had a bachelor apartment on Jones Street in the Village. It was from this apartment that the crowd embarked for the Sunday baseball games and to this apartment that everybody returned to sing, dance, and party into the wee hours of Monday morning. In some strange way, Tony and Harry were temperamentally right for each other, particularly when it came to horseplay.

The baseball games were played at the boat basin on 79th Street and the Hudson River. Since the pickup teams included some of the emancipated Village females, no one took the games too seriously. They were for fun and horseplay. Few participants enjoyed them as much as Tony and Harry, or worked harder at getting laughs.

Tony recalls one game when a batter hit a fast ball straight over Harry's head. Harry was playing shortstop. The ball traveled like a shot. Nobody saw it after it left the bat, least of all Harry Belafonte. But Harry leaped high into the air, acted as if he was losing his balance, managed to right himself and, as he came down to the ground, threw the ball underhand to Tony at first. Tony dove for the ball as the runner streaked toward him. Somehow, he managed to get it, and to dash back to first in time for the umpire to call "Out!" Not until the next batter stepped up to the plate and a mystified pitcher signaled for the ball did anybody realize that the entire play had been a spontaneous dumb show improvised by Harry and Tony. Neither had had even the faintest contact with the ball, which lay somewhere in the outfield.

Harry never missed a Sunday game, no matter how late he played poker on Saturday or The Sage remained open. He seemed to have an inexhaustible reservoir of energy. Tony occasionally stayed away if he worked on Saturday. It meant getting off a job at 4:00 A.M. and, by the time he snacked and simmered down, turning in after 6:00 A.M. Then the word went out to the players that Tony was not to be disturbed.

One Sunday Harry came charging into the Scott apartment. Everybody tried to shush him. "Tony just went to bed!" Harry paid no mind. He headed directly for the bedroom. Without knocking, he pushed the door open and plumped down on Tony's bed. The groggy clarinetist tore his eyes open. He had just fallen asleep.

"Wake up, Tony," Harry commanded. "I've just found the woman for you."

"What in hell!" Tony was no more interested in *the woman* at that hour than in dancing.

"I mean it," Harry said. "I've found the woman for you."

"Lemme alone, Harry. I need sleep, not a woman."

"Wait till you see her." Harry loved to tease.

"I'll wait," Tony sighed, and turned over. "Some day when I'm awake, bring her around."

"She's here—now. She's gonna play ball with us."

"I'm not for jokes this early," Tony growled.

"No joke, man," Harry gibed. "She's in the kitchen. Look!"

The bedroom door was slightly ajar. To satisfy Harry—and to get back to sleep—Tony leaned over to see what he could see through the dim crack. It was a remarkable moment.

"I fell in love with Fran," Tony has said, "in that one glance —just seeing her through that door crack."

But to Harry, Tony burped: "I've seen better heads on cabbages." But he began getting out of bed. "Where'd you find her?" Tony asked.

"In The Sage," Harry said. "After I talked with her twice, man, I knew she was the woman for you."

Fran was—and still is the woman—for Tony. Several years later, when Tony became Harry's conductor, Fran traveled with them and acted as Harry's personal secretary.

"Even in those days," Tony has said, "Harry was the center of things. People depended on him for laughs, for thrills, for excitement, for strength. Not the least amazing thing was his energy. Sheer energy. With him, it always was: 'Who can wear whom out?' And he could generally wear anybody out. He just had loads of energy. And when I say it, you can believe it. Because I can go too."

After the Jones Street apartment, Tony rented a loft at 61 Fourth Avenue, into which Fran and he moved, and which became the hangout of The Sage gang. Here, in two thousand square feet of virtually open space, the song fests and the round-the-clock parties continued.

Below Tony's loft there lived a sculptor, Charles Salerno. His mallet and chisel played a strange counterpoint to Tony's jazz solos. In any event, between the two neighbors, Salerno chopping away at his stone and Scott wailing on clarinet or flute, the Fourth Avenue address was hardly as quiet as a tomb. Nevertheless, Tony recalls that the only time Salerno objected to the noise above him was when Harry and he were trying to work up a number.

It was a folklike spiritual, which involved a solo singer like a preacher leading a congregation. Harry would sing "A Man Ain't Nothin' But a Man," and Scott would act as the echoing chorus. The piece unfolded slowly. When Harry works at something, he likes to go back to the beginning each time. As the number developed line by line, Tony and he kept wandering about the loft, repeating over and over: "A Man Ain't Nothin' But a Man." Meanwhile, Salerno's chisel could be

[85]

heard chipping away. After several hours, suddenly Harry and Tony heard the thump of a broom handle against their floor. For a few moments, they continued singing, uncertain of where the thumps came from or meant. Then it dawned on both of them that Salerno was objecting to their singing.

Later, Salerno told Scott: "I just couldn't stand that voice any longer."

"But there was more than one voice," Tony said. "I was singing too."

"I heard only one," Salerno replied. "And it was not yours. It was strong and full of protest. After a time, it stirred me up so I could hardly go on with my work. I had to protest too."

Although Tony was himself a dedicated jazzman—by 1956 he was recognized as the country's number one clarinetist in trade paper polls—he dug Harry's Sage experiments with folk music. He felt that Harry responded to folk material in a way that he had never responded to pop songs.

The more Harry studied folk song literature, the more enthralled he became. Here, for the first time, were songs that a man could sing with sincerity, with conviction, with feeling. A certain number of successful folk singers had the public's ear at the time. But men like Burl Ives and Richard Dyer-Bennett exploited the archaic beauty of folk tunes. A group like The Weavers emphasized the rollicking lustiness of early American folk songs. Josh White, who occasionally reached into Negro folklore, sang with greater tension but was basically concerned with the visual image he made of himself as a handsome, statuesque bronze. There was no one who dramatized the old folk ballads and responded to them with fire, with excitement, with passion. This was to be the special contribution of Harry Belafonte.

"By the very nature of what folk music is," Harry has said, "you can't or shouldn't treat it in a precious, dull, or cool way. The historical significance of it, the personalities involved, make it dramatic."

Intuitively, Harry determined not to be his own guitarist, as was the case with Ives, Dyer-Bennett, and Josh White. He wanted his hands free to project and exploit the dramatic content of the songs. "I'm a visual singer," Harry has said, "and I never sound as well on records as I do in person."

"When I was a jazz singer," Harry said at the time, "I found that I had nothing to contribute to the field. I couldn't function in it. And my particular function is what I am looking for. In folk music, on the other hand, I can use my voice and my dramatic training and do something for which I've always had much admiration."

Thoughtfully, Harry added: "Going into folk music was originally a study of tradition, of my own people's tradition, an attempt to find a culture in which I could learn and the structure within which I could function successfully."

In all this study and exploration, Harry's newly found associate, Jack Rollins, played a vital and analytical role. By some stroke of good fortune, much of Rollins' own background was in the theatre, and he saw dramatic potentialities in Belafonte, of which Harry could not have been then aware.

What Rollins found when he first began working with Harry was, quite naturally, a singer who was trying to imitate the popular folk singers of the day—Burl Ives, Pete Seeger, Josh White. Rollins' first aim was to help Harry discover a style that was natural to him and expressive of himself. To accomplish this, he rented a small rehearsal studio above the Lyceum Theatre on West 45th Street—and he and Harry shuttled between here and the Music Library on East 58th Street. For a period of five months, according to Rollins, they went over material at the library and then rehearsed it for days at the studio.

"He was a static singer when I first met him," Rollins claims. "I taught him how to move about and make contact with his audience. I taught him the meaning of diction and the power of phrasing. I took him and his folk music, tied them up with a pretty pink ribbon, and made a commercial package of them."

Jimmy Komack, the young songwriter-comedian who starred in *Damn Yankees*, knew both Harry and Rollins in the Village days.

"To those of us who knew Harry at The Sage," he observed one day, "the way he shot up out of nowhere was nothing less than a miracle. Having lost track of him for a while, I just couldn't figure how it happened. Then I discovered that he was being managed by Jack Rollins. Man, that explained a lot. Jack is one of the greatest personal managers of our time."

Komack squinted nervously, as he does periodically, and rounded his mouth in a soft smile. "Harry is a great, great artist. No question. But any artist needs a manager, particularly when he's getting started. He needs someone who will believe in him until the cows come home, who will fight for him, who will help creatively and guide him commercially. Rollins did all these things. You could sense it from the way Harry developed as a showman and traveled as a performer.

"Rollins played it real smart. He would book Harry into places where maybe the coin wasn't so great. But he would get something else that was, maybe, greater. Like, say, a full page ad in the newspapers. Nobody saw the small check. But everybody saw the big ad—and Belafonte began to look important almost from the moment Rollins began handling him. That's what a great manager can do—make you look bigger and more important than you may be. And that's how a guy with talent climbs.

"But Rollins was also great as a creative manager. He worked on Harry's clothes, on his lighting, on his entrance, on his exit, on his handling of encores.

"I wish I had a manager like Rollins. In fact, I tried to get Jack to handle me from way back. When he was doing so great for Harry, he would say: 'I have only one act—Belafonte.' Then, after Harry dropped him, he would say bitterly: 'I don't want to manage anyone any more—not the way I managed Harry. I couldn't ever give as much and you wouldn't be satisfied with less.'"

As Jack's belief and interest in Harry grew, he gave up his own job and devoted himself exclusively to Belafonte's career. Rollins' attachment and dedication to Harry were such that even today he cannot talk of his association with Harry without great emotional disturbance.

"Any man who becomes so dependent on another," Bill Attaway has said, "is heading for difficulties. Any man who allows his personal life to become so mixed up with his professional life must hurt himself."

The Rollins-Belafonte partnership lasted for over three fruitful years while Harry grew in stature and ripened as an artist. "We saw each other every day," Rollins says with pain. "We were like brothers. I was with him more than with my family." It should be added that those years were quite lean by comparison with what happened to Harry immediately after he severed his relationship with Rollins—and lean, perhaps, by any standards.

That what Jack once felt for Harry has now turned to bitterness, and even hatred, was doubtless inevitable. But from late '51, when Harry made his first moves as a folk singer, until Christmas '54, when he was on the edge of world fame, it was Rollins who guided and sweated over Harry's artistic destiny—as more recently he has nurtured the remarkable talents of Tom Poston and Mike Nichols and Elaine May.

STEREO

TEDDY WILSON AND LIONEL HAMPTON

In 1935 Benny Goodman broke all precedents by hiring Teddy Wilson. The appearance of a Negro musician with a white band was then considered a move of such audacity that Wilson was at first not permitted to play with the band. Instead, he was presented as part of a Trio, which in 1936 with the addition of Lionel Hampton on vibes, became a quartet.

In the summer of 1937, after the Goodman band had completed a movie, *Hollywood Hotel,* and was swinging its way back to the east coast, it played a fair in the Southwest. During the second day, band members noticed that a couple of city policemen on duty did not like the attention that Lionel and Teddy were receiving.

"They didn't say anything," Benny reported, "but every time one of the kids came up and asked either of them for an autograph (naturally calling them 'Mr. Hampton' or 'Mr. Wilson') they'd act nasty, because it seems that isn't done in their circles.

"On the third night, after we had finished a session with the quartet, one of the guests thought he'd express his appreciation by sending some champagne back to Lionel. As the waiter got to the stage door, one of these officers stopped him and said, 'Where you goin' with that?'

"The waiter answered, 'It's for Mr. Hampton.'

" 'The hell with that stuff,' this guy yelled, and flung out his arm, knocking the tray, glasses, ice, and champagne out of the waiter's hand."

9. Something of a Sensation

The first night spot that Harry played as a folk singer was not too many blocks away from the defunct Belafonte beanery. Located on Seventh Avenue South, it was a club that had introduced many exciting talents to the entertainment world. Currently pursuing a modern jazz policy, The Village Vanguard then followed a format involving a comedian, a singer (jazz or folk), and an instrumental combo (usually jazz). Professor Irwin Corey, the world's greatest authority (on what?), made his debut at The Vanguard. So did portly comedian Zero Mostel—"What was Pearl Harbor doing in the Pacific anyway?" Also, a zany comedy-singing act known as The Revuers, composed of writer-performers Betty Comden and Adolph Green, and a comedienne named Judy Holliday. Folk singers Richard Dyer-Bennett and Josh White were Vanguard discoveries.

It was natural that Rollins should go after The Vanguard as the first place to showcase Belafonte and his ballads. Max Gordon, the short, soft-voiced, balding owner of The Vanguard, knew Harry. He had been among those who cashed and held some of Harry's slow checks during the Sage saga, and he had twice auditioned him before Rollins sponsored him. Once, he had listened to Harry for The Blue Angel, an uptown club of which he was co-owner. That was in the days when Monte Kay and Virginia Wicks were handling Belafonte.

At a later date, he had considered Harry and a vocal group for The Vanguard. Almost nothing has been written of this group, which was then known as The Belafonte Singers. It bears no similarity to the present male chorus also known by the same name, except that some of the original singers are still with Harry. The Belafonte Singers of 1950 consisted of four men and a girl. They made several appearances on a program emceed by Don Ameche called *Holiday Inn.*

Max Gordon was not sufficiently impressed either by Harry as a single or by The Belafonte Singers as a group to want to book them. The new combination of Belafonte and Rollins—and Harry's new act—were more persuasive.

What happened at The Vanguard is now part of entertainment history. For Harry Belafonte, it was the launching of his legendary career as a ballad singer, a career which was to make him the first folk singer in entertainment history to command a mass audience.

That evening in November 1951, when Harry stepped up to the mike, sans the pencil-line mustache he sported during his jazz-pop singer days, the Vanguard was crowded with what appeared to be an average midweek audience, lackadaisical, noisy and "loaded." For the first time, Harry appeared in the open-necked shirt that was to become his trade-mark. (It lacked the plunging neckline and the tailoring of the thirty-five-dollar silk shirts he now wears. The tight, black, form-fitting pants came later.) His belt, however, was buckled with the two oversized rings that interlocked just over his navel. It could have been a seaman's belt buckle but it came from a smart Village shop. It added a touch of the exotic to a costume, worked out by Rollins and Belafonte, that stressed simplicity and informality. The entire costume was Village inspired.

When the spotlight hit Harry, an involuntary gasp of pleasure burst from the females in the audience. As his appealing, velvety voice rose on the opening notes of a folk song, "Tim-m-m-ber," the noise in the small, low-ceilinged, smoke-filled cellar room died down like a radio station fading off the air.

For twenty minutes, Harry held a startled audience spellbound. Again and again he was called back for encores. As owner Max Gordon puts it, Harry was "an explosion, an unexpected but an instantaneous explosion."

Variety found him impressive despite the "fierce competition" of regulars like Richard Dyer-Bennett and Josh White. "Belafonte has a feeling for the ancient folk tunes," it wrote, "and in addition can vary his offerings with a calypso. He has a tendency to overdramatize some. Other than that, he delivers with authority."

Jazz critic Barry Ulanov, writing in the January 1952 *Metronome*, was unreserved in his comments: "Harry has the most attractive package in the folk music field," he said. "Combining his newly found stentorian tones with the unrestrained guitar of Craig Work, Harry moves and tears his way through a remarkable variety of songs—Negro and Brazilian Negro, American white and European—the best of the music that man has made and hasn't signed, the best of the music of the primitive and untutored. It moves many to tears, this presentation of our international folk heritage; it also makes much of a music that has been prettied and fussed and turned tastelessly indoors in the past. Here, it has a beat and a boom and a fine representative quality, and it's here to stay this way, I think, and more power to it—if there can be any more power to it than what the new Belafonte gives it."

Craig Work, named by Ulanov as the accompanying guitarist, was a talented student of Millard Thomas, today, still Harry's permanent accompanist. Craig worked with Harry in a period when Millard was considering a career as a solo guitarist.

In a whimsical mood, Harry has said of his Vanguard debut: "I didn't have any of the accepted requirements. The audience just accepted Craig and me. He had his open shirt and I had mine."

That Harry's Sage friends had something to do with the success of his opening is undeniable. Tony Scott, his wife Fran, and Bill Attaway hand-addressed and mailed announcement cards to thousands of people. Using the mailing lists of several Negro organizations, they also sent cards to every steady Sage customer they could remember.

Bill Attaway admits, however, that Harry surprised him when he saw him on The Vanguard floor. The female reaction

[93]

did not. Although the Scotts and Attaway were for Harry to the end, no one of them ever dreamed that he could achieve the fantastic success that came to him.

"His art is his own," Bill says, "and we all felt he was a much greater artist than we had realized. Success is, of course, something else. We figured that if he stuck to it, he might climb as high as Josh White and make as much money as he did after a period of years. But then again, none of us anticipated how many people would become Belafonte fans, not only for his talent, but as an expression of unconscious protest over the Negro's position in the American scene."

Booked for two weeks at 75 dollars a week, Harry remained at The Vanguard for fourteen record-breaking weeks, with his salary mounting until he was earning several times the original figure. After a time, Harry's manager suggested that Gordon try the Belafonte magic in his uptown club, The Blue Angel. Max would not give Rollins an immediate answer. Privately, he was not sure that the chi-chi East Side crowd would buy a new, unknown folk singer the way Village audiences had.

But as Harry's drawing power grew, Max and his partner Herbert Jacoby decided to try Belafonte uptown. They waited until they had what they regarded as a particularly strong Blue Angel line-up. As their headliner, they offered Elsa Lanchester, film character actress and wife of Charles Laughton. Also on the bill were comedian Wally Cox and songstress Mary Stevens. Then, Gordon-Jacoby gave the nod to Belafonte.

Their uneasiness was, of course, unfounded and they were in for a surprise. *Variety*, less than excited over Harry at The Vanguard, had this to say about The Blue Angel debut: "The strongest point on the bill is Belafonte, accompanied by guitarist Millard Thomas. He has progressed considerably since he bowed as a balladist downtown a few months ago. He's in a position to develop into an uptown draw. His ballads have style, class, and feeling. The tunes are mixed and include American themes as well as Brazilian and calypso items.

[94]

With a widening catalog, he'll be able to assume concert stands."

Considering what Belafonte did at a concert at the Lewisohn Stadium just a few years later, when he played a one-man program to the largest audience that ever filled the amphitheatre, *Variety* was on the prophetic side. What is to be noted in connection with The Vanguard and The Blue Angel bookings is that both included calypso songs. Not until four years later, however, did the same material find its audience and create a furor in Europe as well as all over the United States.

Harry remained at The Blue Angel for four months, his showmanship and his dramatic style igniting the East-Siders as they had the downtowners. By this time, Craig Work's teacher, Millard Thomas, had replaced his pupil (who went into the Army) as Harry's regular accompanist. From The Angel Harry went to the Rendezvous Room in Philadelphia. Then, early in June, he came back to The Vanguard.

This second Vanguard date proved a remarkable return engagement. *Variety* now joined the thundering applauders: "Belafonte has emerged [this was just six months later] as one of the outstanding practitioners in the folk singing field. Back for a return engagement at Max Gordon's Village Vanguard, Negro balladeer is causing something of a sensation. If the customers had their way, the tall, handsome lad would be vocalizing all night . . ."

Variety added that "the folk singer tag may be a misnomer in Belafonte's case for it usually places the performer in the limited realm covered by the word 'arty.' Singer's appeal, however, is much more widespread."

Despite the glowing notices and the upped pay, Harry was far from earning a solid income. In fact, he and Jack Rollins ate most of their meals at the Automat. Millard Thomas, who had to be paid in accordance with scales set by the Musicians Union, could afford regular restaurants. He came out best while Rollins came off worst financially.

One day Harry and Jack invited Millard to eat with them at their favorite Automat. As they approached the entrance,

Harry suddenly spotted a young comic they all knew. He whispered the fact to Jack. When they reached the entrance, Belafonte and Rollins walked nonchalantly by as if they were headed elsewhere. They nodded to the comic, took a dozen steps forward, glanced back to make sure that they were not being observed, then trotted back to the Automat entrance. Millard Thomas, who never ate at the Automat except when he was dining with Rollins and Belafonte, had walked unconcernedly in—despite the comic—and was impatiently trying to hold chairs for them.

Harry's handling of money even today seems to run to one of two extremes. Either he is unable to spend any at all or he is given to reckless squandering. The pattern was already apparent in the hungry days.

One weekend, at this time, he played a high-priced job in New Jersey. Afterward he drove to New York and came knocking at the door of the Tony Scott's, who lived just off Fifth Avenue on West 52nd Street. It was about 4:30 in the morning, and he wanted them to come for some breakfast. The Scotts are night people, and they were ready. Harry headed his car for the Confucius on 52nd Street, west of Broadway, then a favorite hangout.

When the car pulled up in front of the restaurant, Harry casually asked Tony to pass his wallet to him. It was in the glove compartment, he said. The moment Tony touched the knob, the compartment flew open, as if it were on a spring latch, and a shower of 20-dollar bills shot into the air. In profusion, they fell over Tony and Fran and on the floor of the car. Harry broke into amused laughter at the surprise registered by both Tony and Fran. Tony, who usually could match Harry as a practical joker, was not amused. At 4:30 in the morning, the streets were quite deserted, and he was worried that the sight of the greenbacks might create trouble for them.

Hurriedly he tried to retrieve the scattered bills while Harry sat laughing. After a time Tony was able to force most of the bills back into the glove compartment. At this point Harry got out of the car and came around it to the door near the compartment. As Tony started to climb out, Harry reached in through the open door, tapped the knob and the bills shot out again, this time scattering in part over the sidewalk. Now Tony became real frantic trying to retrieve them. And the more he struggled to put the bills together, the more Harry laughed. This time, Tony bypassed the compartment and stuck the wad of money—at least a thousand dollars—into Harry's coat pocket.

There were few customers in the Confucius restaurant when they entered. As soon as they were seated, a waiter came over to them.

"Would you like a menu?" he inquired.

"We don't need a menu," Harry said, with a grin. He stuck his hand into his coat pocket, pulled out a fistful of 20-dollar bills and flung them over the table.

"We want one of everything," he chortled. "After that, we're buying the joint."

People who knew Harry in this formative period of his career say that the glow of a rising star was quite evident. Talking with hindsight, they assert that no one who came in contact with him even at this time failed to react to the sheer force of his personality.

"He had a charm, despite his comparative lack of poise," Fran Scott has said, "that worked its magic on everybody. The females found him virtually irresistible. There was something so vital and so intense about him that he carried everybody with him like a strong wind. Why, when he went out to Hollywood just about this time—it was his first trip and he was fresh to the dynamics of the movie colony—he made some of the film capital's charm boys look like tired, middle-aged men. You see, he had not only charm, good looks and vitality, but a probing mind. The only man with whom he bears comparison in all these ways—and Harry's better looking —is Frank Sinatra."

Like The Voice, unquestionably a more powerful deity in the firmament of American love gods, Harry has a restlessness that even time has not completely cured. Sinatra has said of his own impatience and nervous tension: "This is something I can't help. I have to go. No one seems able to help me with it—doctors, no one. I have to move." That Harry, too, had to keep on the move was fully apparent to friends and associates of these early days. The end of an evening of hard performing was usually just the beginning.

Even critics of Belafonte agree that few artists in the history of show business give themselves as completely and as consistently to audiences. Max Gordon, who has been watching entertainers for decades, names Harry among the few whose level of performance hardly varies from night to night. "I don't know how he does it," Max has said. "He was in top form all the time—one of the most dedicated performers I've ever known. He never spared himself."

But when Harry came off-stage, he had to move. After the ritual of recovery, he had to move. Bathed in perspiration, all energy and emotion spent, the ritual began with isolation. He had to be left alone. After a time, he would slowly dry his sweat-soaked body, cleanse himself with cold water, and apply copious amounts of cologne to his face. Rejuvenated in a matter of minutes, he was ready to start on a round of clubs that seldom ended before the first soft rays of daylight filtered through the streets of Manhattan. Few friends could keep up with Harry—and Margurite, his wife, saw no point to it. Perhaps Harry didn't either. But there was a seemingly inexhaustible reservoir of energy here that had to be spent before he could retire.

Interviewed some years later, Harry said: "Sleep? Never heard of it!"

1952 was not an easy financial year for Harry—or for Jack Rollins. But it was the beginning. Before The Blue Angel booking was ended, Jack had set Harry for a dramatic role in a new film being produced by Metro-Goldwyn-Mayer. Harry was also signed to a recording contract by the largest of the nation's record companies—RCA Victor, the diskery under whose little black-and-white dog label he still makes records.

As Margurite Belafonte remembers the sequence of things: "It was The Vanguard, The Blue Angel, The Black Orchid in Chicago, the Chase Hotel in St. Louis—and straight to the sky."

STEREO

TONY SCOTT

In 1951 Duke Ellington added white drummer Louis Bellson, now the husband of Pearl Bailey, to his band. In 1953 Dave Black, also white, succeeded Bellson on drums. At about the same time, Ellington hired white clarinetist-saxophonist Tony Scott for his reed section.

After one month Scott was compelled to hand in his resignation. He found the attitude of several band members simply impossible.

Duke Ellington confirms unhappily: "Scott was the only musician who was ever forced out of my band by race prejudice."

[99]

45780

10. Rising Star

The trip to the sky was not without its turbulence despite the auspicious launching. No one could have predicted with certainty, on the basis of the first year's developments after The Vanguard, that the Belafonte rocket would hit the moon.

During that year Harry made his first hopeful trip to Hollywood to play in an M-G-M film *The Bright Road*. It looked like a fulfillment, an unbelievably quick leap toward the career he had sought from the beginning. The Lion had acquired a prize-winning story, *See How They Run,* about a Southern school. A top screenwriter, Emmett Lavery, had been assigned to do the screenplay. David Rose was to score the music. The story concerned a disturbed Negro schoolboy who seemed an incorrigible delinquent until a sensitive schoolteacher discovered a way of using the boy's interest in biology to help him find himself. It was the kind of theme that interested Harry. The two main adult roles, that of the schoolteacher and her principal, went to Dorothy Dandridge and Harry Belafonte.

With all the plus signs, *The Bright Road* did not prove so for Harry, M-G-M, or anyone associated with the production, except possibly the youngster, Philip Hepburn, who played the confused delinquent. Harry's role turned out to be so minor that he was not even mentioned in many reviews of the film. Moreover, he looked too young for the part he played, and his acting all too clearly revealed the limitations of inexperience.

The only song in *The Bright Road* was a blues ballad *Suzanne,* which Harry wrote with Millard Thomas—actually a rewrite with additions of an old folk ballad sometimes known as *Every Night When The Sun Goes Down*. It was used thematically by David Rose as background music throughout the film. Harry recorded it for Victor, and it was released both as a single disk and in the album titled *Belafonte*. But *Suzanne* proved no more of a winner than the film itself.

Whatever its original plans on *The Bright Road*, M-G-M did not treat the picture as a major film nor did Leo the Lion roar very loudly about it. Booked rather quietly in art theatres or as a second feature on twin bills, it did not contribute anything to Harry's acting career beyond a screen credit, nor did it lead to other acting assignments.

Of *The Bright Road*, screenwriter Lavery stated: "We tried to be honest and we tried to be simple and, now that we look at the film again, we realize that we haven't made a so-called 'Negro film' at all."

On being inducted into the Screen Writers Guild, author-schoolteacher Mary Vroman observed: "Oh, I know—we've had lots of angry stories by angry writers. But it didn't change anything, getting so angry. I just thought about how much I loved my children and tried to put it down on paper—that's all."

Bosley Crowther's comment in *The New York Times:* "A certain caution and reluctance to come out bluntly and say the dismal things about racial and economic pressures that are vaguely and overtly implied in the theme and contour of the story, are evident throughout the film. The whole thing has a prettiness about it as though the people who made it didn't wish to open up any problems or tread on any toes."

Was Harry then aware that the film, in Bosley Crowther's words, took "a cozy detour around the fundamental issue it raised"? Four years later he himself was to characterize it as "a nice, bland Lassie-like thing."

Both before and after his trip to Hollywood, Harry cut disks under his new contract with RCA Victor. The first date was on April 3, 1952 at Manhattan Center in New York. With Hugo Winterhalter conducting an eighteen-piece orchestra replete with violins, violas, and cellos, Harry recorded an old folk tune *A-Roving* and a new folk-type ballad *Chimney Smoke.* The disk was, in the parlance of music business, a "dog." It meant so little that it is now among Victor's discontinued single disks as is also the case with the sides Harry cut on his second date: *Man Smart,* a calypso, and *Jerry,* a work song of protest. On this session, Victor used a small five-piece combo, including Tony Scott on flute and Millard Thomas and Mundell Lowe on guitars. Somewhat more satisfactory were the sides produced a few days later (August 5, 1952) on *Scarlet Ribbons* and *Shenandoah.* This time Harry used just Millard and a male chorus. But even this disk sold so poorly that the Victor sales staff began grumbling about the value of Belafonte to the label.

Harry's first important booking, after he had completed the filming of *The Bright Road,* was at the swank Thunderbird Hotel in Las Vegas. His reception as a performer by Thunderbird audiences was not less memorable than the treatment he received from the hotel as a Negro.

On his arrival—it was after dark—he and Millard entered the lobby and asked for their room. A startled clerk tried to say something but did not quite make it. Harry, who was not getting top billing then, explained that he was Harry Belafonte and that his companion was Millard Thomas, his accompanist. At this news the clerk seemed to go completely to pieces. But he managed to reach for a phone. In no time, the manager appeared, welcomed Harry and Millard, and explained affably that the hotel had picked out a lovely place for the two of them to stay.

"You'll like it, take my word," the manager smiled. "Many name acts have stayed there. If you'll come with me, I'll see that you're driven out immediately."

Harry exchanged glances with Millard. He could feel the heat rising in his face. Three years later, as a headliner in Las Vegas, he was to handle the situation differently. But this time around, his first booking in the gambling town, he decided to play it cool.

He and Millard got into the car that drove up for them. It was dark outside. The car sped along the highway, left the concrete road for a tar road, swung off the tar road onto a bumpy dirt road. After a time, the driver braked to a stop and announced: "Here we are."

Millard and Harry stepped out of the car and lifted their cases out. As they turned to get their bearings, the car drove off with a swoosh. With its headlights gone, they found themselves in an almost impenetrable pitch darkness. Slowly they made out a dimly lighted boardinghouse off what was presumably the road. Holding onto each other, they approached it. The floor boards of the stairs creaked in the darkness and quiet as they went up to the porch.

Harry knocked timidly. As he did so, he and Millard heard a growl and the tremendous body of a large dog hit the door. After a time they could hear the scraping of sandals on the wooden floor. The door was opened by an old Negro woman. At this point Harry was confused. Should he fight? Should he accept this impossible situation?

"Come on in," the woman said. "I guess you're the two boys sent by the hotel to stay here tonight."

Slowly Millard and he followed as the old woman dragged herself to their room. When Harry saw where he and Millard were to sleep that night—and presumably for the duration of their booking—he was stunned. The old woman saw it in his face.

"Don't be so surprised, sonny boy," she croaked. "Lots of big people have slept here. Don't know who you are. But if it was all right for them, it sure is all right for you."

Harry felt impelled to rebel. But how? It was dark outside. They had no idea of where the hotel was. They were in a strange but tough Jim Crow town. There was just nothing to do except pass a sleepless night.

Harry and Millard arose late, uncertain of their next move. Harry had almost no cash on him, and he was hesitant about raising a row on his first big booking. After a slow, unhappy breakfast, Harry and Millard went to their first rehearsal. Harry's thoughts were only half on the proceedings. He kept thinking of the segregated "hotel" at which they were staying, unable to resolve his growing impulse to rebel against it and

[103]

his equally strong desire not to lose this important engagement. As he was leaving the rehearsal, feeling confused, unhappy, resentful, he walked unexpectedly into the arms of a manager he knew. It was Pete Kameron, who had handled a famous folk group, The Weavers. Pete, who was driving from California to New York, had stopped at Vegas.

"I sure got a royal welcome," Pete recalls. "I knew in an instant that this was a very troubled man and it took little time to discover that he had two serious problems: money and lodgings.

"Well, I went to the manager of The Thunderbird and wangled an advance on his first week's salary. Then, I drove to the fleabag at which he and Millard were staying. I helped them pack, and loaded them into my car. After that, I drove down the Las Vegas strip until I spotted a likely motel. I played it by ear.

"Out came a guy with a big Texas Stetson, a swagger and, to top it off, an accent that had a faint German sound.

"He had a vacancy. I didn't ask the price, but zoomed around to the cabin and parked my car just outside. Up to this point, he had not seen Harry or Millard, who were in the back of the car. As they started to get out, he appeared out of nowhere and watched them take their luggage out of the trunk. He turned to me and asked:

" 'Schwartze?' That means black in yiddish.

"I played it cool. I answered in my best Yiddish. 'No, they're Latin. They're playing at one of the hotels.'

"In his most charming Yiddish, the motel proprietor responded: 'I don't know from nothin'. You say they're Latin? Okay, they're Latin. To me, it makes no difference even if they're schwartz. I just know what I'm told.'

"Harry and Millard had no problems during their stay at the motel. He went out of his way to be nice to them.

"While they were settling themselves, Harry invited me to their first show. I went—and after it, I went to Harry's dressing room. Naturally, he wanted to know how they did. I said: 'Great!' Harry kept asking and I kept repeating. But he didn't believe me.

"Finally, I gave it to him straight. I couldn't tell him what we both knew. He was scared and he had no stage presence. So I talked to him about his routine. My main point was that he was on a big stage in a big room. Soft, tender, delicate numbers could go only after he captured the audience. It was a matter of pacing. He caught on fast.

"I watched the second show—and there was just no comparison. Harry is a born showman. All he needed was confidence. And maybe I helped restore it."

Harry's opening song at The Thunderbird was the chantlike *Jerry*, the tale of a donkey (*Have You Heard About Jerry?*) who would take punishment only up to a certain point after which he up and did his master in. From the rising and full-toned inflections of this story of rebellion, Harry turned to the softer and tenderer measures of a sailor's love for the daughter of an Indian chieftain, *Shenandoah*. (RCA had just released Harry's recording of the tune.) Then came the colorful and highly visual narrative of the Mississippi riverboat life, *Mark Twain*, a folklike ballad written by Belafonte. Now Harry went for a change of pace and sang the humorous calypso *Man, Smart—Woman Is Smarter*, charming the audience with his pidgin English, inverted accents, and catchy cross-rhythms. As the applause slowly died down, Harry gently segued into the haunting lullaby *Scarlet Ribbons*. The modulation to *John Henry*, the driving tale of the Negro rail splitter who gave up his life rather than his proud status as a workingman, was sharp and overpowering. This was the high point of Harry's program, a song into which he poured all his heartfelt feelings of anger and pride as a Negro. His bow-off song was again a calypso, *Hold 'Em Joe*, that left the audience in a happy, toe-tapping frame of mind.

"Belafonte takes the room by storm," *Variety* reported, "turning out his folk tunes for sock salvos. The Dave Kapp discovery and RCA Victor piper should hit top brackets before too long." Characterizing his style as "highly kinetic" and his showmanship as "sure-fire," the bible of show business added, "He weaves a strong spell with keen perception of drama within his songs."

"It was a very successful engagement," Pete Kameron observed. "But hardly a happy one. Harry could not use any of the hotel's facilities: not the pool, not the casino, not the dining rooms, or the cocktail lounges. Next to his dressing room, which was quite small, the management gave him another room. Here he could eat, relax, receive friends. This was his isolation booth. It bugged him, made him edgy and depressed him.

"All the Negro artists playing Vegas had the same problem. They could entertain the guests. But they could not mingle with them, move about freely, or use the facilities of the hotels where their names were up in lights. To keep Harry's spirits up, I asked the entertainers playing neighboring hotels to visit him backstage. It was like urging people to visit a sick friend in order to keep the guy's mind off his ailments. They co-operated wonderfully.

"Anyway, Harry's first Vegas engagement was the start of a vagrant friendship between us, which has not died. I never know when I'll see him again. But when I do, he knows that I'm a friend. And he always treats me as one. He talks. I listen. I react, usually critically. And he listens.

"He's a very complex guy. But despite what he does—some of it, rough and self-centered and misguided—I feel that he has the one thing that makes a difference. He cares! I mean it. He wants to be good, he wants to grow, and he wants to contribute to the growth of things. How many entertainers can you say that about?"

The story of what happened in 1955 when Harry played Vegas as an established headliner makes an interesting contrast. (See *Stereo:* Las Vegas Taboos.)

In November of '52, Harry returned to New York for an engagement at The Boulevard, a huge dance hall on Queens Boulevard, the heavily traveled artery from Long Island to Manhattan. The booking proved both a test and a triumph. The audience was a younger, more rowdy group than those Harry had encountered at swank spots like The Blue Angel and The Thunderbird.

Tony Scott and his wife Fran attended the opening. To greet an old buddy, Scott bought a new suit of clothes. But when he and Fran went to dress that night, they discovered that their electricity had been turned off. The Scotts were then supporting five people in the large Village loft where Harry had attended many a party. Occasionally, others dropped in to stay for indefinite periods. Electric bills were less important than people. When they realized that they had no electricity, Scott and his sundry roomers repaired to the windows where they sat chanting to passersby: "We hate Con Edison! We hate Con Edison!"

Years later, when police were searching for the mad bomber who was blowing up places because he had a grudge against Consolidated Edison, Tony got a card from one of his former guests: "We won't tell, but we know who the mad bomber is." Having expressed their feelings about Con Edison, Tony and Fran managed to dress by candlelight and to make The Boulevard in time for Harry's appearance.

"The crowd was very impolite," Scott recalls. "The comedienne, a funny chick, couldn't get anything over. Harry came out after his introduction and just stood there. A strange thing happened. He just stood there, waiting. As if he hypnotized them, the crowd slowly settled down. He opened with *Timber* and the crowd stayed with him all through his set."

Reviewer Bill Smith, writing in *Billboard*, reported: "Belafonte has seldom worked better, appeared to better advantage or worked to a more enthusiastic audience than he has here at The Boulevard. From a poor start as a bop singer some years ago, the tall slim Belafonte is rapidly becoming the top folk singer in the business. As he went into familiar items now on RCA Victor, the huge mob rocked with him with such zest that it took on an almost hysterical frenzy more often associated with a Johnny Ray audience . . ."

A "gas" at The Boulevard! But a week later, a flop at The Ambassador in Hollywood. Well, not really a flop. But attendance was so poor at the chi-chi Cocoanut Grove that the reviewers could not avoid commenting on it.

"The small house gave him a big mitt," *Billboard* reported.

"Harry Belafonte has a great new act but he hasn't received enough publicity locally. Crowds have been disappointing since his opening." Sympathetically, *Billboard* pointed out that the Coast, unlike New York, did not have a nucleus of "free-spending ballad *aficionados*" from whom a crowd could readily be drawn. "He really emotes," *Billboard* added. "He's a sort of Frankie Laine of the balladeers," *Variety* observed. In short, as with Harry's early calypso recordings, the public was not ready. And Harry's appearance was that deadly thing—an artistic success and a financial flop.

The success Harry came to enjoy in succeeding years both at The Grove and Hollywood's Greek Theatre is again another story. But late in 1952 Harry was still what *Variety* had called him a year earlier: "A rising star via his cariballads, calypsongs, jungle-rigged chants and folk items."

By Christmas of '52, Harry's own immediate circle, specifically the Village crowd, felt that he had made it. He had not only been accepted at The Vanguard in the Village but had won the plush crowd at The Blue Angel uptown, and he had made a Hollywood movie. It was a time for celebration, and Tony and Fran Scott threw a well-remembered party at their Fourth Avenue loft.

It was a big shindig and brought out, not only all of Harry's Village friends but luminaries from different sectors of show business. Judy Balaban, of the well-known movie family, actress Ruth Attaway, Marlon Brando, actor Frank Silvera, and others attended. Some time before the party, Harry had bought Tony a set of conga drums as a surprise and, with Fran's help, sneaked them into the loft. When the drums were unveiled, Tony took up his flute—and a spontaneous jam session got under way with Tony wailing to the accompaniment of a duo consisting of Harry on one conga drum and Marlon Brando on the other. It became the high point of the evening's festivities.

Sitting in a corner of the loft as they improvised was Margurite Belafonte. Although it was a Village party, and she had anticipated an attendance of Harry's bohemian friends, Margurite came resplendent in a party dress. Most of the crowd came less formally attired, with some of the women cavorting about in slacks. As the evening wore on, Margurite mingled little but sat by—a faintly amused and unsympathetic observer of the proceedings. That she felt herself an outsider, whether she wanted to be or not, was quite evident.

When Tony's longest and most exciting improvisation had left him, Harry, Marlon, and the whole crowd limp, Harry parked his conga drum and went looking for Margurite. The chair she had been occupying most of the evening was empty. After a while he discovered that she had gone home alone.

STEREO

ROY ELDRIDGE

Returning from prejudice-free Paris in the early fifties, Negro trumpeter Roy Eldridge, known as Little Jazz, told a *Down Beat* reporter: "One thing you can be sure of, as long as I'm in America, I'll never work with a white band again!

"It goes all the way back to when I joined Gene Krupa's band. Until that time no colored attraction had worked with a white band except as a separate attraction, like Teddy Wilson with Benny Goodman.

"That was how I worked with Gene at first. I wasn't treated as a full member of the band. But very soon I started sharing Shorty Sherock's book and when he left the band, I took over.

"All the guys were nice, and Gene was especially wonderful. That was at the Pennsylvania Hotel in New York. Then we headed West for some one-nighters, winding up in California. That was when the trouble began.

"We arrived in one town and the rest of the band checks in. I can't get into their hotel. So I keep my bags and start riding around looking for another place, where someone's supposed to have made a reservation for me. I get there and move all my bags in. Naturally, since we're going to be out on the Coast several months, I have a heavy load, at least a dozen pieces of baggage.

"Then the clerk, when he sees that I'm the Mr. Eldridge the reservation was made for, suddenly discovers that one of their regular tenants just arrived and took the last available room. I lug that baggage back into the street and start looking around again.

"When we finally got to the Palladium in Hollywood, I had to watch who I could sit at the tables with. If they were movie stars who wanted me to come over, that was all right. If they were just the jitterbugs, no dice. And all the time the bouncer with his eye on me.

"On top of that, I had to live way out in Los Angeles while the rest of the guys stayed in Hollywood. It was a lonely life. I'd never been that far away from home before, and I didn't know anybody. I got to brooding.

"Then it happened. One night the tension got so bad I flipped. I could feel it right up to my neck while I was playing *Rockin' Chair*. I started trembling, ran off the stand, and threw up. They carried me to the doctor's. I had a hundred and five fever. My nerves were shot.

"When I went back a few nights later, I heard that people were asking for their money back because they couldn't hear *Let Me Off Uptown*. This time they let me sit at the bar."

11. The Lonesome Road

In the early months of 1953, RCA Victor was still wondering what to do with and about Harry Belafonte. They had experimented with several types of instrumental backings. They had released three records. The sales outlook was not bright—and while option time on Harry's initial two-year contract was months off, the renewal outlook was not promising.

Harry had been signed to Victor by Dave Kapp, formerly of Decca Records, now at the helm of his own thriving diskery, and in 1953, chief of RCA's A & R department (Artists and Repertoire). Dave was steeped in folk tradition. At Decca he had worked with such folk artists as Burl Ives, Alan Lomax, Richard Dyer-Bennett, and The Weavers. Despite the fact that no folk singer had ever developed real mass appeal and that the sales figures on most were rather disappointing—The Weavers were an exception—Dave had offered a recording contract to Belafonte, the newcomer.

In the midst of the headshaking among RCA Victor's sales people over Belafonte, Dave Kapp came across a Japanese tune titled *Gomen-Nasai* (Forgive Me). Not a folk song, it had qualities which gave it a folk flavor. Or so Kapp persuaded himself.

When Kapp phoned Harry to tell him that he had a new tune he wanted him to record, there was a momentary silence on the phone. Harry was already working on two songs for his next date. One was the American folk ballad *Springfield Mountain*. The other was *Suzanne*, the folklike tune Millard and he had written for *The Bright Road*.

"It's not a pop tune," Kapp explained quickly, "although it's a new song."

An involuntary sigh of relief escaped from Harry. "I'm glad of that."

"I'll send it over to you," Kapp said.

Again there was a momentary silence. "Dave," Harry said.

"Yes."

"You know I'm not the kind of singer who can look at a song, run it over once or twice and then record it."

"I know that, Harry."

"I've got to live with a tune for a long time before I feel it—to do it right."

"I know that, Harry."

Reluctantly, Harry said: "All right, Dave, then send it over. What's it called?"

"*Gomen-Nasai*. It's a Japanese song." Dave knew of Harry's interest in material that came from different parts of the world.

"That's interesting." That was not what Harry's tone of voice said.

"Harry," Dave said slowly, "the time has come when we've got to show the sales department at Victor that you can sell records. You believe it and I know it. But they keep looking at the figures—and yiping."

"I'm a visual artist, Dave. You know that."

"So is Frankie Laine. But he sells records. So was Al Jolson. But he sold records."

"They weren't singing folk."

"Take a look at the Japanese song," Kapp said. "And let me know what you think." When he put down the phone, Kapp knew what Harry would think.

A few days later they met in Kapp's office on the 36th floor of the RCA Building at 630 Fifth Avenue.

"It's not that I don't like the tune," Harry began. "It's just that I don't think it's right for me."

Folk singers, like blues and jazz singers, worry about their calling. Like any in-group, they are concerned with questions of appropriateness, etc. Today, all singers tend to develop a vocal personality and to select or reject songs on the basis of whether these fit in with that personality. But in 1953 this approach was more typical of folk and jazz artists.

[112]

Kapp well knew how dedicated a stylist Harry was. "This once, Harry," he urged, "let's worry about one thing. How good a job of singing you can do on it."

"You want me to do it?"

"I think it will be a record seller for you."

Harry rose from his chair. He looked out over the city from the window of Kapp's office. Kapp exchanged glances with Jack Rollins, who cleared his throat to speak. Kapp held up a hand and, shaking his head, mutely urged Harry's manager not to say anything.

When Harry turned around from the window, he asked: "Do I have to do it, Dave?"

There was a quaver in his voice. Kapp looked across the room and realized, with a start, that there were tears in the singer's eyes.

"You don't have to do it," Kapp said. "But I would like you to. I think it will be a big seller."

"That's what worries me."

Dave glanced questioningly at Rollins and back at Harry. "Did I hear you correctly?"

Harry nodded and sighed.

Dave started to chuckle. "You're worrying about having a best seller?" Disbelief and amusement were in his voice.

Harry nodded again. "What do I do if it's a hit?"

"I don't understand," Dave said. "Why, you shut up the wise-acres in the sales department here. You earn royalties instead of owing Victor money. And your night club prices go up. It should happen to all of my artists."

"But this song is not my style," Harry said firmly, "and I just could never do it in my night club act. I could never sing those lyrics with conviction."

Dave nervously tamped a cigarette. He took another out of a heavy gold box on his desk and lighted it. "Why don't we worry about that when your record is a hit?" he suggested.

Harry plopped down in a soft chair. "All right, Dave. I'll do it." Rollins started to say something. But Harry waved his manager aside. "When do you want to record, Dave?"

The recording of *Gomen-Nasai* was not a smash. But it was

the biggest seller Harry had during his first contract year at Victor—and it made the masters of the little dog ready to re-sign him when option time approached.

"Belafonte is one of the greatest showmen I've ever known," Kapp said recently. "And like all great showmen, he goes out to his audience. Had he not been flexible on *Gomen-Nasai*, who knows—Victor might not have resigned him." Kapp smiled as he nervously riffled the corners of a pad of paper. "Then I might have had a million dollar artist on Kapp Records."

The interesting sidelight on *Gomen-Nasai* is that Harry did not add the song to his repertoire, not even while his record was being promoted. This was strange and, in some ways, foolish conduct. Harry's disk of *Gomen-Nasai* had to compete with three other versions—Eddy Howard on Mercury, Richard Bowers on Columbia, and Sammy Kaye on Columbia. Even-tually, the Howard rendition outgrossed the others. But in March 1953, while Harry was playing The Black Orchid in Chicago, his record was climbing the popularity charts. It was his first chart-climber. Performances by him in personal ap-pearances might very well have increased its sales—as they did for his later recordings. Nevertheless, Harry stuck to his orig-inal contention that the song was not in keeping with the rest of his act—and he never performed it in person, much to the amazement of people in the business.

Harry's concern about his repertoire and his great care in choosing material are matters that are widely known to all who have ever been associated with him.

"Harry drew a tight wall around himself," Joseph R. Carlton has said, "when it came to material." Carlton, now heading his own record company, just as does Dave Kapp, succeeded Kapp as head of A & R at RCA Victor.

Carlton added: "But Belafonte was one artist who knew what he wanted, and who showed excellent taste in selecting things that were good for him. Extremely articulate and criti-cal, he not only picked his own songs but the arrangers, the arrangements, and the musicians. An indigenous artist, he felt that he had to stay with pure material. And he was skillful in finding, reshaping, and polishing material for himself. On the credit side, also, was his interest and success in discovering new, talented people to work with him.

"There were times, however, when he was hard to take because he made you feel that he didn't need your help or anybody's. Of course, he was fearful of being thrown off his chosen path. This made him suspicious and difficult to reach.

"What I resented, as did others, was his acting as if he was the only person who had ever read a book. He was pedantic and almost babylike in the way he carried on about 'culture.' There was always the question, of what you were talking about meant 'ethnically.' And each problem, no matter how minor, was approached with an intensity as if it were of earth-shaking import. He never really came off-stage."

The Black Orchid booking in March 1953 was crucial for Harry, not because of the audience he faced but because of the singer he followed into the smart North Side Chicago nitery. A new room, The Orchid had opened to SRO business with Josh White. Only two months earlier Harry had been compared to the veteran Negro folk singer and actually suffered in the comparison: "Belafonte has lots of s.a. (sex appeal) for the dames," a *Variety* reviewer wrote of Harry's appearance at The Blue Angel, "but he has a long way to go to assume the authority that Josh White projects with more or less the same kind of numbers."

Anyone who has not seen White perform live may gather something of his overpowering appeal from this passage in Eartha Kitt's autobiography *Thursday's Child:* ". . . Josh White, a man I shall never forget," Eartha writes. "I remember the first day I saw him. He walked into the rehearsal studio with his guitar, went to the piano, stuck a cigarette in the side of his mouth, and plucked . . . I watched his hands, as they told of love and hatred, of sensuous love and faithless women. His mouth moved as though he was making love to the words, but they did not make love to him. His eyes dimmed with 'Come hither, so that I may suck you in. There's no woman I cannot have and any woman can have me.' I went nearer so that I could sense him better and to make him sense me. When his eyes met mine, our senses touched. He finished his song to me . . ."

White had filled The Black Orchid night after night for ten boff weeks. Now, with material that was not dissimilar, it was Harry's turn. In the prospective audience's mind, there could be no question that Belafonte was a brilliant newcomer while White was the recognized old master.

Whatever doubts Harry or anybody might have had as to his ability to fill the room after Josh were quickly dissipated. Not even the usual bistro bugaboo of Lent kept the crowds away.

"Belafonte electrifies the small room with his opener *Timber*," *Variety* reported. "However, he gets the crowd really going with his *Birds and Bees*, a quest on the sex problem of a lad of three who winds up at 93 without the answers. Harry has the patrons chiming in on the endless choruses, pounding the tables and yelling for another verse."

Birds and Bees is a reference actually to a humorous song written in a calypso vein by Harry and his then-manager Jack Rollins. Its correct title is *Man Piaba* and it is to be heard in Harry's first RCA Victor album *Mark Twain and Other Favorites*.

Harry's success at The Black Orchid not only gave him stature. It also showcased the contrast between his style and that of Josh White. Playing the guitar as all early ballad singers did, White presented an arresting picture in repose. It was a lovely still life that he drew, relying on an intense economy of movement, the beautiful blend of his voice and guitar, and the erotic power of his personality.

In contrast, Harry's approach to the folk song was that of the actor. Freed from bondage to the guitar, he used his hands, movements of his body, his face, to create a theatre of the folk ballad. To him, the basic question was: What is the emotion of this song? He seized every dramatic resource at his command to overwhelm the audience with it.

Relaxed, statuesque, contained, Josh White offered an

aesthetic experience to viewers while Harry sucked them into the song and made them laugh, cry, or hurt as active participants. *Variety* made the point in its own way when it said that Harry was "a cross between Billy Daniels and Frankie Laine in his approach."

The sense of satisfaction and elation that Harry felt over The Black Orchid date did not eliminate inner tensions he was suffering at this time.

On the road, Harry was a lonely man. It was true at this time and true in years to come. Traveling salesmen, like traveling performers, tell you that the depressing feeling of being alone in the world is an inescapable occupational hazard. No matter how busy you are all day, there's the long, empty night always stretching ahead. And no matter how difficult life at home may be, there are always the long, quiet, forlorn Sundays.

Harry was never quite able to overcome this lonesome feeling. Never having had very much of home life, he frequently found existence on the road unbearably insecure. At various times, he would invite acquaintances to share his rooms. Cal Lampley, formerly a recording executive at Columbia and now associated with the record division of Warner Brothers, found himself a welcome guest in Harry's suite at the Hollywood Ambassador after a rather slight acquaintanceship with Harry. At other times, Harry would phone friends in New York and pay their fare to wherever he was staying. Bill Attaway, an old friend and collaborator from the pre-Sage days, has spent time with Harry in many different cities. Ostensibly, he was paid to travel wherever Harry was staying so that they could work over some material.

"But it was just an excuse," Bill says. "He was just lonely. You just can't know how lonely this man can get. Why, I've received calls from him at four and five in the morning. The phone would ring. I'd pick it up. And there was Harry calling from Las Vegas or Hollywood or St. Louis. I'd say, kinda startled, 'What's up?' And he'd just fumble. It was nothing, of course. Just that he was lonesome and wanted to talk to somebody. Once in Chicago, I arranged for my sister Florence to meet him at the train just so that he would not feel he was coming alone into a strange city.

"He was the loneliest man after he became quite well-known. And before? Take my word—the road is the most lonesome place in the world for a man who hasn't really made it."

When he was at The Black Orchid, Harry had not made it yet. That created fears and a hunger and a hope and uncertainty. But it also looked very much as if he could earn a reasonable livelihood as a performer. That presented problems, too. Margurite had never been too sympathetic to a show business career. When he seemed to be just wasting time instead of holding down a steady job, when he was reaching for things that seemed unattainable, like a decent role in a Broadway play—one kind of tension existed between them. Now that failure was giving way to success, Harry feared that they were beginning to drift farther apart. The physical separation enforced on them by bookings away from New York seemed to widen the mental rift between them.

In addition, as with all attractive male performers, Harry was faced with the problem of resisting a growing contingent of female admirers. No one outside of show business can really have any idea of how aggressive this contingent can be. Their favors do not necessarily decrease a man's loneliness, tension, or distance from loved ones.

When Sinatra first became the rage of the swoon-and-squeal crowd, his assistants faced the most serious problems in flushing girls out of his hotel bedrooms. Before allowing Sinatra to retire for the evening, they would literally go through his closets to make sure that no adoring and acquiescent females had hidden themselves there.

Some years ago, at the height of Bob Mitchum's rise as a love god, I was walking down Fifth Avenue with him and his wife. Well-dressed women would come rushing at him the moment they spotted him and embrace him, some kissing him or offering their lips for a kiss—completely oblivious of his wife's presence.

Any man has to be rather determined to be able to fight

off advances of this kind. Particularly when he is away from home—and lonely—for long periods of time. That rumors began to fly around Belafonte's handsome head is hardly surprising. Gossip had it that he went for "big blonde showgirls and big white convertibles." Margurite Belafonte was mature enough not to pay attention to the gossip columnists. She disliked it when she read "hot" items about Harry just as she hated the milieu and mores of show business as a whole. For his part, Harry was not only devoted to his family. He was violently afraid of scandal. More than anything else, he would have enjoyed having his family, particularly his daughter Adrienne, with him on the road.

Characteristically, while he was at The Black Orchid, Margurite received a call from him one evening. In a failing voice, he told her that he was very sick and that she had to fly to Chicago immediately with Adrienne.

"I was really frightened," Margurite reports. "When I got to the hotel, the manager was expecting me and he and the bell captain showed me upstairs. Just as we got off the elevator, I could hear a phonograph blasting, *It's been a long time since I've seen that gal of mine.* Harry was sick all right . . . homesick and lonely."

STEREO
WHITE CANARIES AND NEGRO BANDS

In the jazz and pop music fields, the stubbornest interracial barrier of all, according to Leonard Feather, author of *The Encyclopedia of Jazz*, has been the association of the white girl vocalist with a Negro band. But even this barrier fell in the year 1952.

Blonde Helen Merrill, whose white husband played saxophone in the same combo, sang with the Earl Hines sextet. During the following year, vibraphonist Lionel Hampton, a Benny Goodman alumnus, used brunette Janet Thurlow on vocals.

During 1959 a new jazz vocal group, Lambert, Hendricks, and Ross, scored something of a musical sensation. The group consists of two men and a girl. Lambert and Hendricks, the men, are one white and the other Negro. Annie Ross, the girl, is white.

On September 17, 1959 *Down Beat* Magazine, which has always exhibited a healthy respect for the role of the Negro in jazz, scored something of a "first" for itself. On its cover, it carried a full-sized picture of Lambert, Hendricks, and Ross. The two men were touching noses and looking intently into each other's eyes while the girl, whose pretty face jutted up above the two profiles, had an arm draped affectionately over the shoulder of each.

At first it appeared that this might be a "first" in newsstand periodical history. But then I came across an issue of *Ebony* Magazine (July 1953) which featured a picture of three people on its cover—Harry Belafonte, Tony Curtis, and Janet Leigh. Mrs. Curtis had one arm around her husband and the other around Belafonte. Doubtless, *Down Beat* scored a "first" for non-Negro publications.

So far as can be ascertained, no newsstands were overturned and no news dealers, who displayed the *Down Beat* issue, were tarred or feathered.

12. Provoke and Charm

Few people who have ever heard Harry Belafonte do *Matilda, Matilda* on a night club floor—"Seeng another chorus"—forget his rendition or are able to avoid joining in the infectious choruses. It's one of handsome Harry's sure-fire numbers. Before *The Banana Boat Song, Mama! Look A Bubu,* and the other calypso ditties that captured the world's fancy, *Matilda, Matilda* was almost Harry's theme.

Harry recorded *Matilda, Matilda* for the first time in April 1953. It was on his first date after RCA Victor renewed his contract. Henri René arranged and conducted the session. The instrumental backing included three fiddles, three clarinets, three drummers, and a seven-piece vocal group. More than two years later, in August 1955, Harry re-recorded the tune in Hollywood, this time with an arrangement by Tony Scott and an instrumental group that approximated a band of the swing era. A number of the sidemen had, in fact, once played with the big bands of Benny Goodman, Woody Herman, and Stan Kenton. The six-man brass section included Maynard Ferguson, who made a name for himself with the Herman Herd, while the five-man sax section included Jimmy Giuffre, Bud Shank, Ted Nash, and Herb Steward, all swing band alumni. Like Jim Hall, who played guitar, most of these men had become part of the West Coast jazz movement and were making names for themselves with small jazz combos. It's this second version of *Matilda* that was included in the now-famous *Calypso* album.

Harry is one of a limited number of recording stars who are willing to re-record songs they consider important. Since all recording costs are charges levied by the companies against an artist's royalties, re-recording is basically a matter of an artist's own feeling about his material and work. *Eden Was Like This*, a song from the ill-fated production *Sing, Man, Sing*, was recorded by Harry on three different occasions until he got the version he wanted—twice with the same arrangement, though with different musicians, and once with an entirely different background. That he is willing to do this since he hit the bigtime is less significant than the fact that he did it when he was just climbing.

Harry's approach in a recording studio is quite relaxed. He pushes himself mercilessly without pushing the people around him. He is painstakingly meticulous without losing his sense of humor. Occasionally, just before "a take," when every musician in the studio is holding his breath, Harry will let go with a whimsical thought that may cross his mind. It will delay the take and waste precious time. (After three hours of recording, each musician gets time-and-half for each thirty minutes or portion thereof.) But it will, perhaps, bring a sense of ease that may result in a more relaxed and more attractive-sounding take.

The matter of "relationship" is so basic in Harry's thinking and conduct that what happens in a studio depends in large degree on the rapport he is able to establish with his conductor, the musicians, the A & R supervisor, and even the engineers. Harry works at it. Herman Diaz, of the RCA Victor A & R staff, enjoys telling the story of his first date with Harry. Apparently Diaz and Harry did not know each other very well. Some days before the session, Diaz had visited Harry backstage at the Broadway theatre where he was appearing to discuss some songs with him. Harry was neither too receptive nor too friendly.

Came the session, and Harry entered the studio to find Diaz supervising the date. His greeting was perfunctory. As the session progressed, he did not pay very much attention to Diaz' occasional observations from the soundproof engineer's booth nor did Diaz feel free to say very much. The session did not go too smoothly. For some reason or other, Harry was particularly bothered by the drummers.

[122]

In one number, he kept interrupting the take, each time trying to make the drummers use a slightly different beat. Somehow, he could not get his idea across. After he had interrupted the fifth take, Diaz decided that the time had come. He entered the studio, walked over to the drummers, all of whom were of Latin-American descent, and proceeded to explain in a fast, voluble Spanish what Harry wanted. Harry's ears perked up at the rapid flow of Spanish from Diaz' lips. When the drummers confirmed their understanding of the instructions, a smile spread over Harry's face.

"Why, I didn't know you could speak Spanish like that!" he exclaimed to Diaz.

"Why shouldn't I?" Diaz asked. "I'm Puerto Rican."

After that, the session went without a hitch, and Diaz never had another problem with Harry.

I happened to be present at the session at which Harry first recorded *Matilda, Matilda* in April '53. My presence at the date was accidental. I was working as general professional manager of a pop music publishing house. The professional manager is to pop publishing what the music editor is to longhair publishing. He selects material for publication, only since recordings make hits, he's the man who tries to find hit songs and get them recorded.

One day as I was walking through the halls of RCA Victor on 24th Street near Third Avenue, I heard a strange, interesting voice coming out of Studio 2. Although there was a large "No Visitors" sign on the door, I managed to gain entry to the engineer's booth, which is separated from the studio by a thick, soundproof pane of glass. Through it I could see a tall, handsome, young Negro at a mike, chanting with appealing animation the cynical but amusing tale of the girl "who took me money and run Ven-e-zue-la!" It was, of course, *Matilda, Matilda.* I must confess that if I had heard of Harry Belafonte at the time, I knew little about him. But I was charmed by the song and enchanted by Belafonte's singing of it. Apparently, so was everyone in the studio because no one paid the slightest attention to me.

[123]

When the take was over and everybody was momentarily relaxing, a wiry, boyish-looking chap with soft, gray-blue eyes and a crewcut came over to me. It was Jack Rollins. I introduced myself and went right to the heart of the subject: Was *Matilda, Matilda* available for publication?

Rollins hesitated and said "it might be." At that moment, Harry came out of the studio into the engineer's booth. Rollins introduced me as if I were an old friend. Harry said hello in a warm way, but a little bit like a fighter looking over a possible adversary.

When the record date was over, I tried to get Harry and Jack Rollins to come out for a cup of coffee. But they were in a hurry to go somewhere, and the best I could manage was to ride uptown with them in a taxi. There I made my pitch for the publication rights to the version Harry had sung of *Matilda*. Harry listened, joked a bit, said "it might be arranged," and left me hopeful but quite uncertain.

For the three succeeding days, I was on the phone with Jack Rollins or riding taxicabs with Rollins and Belafonte. They were a stimulating pair. Together, they exuded great warmth and displayed an excitement about the work at hand which was catching. There was also an intimacy and interplay between them—at times humorous, at times intellectual—which made their partnership attractive to the outsider. During the course of our negotiations, we had a number of fast sandwiches together. On at least one occasion I went with them to an East Side hospital to visit an ailing girl. She was Virginia Wicks, the attractive blonde who had been Harry's first co-manager and was now simply handling his publicity.

Harry and his manager were obviously trying to size me up during those three days of contact. Presumably, I passed. At the end of that time, Belafonte turned *Matilda, Matilda* over to the firm for which I was working—and on a very reasonable basis. But admittedly something else was going on during those days of negotiation. I can only describe it as a cat-and-mouse game. I was the mouse and Harry was the cat. And I was aware that Harry was getting a certain kind of pleasure out of it. There were times when I almost felt that he could not stop himself from playing around in this way. Most of the time there was nothing malicious about it. But here is where Rollins played his quiet role. As soon as he sensed that the game was beginning to get a little rough—and there were times when Harry's kidding almost provoked the kind of kickback that I could not afford if I was to close a deal with him—Rollins would step in and turn the game from the potentially cruel back to the playful. Like a big cat, Harry had both these tendencies in his make-up.

On a night club floor, you sense similarly conflicting drives in Harry. There is the tenderness—about that little girl in Kingston town, as in *Jamaica Farewell*. But there is also the hostility and the anger, as in *John Henry*. And there is always the ingratiating playfulness, as when he kids an audience about joining him in *Matilda:* "Big spenders, be still! Now, the intellectuals! Everybody, sing!"

A close friend has said of Harry: "His first reaction to people, particularly new people, is to try to get a rise out of them. And he'll work at it. Then, inevitably, he'll work equally hard at charming them, either because he has come to like them or because he does not want them to leave free of the Belafonte spell. That's Harry—provoke and charm!"

By the middle of 1953 Harry began to attract analytical attention in some of the trade publications. *Down Beat* summed up his artistry in one word: *Universality.* "Belafonte hits all kinds of audiences in their emotions," Don Freeman wrote, "hits them with such truth and honesty that the differences in people seem to vanish. Universality is the word."

Nevertheless, the *Down Beat* analyst found that Harry's art was "an elusive quicksilver" to capture in print. The reason: Harry both *was* and was *not* a folk singer. "Belafonte is synthetic in folk singing," he wrote. "His roots are not in regional soil, as Richard Dyer-Bennett's are in Kentucky or Leadbelly's in Texas. Belafonte is a native New Yorker, the possessor of a not-large but extremely flexible voice and a flair for theatre . . . a guy who collaborates with others to revamp different folk tunes . . ."

[125]

Harry's universal appeal was the keynote also of another *Down Beat* article that appeared in November of '53 on his return to The Boulevard. He had been at the Queens nitery just a year earlier and had had the problem of all performers with a rather raucous audience. But he had won them then. Now, after a year, he was to score an even more triumphal reception. So revealing of the strides that Harry had made in a short period is the *Down Beat* review that it deserves to be reproduced in full.

"In two years," critic Nat Hentoff wrote, "Harry Belafonte has achieved an unprecedented power and prestige as a folk singing act for the country's top clubs. Unlike similarly labeled performers, he scores as strongly at The Thunderbird in Las Vegas and the Chase Hotel in St. Louis as in the more subtle rooms like The Blue Angel and The Black Orchid.

"The unusual breadth of his potential audience has been rarely demonstrated more climactically than in this engagement. The Boulevard is a cavernous room populated by a raucous, extremely hard-to-please audience. The two acts preceding Belafonte failed to communicate even minimally—often audience conversation drowned out all activity on stand.

"But at Belafonte's entrance, his command of the audience was electric and complete. Accompanied at first only by guitarist Millard Thomas, the open-shirted folk singer began with the hard driving *Timber* and segued to the softly romantic *Scarlet Ribbons*.

"For his third number *Hold 'Em Joe,* Harry Belafonte had audience joining in the refrain on cue. Belafonte then—like a magician reveling in his skill—threw the room into hushed attention with a musical dramatization of an Alabama preacher chanting a sermon at the death of Lincoln.

"Called back for several encores, Belafonte displayed even more diversity with a rhythmic performance in Hebrew of the Israeli song *Hava Nageela* (*Let Us Rejoice*). The already conquered audience reacted with continuous enthusiasm to *Venezuela, Matilda,* and the Jamaican song about the eternal mystery *Man Piaba.*"

1953 finished in a burst of glory for Harry. *Billboard* chose him as one of the great newcomers for its "Talent Showcase of 1954," and John Murray Anderson signed him for his first appearance on Broadway. As Christmas approached, it was clear that Harry's star had risen. The question no longer was: would he make it, but how big would he be?

Harry showed confidence in his future by moving his family from the fourth-floor apartment they occupied in Washington Heights to a newly purchased, two-story, attached house in Elmhurst, Long Island. The house was not too far from La Guardia Airport, with the constant drone of planes overhead. For young Adrienne, then four years old, East Elmhurst represented a considerable improvement over 156th Street and Amsterdam Avenue, considering the greater play space provided by a private house, a back yard, and traffic-free streets.

Harry found the house through actor Frank Silvera, who was a close friend. Not that Frank recommended it to Harry. What happened was that Frank was driving around with Harry one day, helping him look for a house. In the course of their search, Frank drove to Elmhurst, where he wanted Harry to see a house he was about to buy for himself.

It was at 96-16 Twenty-fifth Avenue. Harry looked it over with Frank.

"What do you think?" Frank asked, when they were back in the car.

"I guess it's all right," Harry said.

"You don't mean that," Frank said. "What's wrong with it?"

Harry proceeded to enumerate. First, it was an attached house. Second, the rooms were not too large. Third, it had very little garden area. Fourth, the price was not that good.

Frank was surprised. But after some conversation, he agreed. He decided to buy another.

"Imagine Frank's amazement," Margurite Belafonte said recently, "when he came to visit us some months later and found that Harry had bought the very house himself.

"It was a white neighborhood," Margurite added. "We were the first Negro family on the block, and as soon as we moved in, a certain number of For Sale signs appeared immediately. We were a little uneasy but there were no incidents.

"In fact, it didn't take too long before a strange thing happened. Harry fixed up the basement for Adrienne so that she had a miniature home down there, completely fitted out with miniature furniture and utensils. In the back yard, Adrienne had a swing, a wading pool, a seesaw and I forget what else. No other kid on the block had anything like it. As the kids found out, they began coming over to play with Adrienne. Before long, our house and yard were like a day nursery.

"One day, after the kids had departed and Adrienne was having her dinner, she explained: 'Mother, we've got to move! We've got to move!'

"I looked at her in surprise. We were in the house only a month or so and everything seemed fine. 'But why do we have to move?' I asked, fearing the worst.

"Adrienne swallowed her bite. Then, as if she were telling me the biggest secret, she said: 'Because there are Niggeroos moving into the block!'

"I stared at her wide-eyed. It was apparent that she was repeating what one of her playmates had told her. And obviously, the playmate didn't understand what she was saying any more than Adrienne did.

"I broke out laughing, the whole thing made such a mockery of prejudice.

"Now, the neighborhood is an integrated one. Most of the people on our side of the street are Negro while the folks across the street are white."

In purchasing the house, Harry had shown confidence in his future. But it was apparent that he, like everyone around him, did not have the slightest inkling of how high he would climb within three short years.

STEREO

BILLIE HOLIDAY

Billie Holiday's experiences with race prejudice were double-barreled. Frequently humiliated because she was Negro, she also suffered the paradoxical experience of being regarded as "too white."

Traveling as the only girl and the only Negro with Artie Shaw's famous band, she first had to endure all the indignities of not being served in restaurants where the rest of the band ate, not being able to stay in hotels where the rest of the band stayed, not being able to use toilets when the bus stopped for the rest of the band, etc.

Back in New York for a stand at the Hotel Lincoln, she was permitted to sing with the band in the hotel but excluded when the band broadcast coast-to-coast from the hotel. The Southerners had at least been honest about their bigotry, Billie felt.

After a time, Lady Day joined the all-Negro band of Count Basie. Appearing at the Fox Theatre in Detroit, she suddenly was amazed to discover that she was too yellow-skinned to sing with the black men in the Basie band. The theatre manager argued that people in the audience might think she was white.

So, as she tells the painful story in her autobiography *Lady Sings the Blues*, the management of the theatre went and got her a special dark grease paint. Each time before she went on-stage, she had to sit in front of a make-up mirror and dutifully apply the dark covering—her hands trembling violently and her heart palpitating with fury.

13. The Crowded Years

Fifty-four was the first of the crowded years for Harry. There were to be four of them. Years exploding, like whirling pinwheels, with critical professional and personal developments. In a glance, in '54 Harry made his first starring movie, was featured in two major theatrical productions, became a father for the second time, "met" his wife-to-be, broke with his dedicated manager, and faced a crisis in his relationship with Margurite.

As the year began, Broadway had its first look-see at Harry. The show was a John Murray Anderson production named *Almanac*. It opened at the Imperial Theatre on December 10, 1953.

Opening night, Harry received a telegram from the girl who is now his ex-wife. It read: "Be brilliant tonight, my retarded one. Love, Margurite." The reference to "retarded one" harked back to the days when Harry was courting Margurite and suggesting that marriage would provide her, as a child psychologist, with "a real good subject since I was a retarded child with lots of problems." The retarded child was brilliant in *Almanac*. But the reference was a little out of date.

Almanac as a whole did not fare quite as well as Harry. It had the promise of bright, successful names like English comedienne Hermione Gingold, comedian Billy De Wolfe, choreographer Donald Saddler, set designer Raoul Pene du Bois, and actor Cyril Ritchard, who staged the sketches. It also boasted the promise of a new team of talented songsmiths, Adler and Ross, protégés of Frank Loesser, who later produced hit scores for *Pajama Game* and *Damn Yankees*. Nevertheless, *Almanac* received only lukewarm notices.

[130]

Harry escaped notice in many reviews. But he was singled out in several in a way that would have made it difficult for readers, who had not seen the show, to figure out what he was actually doing in it.

"What Mr. Belafonte contributes," wrote the dean of dramatic critics, Brooks Atkinson of *The New York Times,* "is so original, imaginative and stunning that perhaps the weakness of the general score is not important. Mr. Belafonte is electrifyingly sincere."

A ready assumption might be that Harry was playing some dramatic part. And that assumption would be given credence by the comments of John Beaufort in *The Christian Science Monitor:* "For style, grave elegance, and authoritative performance, Harry Belafonte makes an outstanding appearance. He appears only briefly in *Almanac,* but he commands the stage whenever he is on it."

Yet all that Harry did in *Almanac* was to sing three songs: *Hold 'Em Joe, Acorn in the Meadow,* and his own composition *Mark Twain,* in which Brooks Atkinson found "a harsh, tense beauty that brings the audience up short."

Two different producers who saw Harry in *Almanac* signed him, one for a starring role in a movie, the other, for a starring role in a new musical. At the end of the theatrical year when awards were being given out, Harry received the coveted Antoinette Perry prize as "the best supporting actor of the year" and the *Billboard* Donaldson Award "for the best supporting actor in a musical show."

To Harry, who still wanted nothing so much as a chance to act, there was something ironic in both these awards, much as he prized them. Here he was receiving dramatic trophies for being a folk singer. "Technically, he could not sing," writer Maurice Zolotow contends. "But he was an actor playing the best role he was ever to get: the role of a singer."

"Instead of bringing me closer to the goal I was shooting for," Harry has said, "I had the oppressive feeling that I might be doomed to go on forever as a singer."

Harry's state of mind calls to mind an observation of John

Dos Passos: "People don't choose careers. They are engulfed by them."

"As a matter of fact," Margurite Belafonte reports, "Harry never went to receive the Antoinette Perry award. He sent me. On the day the awards were being handed out, he suddenly developed a bad case of laryngitis. This ailment has always been a helpful one to Harry. By evening, he could hardly talk. Although I didn't want to go, I just had to.

"When I returned home with the award, the laryngitis had improved considerably. I asked Harry why he had insisted on my going. His response was that he wanted me to accept the award because it was one way of getting me to share in his career.

"I accepted the explanation then. I'm not sure now—although I confess I don't know the real reason for his sending me. One thing is clear. He surely did not want to go to accept it himself."

While he thrilled Broadway audiences with his *Almanac* songs—how far away those nights seemed when he wandered along Broadway yearning to see his name in lights—Harry doubled at the swank, if short-lived, Monte Proser club on East 54th Street, La Vie En Rose. His salary was reported at an astronomical $4,000 a week, which seems rather high, since his work in the theatre made him unavailable for the early dinner show.

Whether Harry's weekly take had climbed to four grand or not, reviewer reaction had risen to the realms of the panegyrical.

"Harry Belafonte improves so much with each hearing," the editor of *Metronome* commented, "that I have run out of superlatives . . . Harry's act is beautifully paced, well acted and wonderfully sung . . . In these continuing days of the cute and/or folksy singers, Harry is a gem."

Nevertheless, Harry was still not over the line. It is one of the enigmas of show business that an artist like Dinah Shore, with a high-rated TV show, is unable to come up with a hit record. For years, Tony Martin has been a sellout in night clubs around the country, likewise has not had a disclick. To score equally in all media an artist has to be at a peak point in his career. While Harry was being showered with accolades for his work in *Almanac* and at La Vie, RCA Victor released recordings of two of the show's tunes. Neither *Acorn in the Meadow* by Adler and Ross nor *Hold 'Em Joe* by Harry and Millard Thomas amounted to anything on disks despite their effectiveness on stage.

During three record sessions in April and one in May of '54, RCA Victor cut twelve sides with Harry, building an LP around his own show-stopping composition *Mark Twain*. While the calypso beat is to be heard in a number of songs, the emphasis in the album is, however, on American, English, and Scottish folk ballads. Harry offers new versions by Paul Campbell of *The Drummer and the Cook* (an old English sea chantey), *Soldier, Soldier, Lord Randall, The Next Big River,* and *Tol' My Captain* (an American chain gang song). Campbell was the writing pseudonym of Pete Kameron, the manager-publisher who proved so helpful to Harry during his first engagement in Las Vegas. In fact, *Mark Twain* and most of the songs included in Harry's first album were published by the firm with which Kameron was then associated. Harry had not forgotten. But unfortunately, the sales of *Mark Twain and Other Favorites* were little more than satisfactory on its initial release. In '55, when Harry went on tour with *Three for Tonight*, the album began to move. But after the *Calypso* album broke for a runaway hit in '57, *Mark Twain* suddenly turned into a fast seller, along with practically everything that Harry had recorded before it.

Hardly satisfactory were developments in the Belafonte household. Courtrooms cover such situations with the word "incompatible." The deepening rift between Margurite and Harry was not even verbalized at this stage. Many a night during the run of *Almanac*, Harry slept at the fourth-floor walk-up of Tony and Fran on West 52nd Street.

But an intimate friend of Harry's recalls one evening when he drove Harry home late at night. Instead of going in immediately, Harry sat in the darkened car trying not to talk and not being too successful at it.

"He was pained beyond words," a friend reports. "He had no desire to break up his marriage and yet he felt he was powerless to prevent it. Margurite and he were just drifting—and the drift was apart. Each had accepted the other's position and come to recognize that it was beyond alteration. Margurite still cherished her own concepts of the home. She still did not think it was right for her to be a working mother or for Harry to be away for long periods of time. For his part, Harry was committed to the showman's way of life, which Margurite regarded as bohemian.

"By this time, I think Harry had given up the battle to win her over. In fact, what pained him so much was that he didn't care any more. Just didn't care. The amenities and the courtesies of living together were observed. But the feeling was gone.

"What made the situation even more delicate was that a second baby was on the way. Presumably, the idea was that this baby would bring them closer together. You know, it would cement in the absence of feeling. As with many couples, by the time Shari arrived in September, their relationship was virtually at a breaking point. In some way, I don't think Margurite sensed how far Harry was drifting.

"You see Harry is basically a lonely character. He needs affection. He needs companionship. He had very little of either of these in his youth so that they are a constant hunger with him. How do you get companionship out of a woman who disapproves of your friends? How do you get companionship out of a woman who does not agree with your outlook on things and is not interested in the things that interest you? That's why Harry turned to me and to other friends and acquaintances in New York and on the road.

"But he was ripe for a female that could give him companionship when he ran into Julie Robinson in Hollywood during the filming of *Carmen Jones.*"

Despite the spiraling success he was enjoying as a singer, Harry still felt full of frustration about his acting. Interviewed by *Newsweek* at this time, he said of his singing: "It's like having a big brother overshadow you all the time."

But it was "the big brother" who opened the door to an acting assignment. Into a performance of *Almanac* one evening came Otto Preminger, the Hollywood producer. Preminger was then occupied in casting *Carmen Jones*, Oscar Hammerstein II's modernized, all-Negro version of the famous Bizet opera. One look at the "singing actor" and Preminger knew that he had found his male lead. On April 29th, while he was completing the *Mark Twain* LP for RCA Victor, Harry was signed to play Joe, the soldier boy who falls tragically in love with Carmen, the cigarette girl.

A month later, Harry headed out to Hollywood. This was his third visit to the movie capital. A little more than a year earlier, he had been the first Negro to play the posh Cocoanut Grove in the Hotel Ambassador. Two years earlier, he had made *The Bright Road* for M-G-M.

But his visit in 1954 was much more important. Now, for the first time, he had a dramatic role in a major production, something for which he had been hungering since that dramatic night in 1946 when he had seen a flop play at the American Negro Theatre. Interestingly enough, Harry did no singing in *Carmen Jones*. Levern Hutcherson, one of the Broadway Porgy's in *Porgy and Bess*, dubbed in the exciting music while Harry mouthed the lyrics.

Without anticipating it, Harry's '54 visit to Hollywood took on a personal import far exceeding any professional promises it posed. One day on the set of *Carmen Jones*, he met the girl who was to become the second Mrs. Belafonte.

Julie Robinson, the second child of a libertarian Jewish couple, Clara and George Robinson, was born in New York City almost ten years after her older sister. Growing up during her parents' middle years and when she could not establish much rapport with her sister, she was a rather lonely child. Early, she revealed two tendencies which were to become prominent motives in her life. The artistic impulse took her to the High School of Music and Art, after she attended The Little Red School House in Greenwich Village. Later it

[135]

launched her on a career as a dancer. The humanitarian impulse expressed itself first in a fondness for stray animals, later in a deepening friendship for all outcasts, and eventually in concentrated activity in behalf of the NAACP. Wedded to these two impulses was a carefree, fun-loving Bohemianism, which could well have had its origin in the Village where Julie went to school and lived for twelve of her formative years.

Friends of Julie's say that by the time she was twelve, all her closest friends were Negroes. Something in the lonely Jewish girl apparently responded to the problems of ostracism and discrimination endured by her Negro playmates. Just as Harry could not early identify with members of his own family, Julie more easily identified with an alien culture.

As she grew, this cultural alienation developed into a far-ranging interest in other cultures. When she began to travel, she displayed an unusual knack for participating in the ways of other peoples and identifying with them. Languages came easily to her. This deepened the degree of her rapid immersion in a new culture.

Julie's father, George Robinson, contends that her young friendships were not all, or even mostly, Negro. According to him, comparatively few Negro families lived in the Village from '35 to '47, the years in which they dwelled there, and her classmates at The Little Red School House included only a few Negroes.

"What is true," George Robinson said recently, "is that Julie had a feeling for all people. Once, she told me that she just did not see skin color, that it had no more effect on her than eye color. But her intimacy with Negroes was not a deliberate choice. It was a natural result of her interest in dancing and her studies with The Katherine Dunham Dancers."

Although she had a good musical ear and an ability to draw —her father thinks she was a better artist than a dancer—it was the dance that became a consuming passion with Julie by the time she was in high school. Nor was it long before that passion defined itself as a determination to become a member of a leading dance group of the day, The Katherine

Dunham Company. Nobody who knew the small, dark-complexioned girl, with the long black braids—she still wears a pigtail or one braid over each shoulder—ever escaped knowing that this was her one most encompassing desire. And, of course, the members of the Negro Company itself were well aware of the intensity with which Julie Robinson, white and Jewish, studied, practiced, and yearned to be one of them.

Competition among students at the Dunham School for acceptance in the Company was quite keen. But Julie was not only a fine, dedicated dancer. She was quite resourceful. When the Company left for Mexico to give a series of dance recitals, Julie followed them at her own expense, presumably just to be near them. According to dancer-singer Eartha Kitt, who was to become Julie's closest friend in the Company, along with Walter Nicks, this action was what finally broke Katherine Dunham down. On their return to New York, Julie was accepted as a full-fledged member of the troupe. It was the happiest day of Julie's youth—although it was also not to be without its difficulties.

As the only white girl in the Dunham Company, she was to face the same problem of acceptance which once troubled Tony Scott as a white clarinetist in the Ellington band. With all the Negro girls who wanted to join the Dunham Company, there were members of the troupe who resented Julie. Her competence had nothing to do with the fact that she was depriving a Negro—with more limited employment opportunities—of the chance to be, and to earn a livelihood as a dancer. Of course, most members of the Company felt that an integrated troupe was a good thing artistically and socially.

The resentment was short-lived. Julie's animated personality, her complete ease, and, perhaps, most of all, her willingness to share the problems as well as the pleasures of a Negro dance group—soon broke down the few Dunham dancers who had reservations about having a white girl in the Company.

By 1947 Julie's name was to be found in the mimeoed brochure of The Dunham School of Dance as one of the teachers of the basic course: "Dunham Technique and Primitive Rhythms." In the same year, when the troupe went to England, it was Eartha Kitt with whom Julie shared an apartment. And it was through people whom Julie's parents knew in London that the two of them managed to find a four-room flat at 10 Manchester Square.

"It cost more than we could really afford," Eartha said recently. "But we were taken with the place, particularly because it had the largest bathroom we had ever seen. It was just enormous. And all of the rooms were bigger than a similar apartment in New York. So you can just imagine. We decided, after one look, that even though there was an attractive fireplace, it was the bathroom that was worth all the careful budgeting it would take.

"We got along beautifully during the six months we lived together, not only because Julie is very sensitive and full of understanding, but because we were most sympathetic to the problems of each other's people and, in an over-all way, to the problems of the relations of different peoples all over the world.

"Julie is a very methodical person and we worked out a routine. I took care of the shopping and Julie took care of the apartment. We alternated in cooking although Julie was particularly good at it and loved to cook for friends who came over. Every Sunday was open house and we used to have a constant flow of people—friends and people from the theatres we played—who would come up for talk, tea, and food.

"One of the things that bothered Julie was that we might be depriving British people of food rations. You see, even though we were American visitors, we were on rations just like the rest of the country. And we got exactly the same amounts of butter, meat, sugar, etc., as the English. Julie and I used to discuss this problem constantly. In her concern over the relations of different peoples, she was troubled that the English might resent Americans who took their rations. The truth is, despite all the entertaining we did, we usually succeeded in saving some of our weekly rations. Each week we would turn over our surplus to people around the theatre, the ushers, the maintenance workers, the ticket sellers.

"But not all of our days were 'problem' days. Julie was a very gay person, full of life and excited about living so that it was fun living with her. Ours was a wonderful friendship and we still enjoy its fruits and good feeling."

By 1950 Julie appeared as a featured dancer in three numbers of The Dunham Company repertoire. A program of The Broadway Theatre for May 1 of that year lists her as one of four soloists in a 19th-century Brazilian Quadrille and as one of three featured dancers of the Bamba in *Veracruzana.* The Bamba is described as a native South American dance in which participants tie a knot using their feet alone while they lie on the ground. On the same program, Julie also danced the Tango, as the first part of *Jazz in Five Movements.*

All in all, Julie remained with The Dunham Company for almost six years, traveling around the world with it and winning the respect and admiration of its members both for her dedication as a dancer and her complete identification with its problems. When the Dunham troupe faced discrimination, Julie refused to separate herself, as she could have done, and shared the humiliation to which the color of her associates subjected them.

By the time Harry met her, she was settled in Hollywood, where her father had gone into semi-retirement and moved his family. She herself was involved in some motion picture work, and was known to be one of the girls whom Marlon Brando was dating steadily. Apparently it was Brando who took her onto the set of *Carmen Jones* and introduced her to his friend of the New York Drama Workshop and Village days.

Of his contact with Julie at this time, Harry has said: "From the very beginning, I found conversation with her wonderful and easy. We talked about the struggle of the Negro against second-class citizenship and of the revolt against colonial rule going on among millions of dark-skinned Africans and Asians. We talked about jazz and folk music, politics and baseball."

When the conversation got around to books, Julie offered to lend Harry several that she had recently found exciting.

[139]

Harry remembers the titles of two: *African Folk Tales and Sculpture* and *Slave Songs of the Georgia Sea Islands*. A few days later, he dropped by the Robinson home to pick up the volumes. It was his first meeting with Clara and George Robinson, Julie's parents.

Harry recalls that they sat and talked in a very relaxed fashion. That he was impressed by their cordiality is clear. "To them," he later wrote, "I was a practically unknown actor-singer. Things were just getting started for me and the hot records were many months away." What also moved Harry was the lively and warm atmosphere of the Robinson home. It was the kind of home he had never known as a boy.

When Harry left the coast that summer, he was filled with strange inner stirrings.

Although *Carmen Jones* was a hit as a Broadway operatic musical and became a solid box-office success as a movie, it far from satisfied the movie critics. *New York Times* reviewer Bosley Crowther felt that "the Joe of Harry Belafonte is an oddly static symbol of masculine lust, lost in a vortex of confusion rather than a nightmare of shame. He is the hero, but he is oddly unheroic in this noisily ridiculed role." Nor was Crowther entirely pleased with the handling of some of the Negro roles. "Around the fringes," he stated, "there are numerous and assorted Amos 'n' Andy characters."

On the other hand, some reviewers greatly admired Harry's acting. The torrid love sequences were singled out for praise. One writer compared the scene where Harry kisses Carmen's big toe with such famous scene stoppers as Lauren Bacall's line to Bogart, "If you want me, just whistle," and an earlier socko scene where Jimmy Cagney squashed a grapefruit in Mae Clarke's face.

In an interview only recently over KRHM of Los Angeles, Harry indicated that *Carmen Jones* served an important historical purpose.

"It was the first all-Negro film," he said, "that became a great box-office success. It established the fact that pictures with Negro artists, pictures dealing with the folklore of Negro

[140]

life, were commercially feasible. This was a sign of growth that had occurred both in the United States and throughout the world."

Harry threw himself into his role with his usual zest for work and the restless energy that frequently has driven him to record right through the night. So impassioned was his playing that in the final scene where he murders Carmen for her faithlessness, Otto Preminger became worried lest he hurt Dorothy Dandridge, who played Carmen.

"When you strangle the lady," Preminger warned, "don't put wrinkles in her neck."

This was the second film in which Dandridge played opposite Harry. It was not the last. But during the filming of *Carmen Jones*, the story was that they were fighting.

"I hate the way these things get started," Harry said at the time. "Dorothy and I are supposed to have fallen out over who got top billing in *Carmen*. In the first place, the dispute was between our representatives. In the second, the outcome was a tie. She got top billing in advertising and I got it on the screen."

When he completed the shooting of *Carmen Jones*, Harry made his second appearance at the Cocoanut Grove. This time (August '54), the balance between artistic and financial success was more neatly maintained. In fact, business was good and the reviews were even better.

"Return of Harry Belafonte to this hotel's after-dark retreat," wrote *Variety*, "has all the makings of a solid three week stand . . . Opening night crowd was pounding for more." Singled out for special praise was *Noah*, a gospel shout in which he was accompanied only by the mesmerizing beat of the drums.

Harry's second child, christened Shari Lynn Belafonte, was born at French Hospital in New York on September 22, 1954, after Harry's return from the filming of *Carmen Jones*. During that week, Tony Scott received a phone call from Harry inquiring whether he and Fran would be home on Sunday.

"Sure thing," Tony said.

"I'll be over at about eleven A.M.," Harry promised.

[141]

Close to the hour, the bell of their fourth-floor walk-up rang, and there was Harry.

"How soon can you get ready?" he asked.

"Where are we going?" Tony inquired.

"Out to Elmhurst."

"I'm ready now," Tony said. He was wearing an informal sports outfit. "But Fran can't come."

"Oh, we can't go without Fran," Harry insisted.

"She can't. She's in bed with the grippe."

Harry needed convincing. Even after he saw Fran lying in bed, surrounded by the usual medical bottles and Kleenex, he was not ready to take "no" for an answer.

"I'll drive her there and back," Harry urged.

"The doctor says she has to stay indoors," Tony said.

Harry was disappointed. "All right, then, let's go."

It was only when they reached Harry's home in Elmhurst that Tony discovered the surprise in store for him. He was to be godfather to Shari. Thus, Shari Belafonte became the first child in history to be attended by a godfather dressed in slacks, sports shirt, and sneakers.

The baptismal ceremony took place at St. Gabriel's Roman Catholic Church in Elmhurst. Ann Silvera, the wife of actor Frank Silvera, was godmother.

When Margurite returned home after Shari's birth, she opened the drawers of a little used closet. There, tucked among a stack of music, was a little stack of letters. At first Margurite thought they were old letters she had placed there for safekeeping. She took them out, planning to transfer them to another place. Now, with another child in the house, the extra space could be used.

Suddenly she realized that there was something strange about the handwriting. For no reason, she felt her heart beating wildly. As she began glancing through the letters, it all seemed like a bad dream. She did not have to finish any missive to know it was from a girl. So were all the letters. They had all been sent to Harry at an address other than the house. They all bore the same signature.

At first Margurite decided to act as if she had not seen them. She tried to think back over the events of the past months. There was nothing in Harry's conduct to suggest that he was interested in another girl. Away from New York, he had phoned regularly to talk to her and Adrienne. In New York, he had treated her with consideration and affection. Sometimes he seemed distracted. But she had attributed it to all the new things that were happening to him.

Still, it was impossible to brush aside the letters or the name "Julie." Who was she? Here Margurite's lack of contact with Harry's circle of theatrical friends stood her in poor stead. She thought about it for a while. Suddenly she remembered little things that had been whispered to her over a period of time. She was not given to jealousy and she had dismissed the gossip as idle rumor. But now she had to know.

"Who's Julie?" she asked, the following morning. She tried to make it sound matter-of-fact.

"Julie who?"

"How many Julie's do you know, Harry?"

Harry looked at his wife nonplused. "If you mean Julie Robinson. She's a dancer. Used to be with Katherine Dunham."

"What's she to you?"

"Just a friend. Why?"

"I accidentally saw some letters she wrote to you."

"You did? How could you?" Harry glanced involuntarily at the closet where he had put the letters.

"It was an accident. I'm sorry."

"I am too."

"Are you serious about her?"

There was a noticeable pause before Harry replied. "I'm serious about my work."

"Are you planning to see her again?"

"I'm planning to do a Negro folk musical this winter."

"You didn't answer me, Harry. I think an answer is in order."

"I have no answers—for a lot of things any more."

"Oh . . ."

[143]

"I have no answers for what's happened to us."

"And I thought things were going nicely for us."

"That's not what I mean." Harry could not keep the tension out of his voice. "For us—yes. I'm talking about *with* us, Margurite."

Now Margurite's self-possession began to crack. "Harry," she said, "you're just beginning to be somebody. It's taken a long time. Scandal can wreck a man's career. Don't let yourself get involved. It could hurt you real bad."

Harry rose from his chair. "Still the retarded child," he half mused to himself. "And you're still mothering me."

"I'm trying to protect you. I'm trying to protect your family —*our* family." Her voice rose involuntarily. "Harry, is there something wrong in that?"

"No, there isn't," he murmured, as if he were talking to himself. "No, there isn't." The turmoil was in his face. "Or is there?"

The Negro folk musical mentioned in his talk with Margurite was an idea that had evolved in discussions with theatrical producer Paul Gregory. As far back as July, they had agreed that they would call it *An Evening of Negro Folklore with Music.* Harry would star. Gregory would produce. Charles Laughton, the actor, would direct.

Because Laughton did not know Belafonte's work too well, Paul Gregory had taken him to hear Harry at La Vie En Rose. The evening that the two were due, Harry suddenly developed an attack of laryngitis. By the time he reached the club, his voice was so hoarse he could hardly do more than squeak. He tried the usual home remedy—hot tea. The warmth brought only slight improvement. In desperation, he had the club manager phone for a neighborhood doctor. It took time before a doctor was found who would make a call that late— it was almost midnight by then. While the doctor was ministering to Harry, the emcee made an announcement regarding the delay.

Finally, the club darkened. The orchestra played the opening fanfare. A beam of light cut through the darkness. It picked out Harry's face, and he opened his mouth to sing. But his voice had the cracked waver and hoarseness of Louis Armstrong with a heavy cold.

When he was twenty seconds in his opening song, Harry suddenly paused. The orchestra leader glanced up in surprise. Harry motioned for him to cut the band. The management was aghast. The audience was nonplused as Harry stepped to the edge of the stage.

"Ladies and gentlemen," he announced through his hoarseness, "as you have probably heard, I had a sudden attack of laryngitis a short while ago. A doctor helped. But as you can hear, I am still quite hoarse. I was determined to go on in the accepted tradition of the audience comes first. But I am sorry to confess, I will not be working at my best. And I would rather disappoint you than give you second-rate Belafonte. Will you bear with me?"

Harry looked around the room and, as his eyes traveled from table to table, spontaneous applause broke out wherever his glance traveled.

Charles Laughton's eyes grew bigger and bigger in amazement. "By jove," he exclaimed, unable to restrain his admiration. "Magnificent! Magnificent!" And he and Paul Gregory stood up in appreciation and joined the applause.

It was, perhaps, the first time in Harry's career that he had scored at an audition without doing a single number. His mere manner had carried the day.

Despite Laughton's enthusiasm for the Negro folk musical, the year came to its end without the production getting under way. Instead, Harry was starred by Paul Gregory in an unusual production called *Three for Tonight*. Just before he left on a fifteen-week tour of one-nighters with Marge and Gower Champion, his co-stars, Harry described his future plans to *Down Beat*.

His most ambitious project, he indicated, was to be what he now called *The Negro Anthology*, tentatively set to begin its travels sometime in the fall of '55. Still to be produced by

[145]

Gregory and staged by Laughton, it would have a company of fifty and feature readings from such Negro authors as James Weldon Johnson and Paul Laurence Dunbar.

"It'll be as authentic as I can find and interpret it," Harry said. "We plan to go into and visit the chain gangs and prison camps in the South." Harry added: "I hope that by the time I'm forty that I'll be sufficiently established so that I can perform material that's even closer to the ethnic base than I do now."

The Negro Anthology was an interesting idea. But it never came to be.

As he was leaving New York with the touring company of *Three for Tonight*, the magazine of female sophistication, *Vogue*, appeared with this comment in its special section—*People Are Talking About:*

"Harry Belafonte, a tall, relaxed young man with long, delicate bones, golden brown skin, and a voice like a strummed guitar, warm and resonant, at 28, an unflustered success in the movies, in night clubs, and on records . . ."

STEREO

LESTER YOUNG

When the late Lester Young, founder of the cool school on tenor sax, was in the Army, he tried to join the band. The warrant officer, an Atlanta man, rejected Young, despite his known musicianship, on the ground that "he'd be too hard to manage."

A sensitive man with virtually no interest except his music, Young went to pieces. Soon a move was under way, initiated by two sympathetic officers, to have him discharged because of "maladjustment to the confines of the Army."

While this was in process, Young entered the hospital for rectal surgery. In answer to a question on the medical forms all surgical patients had to fill out, Lester stated that he smoked marijuana. When he was discharged after the operation, a search was conducted of his belongings.

"In charge of the search," Nat Hentoff writes in *The Jazz Makers*, "was a major from La. who was Jim Crow. In going through Lester's locker, the major found pills (given to Young to relieve postoperative discomfort). He also found a picture of Lester's wife. Lester's wife—they were later divorced —was white . . . Pot [colloquial for marijuana] was probably found . . . The major brought charges against Lester."

Young was given a sentence, after a trial, of five years. Later this was reduced to one year, which he spent in trauma at the detention barracks at Camp Gordon, Georgia.

A friend of the tenorman has said: "Lester has yet to talk in any detail of that year. He'll say a few words once in a while, but then he'll stop. It was a horrible time."

D.B. Blues, which Lester recorded after he got out, provides a musical picture of the nightmare experience.

14. The Trauma of Success

In *The Trouble with Cinderella,* bandleader Artie Shaw tells of how his overnight fame, after the release of his record of *Begin the Beguine,* brought him to the verge of a nervous breakdown. Two things troubled Shaw. One was the gulf that opened between him and men with whom he had worked for years. Suddenly he was alone, isolated, separated from associates by the very fact that he had become a celebrity.

Equally troubling was the blinding and garish glare of publicity in which he found himself floundering. As suddenly as friendships of years' standing, all privacy evaporated overnight. Everything he said, everything he did, was a matter of public interest. Shaw just would not take it. Unnerved, depressed, and resentful, he fled in desperation to Mexico to recuperate from the strain and stress of success.

"They can try and put me in a goldfish bowl," Frank Sinatra has said, in a more and a constantly belligerent mood, "but I don't have to co-operate."

The sudden loss of privacy was equally trying to Harry Belafonte. He hated the feeling of having the press and the public constantly looking over his shoulder. Occasionally, in a spirit of taking revenge, he circulated whatever stories suited his fancy. Queries concerned with his personal life angered him, as they did Frank Sinatra. It was almost four years before he could say with equanimity in a by-line article explaining his second marriage: "I used to think that it should not be necessary for a man to publicly discuss his personal life . . . But things have changed a lot since then. I have changed. I've discovered that an awful lot of people are interested in what happens to me and what I do and feel and think."

The more explosive impact of success had to do, not with Harry's loss of privacy, but with his ambiguous social position. Like other Negroes, he had been refused admittance to various clubs and restaurants, in New York City as well as elsewhere. Of a sudden, the doors of these places were open to Belafonte the performer. The proprietors now were willing to pay large sums of money to book the man they had once barred.

"How do you bridge that gap emotionally?" Harry has asked.

But it was not as simple as all that. There was still a gap of humiliation between Belafonte, the successful artist, and Belafonte, the Negro. Accepted and admired on stage, Harry might immediately thereafter encounter harsh discrimination off-stage. Applauded one moment as a performer, he might face rejection as a human being moments or hours later. How does a sensitive man put these paradoxes together?

Trumpeter Roy Eldridge, known as Little Jazz, tells an almost unbelievable story of how in the days when he was playing with Artie Shaw, he literally could not gain admittance to the hall where he was scheduled to perform.

"This is a white dance," they said.

"And there was my name right outside," Roy (Little Jazz) Eldridge says. "And I told them who I was.

"When I finally did get in, I played that first set, trying to keep from crying . . . I don't know how I made it. I went up to a dressing room and stood in a corner crying . . . Artie came in and he was real great. He made the guy apologize that wouldn't let me in and got him fired.

"Man, when you're on the stage, you're great. But as soon as you come off, you're nothing. It's not worth the glory, not worth the money, not worth anything!"

As time went on, Harry himself was to run into similar situations—once, even, where he was not recognized by a maître d' and told in menacing tones to leave the hotel room where he was scheduled to go on in a few moments.

"Success was traumatic for me," Harry said once. "Here I was, a Negro, being accepted by people of all denominations, in all walks of life, by millions as a performer and an artist.

Yet in my personal life, I was nowhere, not ready for it. I have a swell group of friends of mixed color and denomination—but a small group. I wasn't prepared for this universal acceptance."

"It takes a terribly long time," Sammy Davis, Jr., has said, "to learn how to be a success in show business. People flatter you all the time. You are on all the time. And if you're a Negro, you find yourself using your fame to make it socially. Let's face it. The biggest deals with the moguls are made in a social way around the pool, that sort of thing. If you're not there, well, you're not there. So I used to think the greatest thing in the world was to be invited to a movie star's house."

Harry's new situation made him tense and uneasy. Once, in a sense, he knew who he was, where he stood, and what to expect. Now he could not be sure of anything. He was two people at once. The performer could count on acceptance. The man did not know—he just could not be sure.

"All of a sudden there are crowds coming to see you," Harry has said, explaining his bewilderment, "hundreds of faces looking at you wherever you go, other performers coming to see you work. You're suddenly this special kind of thing. I was too strong to collapse physically. So I collapsed mentally."

Shortly after he broke into the bigtime and the doors of Broadway, Hollywood, and the entire entertainment world began to open wide to him, Harry did what many a celebrity has done before him. The success he hungered for so avidly and struggled for so tenaciously proved temporarily too much of a burden. He felt in need of psychiatric care. He considered several psychiatrists. Eventually, the person he turned to was Dr. Janet Alterman Kennedy, a white analyst and the wife of the man who was to replace Jack Rollins as his manager.

Harry met the Kennedys sometime during the summer of 1953. Ironically enough, he met them through Rollins. Harry was playing a series of one-night stands set up for him by Rollins, which took him to hotels in the White Mountains of New Hampshire, among them Mt. Washington at Bretton Woods and Lake Tarleton Club at Pike. Margurite drove the car from place to place. At one time Millard Thomas had participated in the driving. But Harry and he had had an accident on a trip to Cleveland. Thereafter, Thomas did no driving on their trips.

The Tarleton Club annually runs a summer Festival of the Arts. It invites luminaries from different fields to talk about their work. J. Richard Kennedy, a stockbroker and sometime agent, was present to discuss his new novel *Prince Bart,* then on best-seller lists. Harry had been invited to present a program of folk songs. It was in this setting that Harry met his future analyst, Kennedy's wife, and his future manager, Kennedy himself.

Dr. Janet Alterman Kennedy, a teacher in psychiatry at Columbia University, was known for her interest in the psychotherapy of Negro patients. By the spring of '54, it is reported, Harry was visiting her couch as often as five times a week. If nothing else, this demonstrated, according to contemporary standards of artistic progress, that Harry was on the road to success.

In May 1954, while Harry's visits to Dr. Kennedy continued, he entered into a written agreement with Dr. Kennedy's husband whereby the latter undertook to serve as Harry's business manager and to handle his finances. The agreement extended to August 31, 1957. At the time that it was signed, Jack Rollins was still intimately associated with Harry, his contract as manager being in effect until the end of 1954.

For the better part of a week, I recently attempted to get Rollins to talk of his relationship with Belafonte, both before and after the entry of Kennedy on the scene. For hours at a time, Rollins would patiently explain to me why he could not talk of his days with Belafonte. He felt that going over the past would only revive painful memories.

"What hurt most," Rollins finally admitted to me one day, "was the way I was let out. He threw me away like a used paper cup. He never came right out and told me himself. Instead, he had his new manager phone me and ask me to come down to his office. Of course, I suspected what was happening, but I just couldn't believe it. There had been hints about his needing a business manager to handle big deals. There had been intimations that, perhaps, I would be happier just handling the artistic side of Harry's work. But there had been no suggestion that our association might cease.

"As soon as I was seated in his office, Mr. Kennedy told me he had a letter to read me. Then he proceeded to read this letter, which presumably Harry had written. The gist was that Harry had decided not to renew my contract. He was legally within his rights. I had drawn that contract myself at a time when it seemed silly even to have a contract. Who needed a contract, I thought, when we were brothers—like Damon and Pythias?

"Even though I sensed what was coming, it hit me so hard that I didn't have the strength to rise from my chair. I just sat there speechless and I had the strangest feeling. It was as if I had suddenly been shot into outer space. I was completely detached from everything. I still don't know to this day how I left Mr. Kennedy's office or where I went. Hours later, I found myself at home. Then the realization struck me with hammer blows. I had no money. Although Harry's weekly take had been increasing, he wasn't making enough even in 1954 for my commissions to amount to anything. Furthermore, I had no clients. I had been so immersed in Harry that I hadn't bothered with anyone else.

"The fact that Harry fired Kennedy two years later before the expiration of his contract does not make me feel any better."

"I never knew anybody in this business," said Virginia Wicks, Harry's first co-manager and his praise-agent during Rollins' managership, "that worked for a client as Jack Rollins did for Harry. He slaved for him twenty-four hours a day. And he wasn't getting fifty per cent like some managers. Just a straight ten per cent. Jack got Harry his deal with RCA Victor, his first date in Las Vegas, and his first movie contract. He raised him from two hundred dollars a week up to thirty-five hundred a week, in less than three years."

One of the best personal managers in the entertainment business who knows Belafonte and Rollins said to me: "Any artist who rises as fast as Belafonte did is likely to do what he did. It's partly a matter of ego. But also he may have come to believe that Rollins could not move him beyond the point he had reached. He may have felt that he needed somebody with a bigger front. I'm not saying it's right—but all of us have had our bad experiences. Look at how Jerry Lewis and Dean Martin treated Abbie Greshler after he made a million-dollar act of them. There aren't too many lasting associations in the entertainment field like the Patti Page-Jack Rael partnership."

In a more classic vein, Spanish philosopher Ortega y Gasset has said: "Triumph cannot help being cruel."

Rollins lashed out with lawsuits against both Harry and the Kennedys. The suit against Belafonte was simply for money owed to him on bookings previously secured by him. Against J. Richard Kennedy and Dr. Janet Kennedy, Rollins filed what amounted to a $150,000 alienation suit. He charged that Dr. Kennedy, as Harry's psychiatrist, had secured a disclosure of his business affairs, then had persuaded Harry that his condition would not improve unless he severed his relationship with Rollins, and had finally touted her husband to Belafonte as a prospective business manager. Dr. Kennedy's attorney responded that Rollins' accusations "outrageously libel her integrity, professionally and as a human being." Court records indicate that neither suit ever came to trial. Rumor has it that an out-of-court agreement, reached by all the conflicting parties, involved payment to Rollins of a sum in the neighborhood of $30,000.

Of Harry's parting with Rollins, the ex-Mrs. Belafonte has said: "There's no denying Jack Rollins' contribution to Harry's rise even though Harry himself may occasionally talk or act as if he made it alone. No one makes it alone. Yet I believe that Harry had outgrown Jack at the point where he parted company with him. Jack was a shy, gentle, retiring man, almost on the apologetic side. He found it difficult to approach people with big names. By contrast, Kennedy is a pushy, aggressive type of person. He established a kind of father-son relationship with Harry, taking care of Harry's money while Mrs. Kennedy took care of Harry's emotional life. Kennedy was quite astute when it came to money matters and rather successful in getting Harry into places that had never previously booked Negro performers—places like the Palmer House in Chicago and the Eden Roc in Miami.

"Of course, I don't think that Harry is entirely happy about the way he parted with Jack and I'm sure that he wouldn't handle it that way again if he had it to do over. But the fact that Rollins has not gotten over his break with Harry right up to the present time is, perhaps, an indication that he was not strong enough for Harry."

Margurite Belafonte thought for a moment and added: "Of course, the fall of 1954 was an extremely trying time for Harry—also for me. To the outside world, the birth of our second child doubtless must have seemed like a symbol of connubial bliss in the Belafonte household. What the outside world could not know was that we were both quite upset about the future of our relationship."

In point of fact, the outside world was not as unknowing as Marguerite suggests—although it did take a little time for the truth to come out. On February 12, 1955, a columnist in *The New York Amsterdam News* item-ed: "The Harry Belafontes are busy denying those rift rumors . . ."

STEREO

JANICE KINGSLOW

Janice Kingslow, who starred in the Hilda Simms role in the Chicago company of *Anna Lucasta,* came to New York when the play closed. With her scrapbook of press reviews under her arm, she went the rounds of Gotham casting offices, seeking not Negro roles, but any role. The routine was always the same:

"What have you done?"

"*Anna Lucasta.*"

"Wasn't that an all-Negro show?"

"That's right."

"Sorry, we have nothing for you."

"But I'd simply like to audition for what you have."

"Sorry."

Back in Chicago some time later, a young TV director Greg Garrison wanted to use Janice in a mystery series. He was immediately told by his superiors that he could not "put a Negress in a white part."

"I'm putting an actress in the part," Greg argued.

"But not that actress," they announced.

That was the closest Janice ever came to acting in television.

The story was the same in motion pictures. Otto Preminger flew her to New York to audition for *Carmen Jones.* Allegedly, her skin was too white and her eyes too green. Called by Richard Wright to test for a lead role in his *Native Son,* she was ruled out by a French director who felt as Preminger did.

And so Janice Kingslow's struggles to make a dramatic career went from frustration to frustration. "When I auditioned for Negro roles," she wrote in *Ebony* recently, "I was told I did not look like a Negro. When I auditioned for white roles, I was told, 'But you're a Negro!' "

Eventually Janice suffered a breakdown, which put her in a mental institution for four years. "Many things contributed to the blowing of the fuse," she has said, "of which my attempts to survive as a Negro creative artist in white America are just one."

15. The Color Line

Harry was in St. Louis with *Three for Tonight*, the musical in which he co-starred with Marge and Gower Champion, when Sammy Davis, Jr., met with the automobile accident that cost him an eye. Harry phoned Sammy to ask him how he was getting along.

Harry and Sammy were good friends then and remain so today. At the *première* of *Island in the Sun* in June '57, Sammy escorted Harry's new wife. The following January, Harry was Sammy's best man at his Las Vegas marriage to Loray White.

After joking about the accident and the vexations of hospital life, Sammy inquired: "Where are you calling from, Harry?"

"I'm in St. Louis," Harry replied, "and we're going farther south."

Sammy began chuckling: "Why are you asking me how I feel? Man, I should be asking you."

It was the winter of 1955 and the South was brooding over the desegregation of schools decision just handed down by the Supreme Court. Harry knew the possible embarrassments, humiliations, and even dangers facing him in touring with a mixed company. Nevertheless, he felt called on to accept the challenge presented by 94 one-night stands, which would take *Three for Tonight* into the prejudice-ridden areas of the Deep South.

"My motivation," Harry explained, "was to help bring about as much as anyone could, a greater feeling of respect for my race. I was determined to face whatever conditions existed in order to go out there on the stage and cause white Southern audiences to accept a Negro performer in a mixed cast."

The *Three for Tonight* company played every town where

they could find an audience. And there were threats. There were incidents. There were unpleasant and humiliating situations. But Harry and the dancing Champions stuck doggedly to their schedule. They played towns where there were no theatres—just concert halls, school auditoriums, and gymnasiums where hard-working stagehands created fake stages on table tops. Harry used Negro bathrooms, Negro water fountains, slept in Negro hotels, and sat in the segregated sections of airports and rail terminals.

In Petersburg, Virginia, Harry trotted accidentally into a white washroom. A state trooper defended the sanctity of the segregated toilet by ordering him out. In Spartanburg, South Carolina, accompanist Millard Thomas tried to register in a white hotel.

"With his lighter skin," Harry explained, "it was often hard for them to be sure he was a Negro."

Nevertheless, a sheriff appeared to eject Millard. Whether word spread about the guitarist's audacity, or the mere presence of a mixed cast caused tension, the police became uneasy. After the show, they whisked Harry, Millard, and others out of town by car. A private plane flew them to their next date.

The farther south the company went, the tenser the atmosphere became. In Houston, Harry found himself in a situation which was more destructive to him, precisely because it was more subtle. Wherever possible, Harry's manager arranged for him to stay overnight at the home of a local Negro leader. Since the company had expected to fly out immediately after the Houston performance, this was not done. Last-minute efforts to find sleeping accommodations did not work out. Harry remained in the airport through the night.

In the morning he went to the check-in counter to ask how soon his plane would arrive. The ticket agent glanced up at him from his work. All he saw was a young Negro, handsome but tired-looking. Instead of giving Harry a simple answer, he replied that the plane would arrive when it was "damned good and ready." Then he turned back to his work and proceeded completely to ignore Harry. Unwilling to create a rumpus but equally unwilling to yield ground, Harry re-

[157]

mained at the counter while the agent, pretending to be oblivious of his presence, busied himself with various clerical details.

After about twenty minutes of this silent fencing, a group of high-school students came through the air terminal. One youngster recognized Harry. In an instant, the white teen-agers descended on him, clamoring for autographs.

"Here I was, pinned in a corner," Harry says, "signing auto-graphs. Then I saw this man looking at me. He was trying to figure who I was. He decided that I was somebody. Then he found my ticket. He still hated me but now he was holding it in. And as I looked at him, I thought I ought to explain that I was Ralph Bunche's son or the Arab delegate to the UN."

Here was the pattern that was to baffle and confuse Harry. And the confusion was to grow into consternation, disbelief, and overpowering frustration, the more celebrated and wealthy Harry became. Neither money nor renown was to change the constant alternation of admiration on stage, humiliation, off. Acceptance as an entertainer. Rejection as a human being.

Yet despite the incidents and the situations, despite the repetitive pricking of his racial pride and the undercurrent of resentment that flowed through him, Harry was still able to say of his *Three for Tonight* tour: "It definitely was not a series of humiliation after humiliation. Certainly, I didn't feel happy that Millard and I had to sneak into 'white' hotels by hiding in the middle of a group of white cast members. Nor were we happy at the Jim Crow rules in restaurants and else-where.

"But the situation is not a static one," Harry mused. "Why, not too far from where I had that difficulty at the airport, a group of Texas University students invited me to their frat house. That's something." And Harry laughed huskily.

At Texas A and M, a white student in a ROTC uniform came up to him in the college cafeteria and extended his hand. "My name is David O'Daniel," he said, "and we're mighty proud to have you down here."

Of the Negro leaders who were his hosts throughout the South, Harry said that he "had never before thought of them as heroes. But they are the men who sat there for years trying to get their case before the Supreme Court. They sit there now with time-worn faces and patiently wait and roll up their sleeves and go through what they must go through. Seeing them, I've got to go back and go back and go back."

Lest anyone assume that it is only the South that caused humiliation to an entertainer like Harry, here is what happened in the North. It was the same year, and he was opening the Palmer House's glittering Empire Room for the fall season.

Waiting for the preceding act to finish, Harry stood behind some drapes. He was wearing a jacket over his well-known floor costume. At that moment, the maître d' happened by. In the dim light, he did not recognize Harry.

"What the hell are you doing there?" he snapped. "Don't stand there! Move!" To the busy host, Harry was an unwelcome Negro boy.

Harry studied the maître d's face. Inside, he was aflame. "It took all the strength I had to prevent me from belting the guy. He wasn't insulting me. He was humiliating every guy of my race."

Instead of lashing out with his fists, Harry left the room and went into the hotel lobby. He sat down, his head throbbing with hurt but also with hatred. He had to pull himself together, to overcome the injury to his pride. Through him raced a mounting desire to hurt in turn, to strike back at what had hurt him without provocation—a feeling well described by James Baldwin in his *Notes of a Native Son* when he writes:

"There is, I should think, no Negro living in America, who has not felt briefly or for long periods, with anguish sharp or dull, in varying degrees and to varying effect, simple, naked, and unanswerable hatred; who has not wanted to smash any white face he may encounter in a day . . ."

After a time, Harry heard the fanfare announcing his entrance. He just remained sitting in the lobby. He had no heart to go on the floor. But he also wanted to punish. The waiters, and in particular, the maître d', did extremely well when he appeared at the hotel. Reservations were at a premium and tips ran high. As the audience waited for Harry to appear, and he was nowhere to be seen, uneasiness spread through the staff.

After some frantic minutes, somebody spotted America's foremost balladeer where he sat. Spurred by the almost prostrate maître d', who had somehow discovered his mistake, a group of waiters came to Harry and obsequiously escorted him back into the room. After the show, the maître d' came to Harry and made a humble, unsolicited, and unsatisfying apology.

For purely personal reasons, a minor incident during the *Three for Tonight* tour proved a source of great amusement and satisfaction to Harry. After a performance at a Southern college, the President was showing Harry about the grounds. As they wandered around, the President enjoyed calling Harry by his first name just as Harry derived pleasure out of calling the President by his. At one point, a member of the faculty approached them and, quite naturally, addressed Harry's august guide as: "Mr. President . . ." It took all the control Harry could muster not to give out with the biggest horse laugh of his life. The faculty member happened to be one of Margurite's brothers—one whose college degree had, in the early years of his marriage, added to the tension between himself, Margurite, and his mother-in-law.

For some time afterward, Harry could not resist telling friends how his brother-in-law with his college degree had to address his guide as "Mr. President" while he, Harry Belafonte, without a college degree, was calling the college official by his first name.

Three for Tonight opened on Broadway in April after playing 94 performances on the road and after Harry had completed his first booking at the Copa. Produced by Paul Gregory, with such hits as *The Caine Mutiny Court Martial* to his credit, the offbeat musical was highly successful as a show and as a vehicle for Belafonte.

The birth of *Three* is interesting. In a curious way *The Caine Mutiny Court Martial* was responsible for it. The night that the dramatization of the best-selling novel by Herman

Wouk opened on Broadway, producer Gregory was in a highly excitable state. Openings may be electric for first-night audiences. They are merely nerve-wracking for people of the theatre. As the play about the neurotic captain of the *Caine* unfolded itself, Gregory became more and more jittery. After a while, he left his very desirable seat in the orchestra and stood in the rear. Even this did not help. Before long, he was out on the sidewalk, chain-smoking, pacing, and unable to contain himself.

The Plymouth Theatre, where *The Caine Mutiny* was being presented, is only a few doors east of the Imperial. Here Harry Belafonte was appearing in his first Broadway production, John Murray Anderson's *Almanac*. In a desperate effort to distract and quiet himself, Paul Gregory wandered into the Imperial. It was just at the moment when Harry was performing his own show-stopping composition *Mark Twain*. In an instant, Gregory forgot the *Caine* and sat enthralled by the folklike ballad of the gaugers on the Mississippi River boats who used a lead weight on a ball of twine to gauge the river depth and who sounded the fathoms in a colorful chant that was shortened, as time went on, from "markin' the twine" to the title of Harry's song.

After *The Caine Mutiny* was comfortably ensconced for a hit run at the Plymouth, Gregory came back to hear Harry in *Almanac*. On the sixth or seventh visit, he went backstage and introduced himself to Harry. They decided to do a show together. At first they considered a musical of Negro folklore.

That's how *Three for Tonight,* starring Marge and Gower Champion and Harry Belafonte, came to be born. Played before drapes, with half a dozen stools and a music stand for props, the musical included the Voices of the late Walter Schumann, Hiram Sherman, and Betty Benson. While there were one or two dissenting votes among the New York critics, most reviews were raves. For his part in singing fourteen of the best-loved songs from his folk repertoire, Harry received superlative notices.

Reviews spoke of him as a "magnetic singer" whose arrangements were "hypnotic." They said he sang "with tension and ecstasy" and that his delivery had "immense style and authority." He was characterized as a brilliant performer, a masterly showman, and an artist of great and growing consequence. "His husky voice," wrote William Hawkins, "has the soft and certain traction of crepe soles." One reviewer indicated that he "sent" the audience. Another announced that he "pulverized" it.

Walter Kerr, dramatic critic of *The New York Herald Tribune,* stated simply: "Producer Paul Gregory doesn't need three for tonight so long as he's got Harry Belafonte for tonight." And the dean of New York critics, Brooks Atkinson of *The Times,* began his review: "Why is Harry Belafonte so magnificent in *Three for Tonight?*" His answer: "Because he represents the fanaticism of the dedicated artist. Eliminating himself, he concentrates on the songs with fiery intensity. Although his manners are simple, his singing personality is vibrant and magnetic. Mr. Belafonte never makes a mistake in taste or musicianship, for he is all artist and a rousing performer . . ." A few days later, in a special Sunday article, Atkinson dissected Harry's art as that of the evangelist, and characterized him as "apocalyptical."

Among the loud chorus of yea-sayers, there were a number of voices that chanted a countermelody to Atkinson's sustained organ chords. They did not feel that Harry eliminated himself or that his manners were simple or that he was without mistakes in taste and musicianship. One critical reviewer suggested that Harry's sense of drama occasionally got the better of him. Another mocked "his stance of crumpled power, half Radio City Atlas, half Ed Sullivan." Still another objected to "the pretentiousness of his delivery" and contended that "pleasure in his singing is diminished by irritation with his manner." The late Wolcott Gibbs of *The New Yorker* summarized this choir of criticism when he wrote that Harry was "in danger of acquiring certain theatrical mannerisms that he may live to regret. The most notable of these is a sort of clenched, Rodinesque posturing that suggests that whatever he is doing has a nearly supernatural emotional significance."

What is interesting about these comments is that the accusation of pretentiousness has come back to haunt Harry on more than one occasion. In '56, for example, one of Harry's many return engagements at New York's Waldorf elicited a *Variety* review that lamented the loss of simplicity and sincerity in his act. The song is lost "in an over-arrangement or an over-dramatic emphasis." In place of the tension and excitement he used to communicate, wrote Herm Schoenfeld, "there is now an air of slickness and smugness," and his intrinsic style has become "so overladen with mannerisms" that Harry no longer seems to know the boundaries of his talent.

In December '57, Hy Gardner observed in his *Herald Tribune* column: "I'm afraid Harry Belafonte, long one of our favorite entertainers and friends, has been caught in the same trap other great artists fall into once their artistry becomes recognized and respected. In his current Waldorf Empire Room engagement, the singer practically discards all the songs which made him famous and replaces them with numbers, which are so-so arty his routine is a singing tranquilizer."

As recently as April '59, jazz critic John Wilson of *The Times* leveled similar charges against Harry with regard to a benefit concert at Carnegie Hall. In this instance, Harry was damned for using an orchestra of fifty musicians to accompany a program of simple, unpretentious songs. "It lent the occasion," Wilson concluded, "an air of pompous formality that, supplemented by Mr. Belafonte's mannered solemnity, raised a wall between singer and audience on many selections."

"Technique has begun to triumph over talent," Brooks Atkinson, an early enthusiast, wrote in December '59 of "Belafonte at the Palace."

Apart from the fact that Harry has not been able entirely to eliminate this shortcoming from his work—what Ovid once referred to as "art hidden by artifice"—there is the matter of the extent to which he is mannered, pretentious, or pompous in his dealings with people generally. There is no agreement on this among Harry's friends or his business associates.

If '55 brought humiliation and hurt to Harry for the color of his skin, it also yielded moments of triumph. One of these was his first appearance as the headliner at the Copa.

Properly to understand what this engagement meant to Harry, one should bear in mind that the Copa is something more than just another night club. It is, in fact, to the nitery circuit of today what the Palace once was to vaudeville. Until a performer plays the Copa, he has not arrived. Once he has played it, he enters the select company of such entertainment celebrities as Joe E. Lewis, Sammy Davis, Jr., Jimmy Durante, Martin and Lewis, Frank Sinatra, and other show biz immortals.

To Harry, it also meant something else. During the war years, he had once tried to go to the Copa with several other Negro couples. The rope was up. The Copa is almost always a sellout. When Sinatra plays it, there are no reservations generally for any show during the entire length of his engagement. The Copa could have been sold out the evening that Harry arrived with his sailor friends. To him, it meant only one thing. What Big Bill Broonzy, one of Harry's early idols, has said so pointedly in his *Black, Brown and White Blues:*

> Now, if you're white, you're all right,
> And if you're brown, stick around.
> But if you're black, oh, brother,
> Get back! Get back! Get back!

To be the headliner at the Copa? It was fame, fortune, excitement, publicity, talk-of-the-town stuff. But most of all, it was what Harry had cried for in his first song—*Recognition!*

Of course, being booked at the Copa is one thing. Making out with Copa audiences is quite another. This is a supper club. Customers eat, drink, and talk. Many a headliner has found that keeping the customers quiet can be quite a struggle. Many a performer has had to resort to the Jack E. Leonard type of humor—insult—in order to shut up a boisterous table. That's not too difficult for a comedian. But what does a folk singer do, especially during some of the more tender and delicate ballads?

On the same bill with Harry was zany comedian Morey Amsterdam. There were many evenings when Amsterdam simply could not annex the attention of the noisy dinner hour crowd. But from the very first show of his appearance, Harry Belafonte commanded the kind of attentive silence which gave him scope for shading and nuance in his most gentle songs. It was awe-inspiring. And the reviewers chanted, as one of their number wrote: "The ascent of Harry Belafonte to the uppermost levels of show business continues at sports car speed."

Artistically, '55 was partly a year of re-evaluation for Harry. Unlike many performers, Harry has a sharp, analytical mind as well as an excitable temperament. Reading the reviews—he does, and with care—he detected something that bothered him. The superlatives were there. "Harry Belafonte took the Empire Room by storm opening night . . ." "Belafonte blends a vital animal magnetism with savvy showmanship, charm, and a sonorous voice for a sock parlay . . ." But midst the rhapsodic rhetoric, he heard a new note. He did not agree with comments that criticized him for being pompous and pretentious. But he was concerned about something that a friend, jazz critic Nat Hentoff, had said to him. It had to do with his becoming too stylized, too routine, too pat.

This is a problem that all performers face. Slowly, they develop an act, discover what things work, what material is good for them. Then they go through a stage of polishing, sharpening, perfecting. Beyond this point, the worry is to retain sharp-edged impact without sacrificing excitement and spontaneity. This is the crossroad at which Harry found himself in '55. A related problem was posed by the fact that Harry had moved from floors of the smaller, more intimate boites onto the stages of the big swank clubs. Something more was needed occasionally than the sweetness and delicacy of Millard Thomas' tender guitar.

Spurred on by his new manager, Jay Richard Kennedy, who was responsible for some of the new, swank bookings, Harry called in an old friend of his Village days, jazz clarinetist Tony Scott, and had him rewrite his "book." On the face of it, what Scott was doing, during the ten months in which he served as Harry's musical conductor, was writing new arrangements that enlarged Harry's accompaniment from guitar to orchestra and/or chorus. But the change in accompaniment was not merely a quantitative thing. Admittedly, on the basis of the bigger prices Harry was receiving for personal appearances, he could now afford the backing of a band instead of just a guitar. The new arrangements represented a qualitative change as well. New colors, new sounds, and fresh feeling were being added to the material in Harry's repertoire.

"Harry wanted to inject some jazz into the accompaniment," Scott explained. "Folk material always has a pronounced rhythmic beat, partly because much of it is sung by groups of people. Distinct rhythms make it easy for them to keep together. Also, some folk material is sung in connection with dances. What I did, with Harry's active collaboration, was to introduce, wherever it seemed natural and spontaneous, a jazz feeling."

The effectiveness of this freshening process was apparent, not only on the floor. It may be heard in two of Harry's RCA Victor albums. One is the fantastically successful *Calypso* album released during the following year. The other is the LP, also released in '56, simply titled *Belafonte*. Consciously, and with Harry's consent, musicians with jazz backgrounds were chosen for recording sessions of both albums.

The Copa date was one of the first that Tony played with Harry. Naturally, Harry was very tense about it. He felt that the opening theme was crucial, and he spent hours discussing it with Tony. The Copa's setup is such that a performer must pass through part of the audience before he gets to the floor. The problem was to keep the audience's interest fixed on the band. Then Harry could sneak through in his striped silk shirt and come on with the shock of surprise that snapped customers to attention. There was also the problem of the audience mood that the band's fanfare and introductory theme would create for Harry.

Tony worked over the opening for days. He was determined to concoct something so impressive, so startling, so attention-getting that no one would forget it. Came the day of the first rehearsal. Harry was well pleased when he saw the band.

To the Copacabana's regular white complement of sidemen, Tony had added six musicians. The additional men were all Negroes.

For many years the canard circulated in musical circles was that Negro musicians could not read. It was said that Negroes were great at improvising and playing "head arrangements," that is, arrangements worked out and not written down. But when it came to radio, TV, recording, night clubs, Broadway shows, or movie backgrounds, all assignments where a man had to read well on sight, you could not rely on Negro musicians. This was presumably "the justification" for the color line—not prejudice. Well, Harry and Tony were going to break the color line and expose "the justification" as well. They did.

Harry stood to one side of the room as Tony distributed the parts for his entrance theme. Pretending he was the emcee, Tony mimicked: "Introducing Harry Belafonte. And here he is!" Then the augmented band blew the opening fanfare and swung into the introductory theme. It was a slow jazz motif with a blues feeling. The rhythm section pounded a stately, throbbing beat. The saxes and brasses punctuated with big, blasting chords and a strong after-beat feeling. Over it all soared a sexy blues theme on trumpet. The blue trumpet yielded to a jazzy, excited, wa-wa trumpet, which in turn gave way to a low, growl trombone. As they say in modern jazz circles, "the opening was a gas."

Instead of popping onto the floor, as he would at a regular performance, Harry walked slowly to a position in front of the band. Tony was waiting for his reaction. It was the first time Harry had heard the full theme. Harry turned his head and looked at Tony through the corners of his eyes, the glimmer of a wry smile playing around his lips.

"That was my opening?" he asked.

Tony nodded, trying to figure Harry.

Belafonte shook his head in mock desperation. "Okay, that's my opening," he said. "Now, you tell me, how I'm going to follow it. How great can a man be?"

Once he had played the Copa, Harry's associates decided that his act was more suited to the relaxed atmosphere of the

Empire Room or the Cocoanut Grove than the Copa. Harry's style, pacing, and material demanded a kind of audience attention and response, which, they felt he could more readily command in a hotel room or a theatre than in a boisterous night club.

In August '55, when he was playing The Fairmont in San Francisco, Harry invited Fran and Tony Scott for a trip to Muir Woods, the awesome forest of giant redwood trees that go back for centuries. As they were driving along, Fran sat opening the morning's mail. She acted as Harry's personal secretary while her husband served as Harry's conductor.

"Anything?" Harry asked, after a time.

At that moment, Fran was opening a letter from the National Association for the Advancement of Colored People, which pointed out that Yellow Cabs refused to hire Negro drivers. NAACP members and friends of the Negro people were urged not to rent Yellow cabs.

Harry glanced at Fran and Tony. Then he turned to the driver.

"Is this your own cab," Harry asked, "or is it owned by a cab company?"

Before the driver could reply, Harry's mouth froze into a look of self-criticism, and he nodded to Tony and Fran as if he expected the worst. It came.

"No, this is not my cab," the driver said. "It's owned by the Yellow Cab people. Why?"

Harry half laughed. "Oh, nothing," he said. "We just stopped using Yellow cabs."

A few days later Tony and Fran made a swing around Frisco visiting the disk jockeys in behalf of Harry's records. They were traveling on the outskirts of town when suddenly they heard someone calling to them. They asked the driver of their cab—not a Yellow—to pull up. After a moment they realized that the two slightly bedraggled figures approaching the cab were Harry and Millard, the latter lugging one of his guitar cases.

Harry and Millard had been visiting a local station. They had been trying to find a cab—and the only cabs that had passed them for almost an hour, were cabs of the company they were boycotting.

Toward the end of '55, Harry played the Waldorf in New York. It was the last date at which Tony served as Harry's musical conductor. In the months in which they worked together, there had been a normal number of disagreements. But Tony, who was to win the *Down Beat* poll of the year as the nation's number one clarinetist, had decided that he wanted the freedom and the limelight he could get out of leading his own jazz combo.

One evening, after Harry had finished his regular program and customers were calling excitedly for encores, a large table requested *The Wedding Song*. They were referring to a number written by Harry and Bill Attaway—*Will His Love Be Like His Rum?* Harry was about to pass up the request when the people at the table indicated that they were celebrating a twenty-fifth wedding anniversary.

After Tony gave the downbeat to the band, Harry motioned for Tony to join him on the floor. Scott came down, nonplused.

"Let's make it a duet," Harry said, his eyes on the customers. "I seem to have forgotten some of the lines."

As the number proceeded, they locked bodies side by side so that Tony could whisper occasional key words during instrumental interludes. By that time, Tony knew Harry's repertoire as well as his own name. Although they had never done the number together, Tony, who has perfect pitch, was able to sing harmony, phrasing perfectly with Harry.

Whether Harry had actually forgotten the lyrics or merely sought to break the color line, the proximity of white and Negro faces on the Waldorf floor added a piquant touch to the evening's proceedings. As Tony returned to the bandstand, Harry called for the entire band to rise and acknowledge the audience's applause.

"And now—my orchestra," he said, "in technicolor."

As on the Copa date, Tony had added a group of Negro musicians to the Waldorf's regular white band.

Another moment of triumph that helped soften the memory of the indignities suffered during his *Three for Tonight* tour, came at the end of the year. Christmas 1955 marked the *première* season of Miami's newest million-dollar monster hotel, The Eden Roc. Harry was selected to open the opulent and fashionable Café Pompeii.

Only five years earlier, and little more than a mile from the Eden Roc, Harry had ostensibly written finis to his career as a singer. Through his unhappy stay at the Five O'Clock Club, he had had to endure all the humiliations of being a Negro in a tough Jim Crow town. Segregated hotel. Segregated transportation. Segregated restaurants, water fountains, and toilets.

Now, five years later, during his engagement at The Eden Roc, Harry was to break a color line that had existed from the Civil War on. He was to become the first Negro in Miami's history permitted to use all of the "white" hotel's facilities. Fully to appreciate the significance of this, here is what jazz bassist Milt Hinton has said of the days when he toured Florida with Cab Calloway: "Do you know that in Miami, after nine o'clock at night, Negroes had to be off the streets unless they carried a note from their boss saying something like, 'This boy works for me.'"

Harry Tobias, songwriter and bright-eyed emcee of The Eden Roc, always says with pride in his voice: "My boss, Harry Mufson, was the one who broke the taboo against Negroes on the lily-white beaches of Miami. Belafonte was the first."

There were other things that Belafonte did, which Tobias talks of with less satisfaction. "I'm a very nervous cat," Tobias reports, "and when I'm emceeing a show, I like to know that my acts are on hand before I announce them. You can't pace a show unless an act comes on fast after your announcement. And how can you do your own bits and set the coming act up unless you know they're ready to go on when you call them.

[170]

"Well, Belafonte played hide-and-seek with me almost from the start. I guess the first or second night, he didn't show until the last minute. I was frantic. And when he discovered how upset I could get, he went to work on me.

"Let me say this. He was never late for a show and he never missed his entrance. But many a night, he would wait until the last split second. I'd be biting my fingernails waiting to spot that tall, handsome figure of his. In desperation, I'd announce him with the necessary flourish—and close my eyes.

"When I'd open them, there he was. As I'd pass him coming on-stage, he'd give me a sharp, sidewise glance and a lip curled into a triumphant little smile. Like he was saying, 'Gave you heart failure, didn't I?' Well he did. And he knew it. And that's why he did it. Playful, you know, like giving a guy a hot foot."

Before the Eden Roc date, Harry made a number of appearances on TV. These were his first exposures on the medium. In two of them, he sang. The third appearance, and to Harry, the most important, was in a purely dramatic role on the General Electric Theatre. *Winner by Decision* was the name of the play, and it was the work of Harry's friend of the Sage days, Bill Attaway, writer of more than 400 TV scripts. Playing the part of a prize fighter, Harry co-starred with Ethel Waters.

"No author's script was ever handled with greater care," Bill Attaway has said. "As the mother, Ethel milked every line. As the son, Harry likewise allowed no line to get away from him. I couldn't have been more satisfied except for what happened at the end. As a result of this effort on the part of both principals to outdo one another, the show ran long. I was watching the play proudly with a group of friends.

"Perhaps you have guessed it. *Winner by Decision* ran so long that there was no time for Ronald Reagan's closing commercial. Nor was there any time for the credit chaser. That one moment—'Script by Bill Attaway'—which I had been waiting for all during the hour never came.

"I received an apologetic telegram from the director of the show and I had my first, and only, argument with Harry. I guess I was being as big a ham about the credits as Harry about his role. Still, he had more reason than I. It was not my first script. But it was Harry's first dramatic role on television—and you know how much acting meant to him."

For Harry, 1955 ended on a high point. It had been a good year for him artistically and financially. In addition to the big, swank hotel rooms that he had played for the first time—breaking down color barriers—he had made several appearances on TV, a medium not too receptive to Negroes. A TV version of *Three for Tonight* had brought him accolades as "the most compelling new artist of the TV year." During the year he had signed a deal with the Waldorf, reputedly at the highest salary ever paid a performer, providing for two bookings annually—in the fall, at the posh Empire Room, and in the spring, at the large, glittering Starlight Room. As the year came to a close, *Variety* reported that Harry's earnings were soaring over the $350,000 a year mark.

1956 was to be even greater—also more difficult.

STEREO

DUKE ELLINGTON

At one time when Duke Ellington and his band were appearing in St. Louis, he and his men discovered that they could not get service in any of the restaurants near the theatre. Since there was not time enough to go across town to a segregated district, they returned to the theatre and sent a white man out to buy sandwiches. He came back empty-handed. Somehow, the drugstore owner learned that they were for the "nigger band," and refused to make them up. While the hungry musicians were milling around backstage, their cue sounded. The curtain rose. From the white audience out front, composed in part of men like the druggist, there came a burst of applause.

"The crowd cheered, whistled, and stamped its feet," wrote Richard O. Boyer in *The New Yorker*. "As the curtain was going up, the dejection on the faces of the players vanished . . . The music blared. Duke smiled . . . Rex Stewart took off on a solo that was greeted with fervor. As he bowed, the musician next to him muttered out of the side of his mouth, 'Bend, you hungry bastard! Bend!' "

16. Eden Was Not Like This

In 1956 Harry was to endure his first flop in a career still soaring to new heights. It was a crucial year in other ways. Hanging in the balance were his relationship with his third manager, Jay Richard Kennedy; also, his relationship with his wife and family; and, indirectly, his relationship with his own people.

Expressive of the conflict that developed between Harry and his third manager was a musical production *Sing, Man, Sing,* with which Harry was preoccupied during the early months of the year. Starring Belafonte, it was subtitled: "A New Musical Odyssey as Big as Life." It used a company of twenty-six. The score was by Harry Belafonte and manager Jay Richard Kennedy. The book was by Kennedy. And so were the lyrics.

During 1955 The Museum of Modern Art held an exhibition assembled by the famous photographer, Edward Steichen. Titled "The Family of Man," it consisted of 503 photographs chosen by Steichen and his staff over a period of 3 years from over 2 million pictures taken in 68 countries by 273 photographers, amateur and professional, famous and unknown. The emphasis in the exhibited photographs was on the "daily relationships of man to himself, to his family, to the community and to the world we live in." Few things, outside the world of music and the theatre, moved Harry as deeply as this exhibit, whose photographs were later embodied in a book, published under the title *The Family of Man.*

Harry not only made many visits to the exhibit. He bought innumerable copies of the book to give to friends, among them Bill Attaway, who treasures a copy with the following inscription: "Never can I ever think of you but in the warmest terms.

[174]

Never even will I be able to tell you all you have meant and will always mean to me. Perhaps, however, through my art, whatever strong, positive things you may see, know that you have through your understanding, your strength, and your great kindness contributed to that art and therefore to me and therefore to 'The Family of Man.'" The inscription, dated August 1955, was signed: "Your devoted brother, Harry."

Out of this exhibit and book, according to Attaway, came the initial impulse for *Sing, Man, Sing*.

A number of people were involved in the creation of material for the production. Bill Attaway was one. Norman Luboff, the conductor and choral director, was another. Will Lorin, ditto, was a third. And Lord Burgess, the calypso songwriter responsible for most of the material in Harry's *Calypso* album, was a fourth. All of these contributed and/or collaborated on lyrics, music, script, or production ideas. Nevertheless, the major share of the credit—and eventually the blame —went to J. Richard Kennedy, who had succeeded Rollins as Harry's mentor. There is no agreement on how the two came to be associated. Each claims that it was the other man's idea.

"Belafonte began romancing me," says Kennedy, "and urging me to take over his management and handle his business. I didn't know anything about his background with Rollins. I didn't want Belafonte's business but he turned on all his charm and talked me into it."

To a *Time* reporter, Harry said flatly: "The husband of Dr. Kennedy [his psychiatrist] took me over."

Magazine writer Maurice Zolotow has published the following apt observation: "Belafonte was simultaneously being treated for emotional problems by her and for fiscal problems by her husband—one of the strangest cases in the annals of medical science and modern business."

What Kennedy, as Belafonte's third manager, contributed to his career in addition to the "Musical Odyssey as Big as Life" is not easy to assess. A small man in stature, Kennedy had big ideas and a big selling style. Many have commented on his persuasive, almost hypnotic, power as a talker.

Others tell stories depicting a man of extreme, if not theatrical, emotionalism. One of the musicians associated with Harry during Kennedy's tenure, recalls a telling incident that occurred on an evening after a very successful show.

Harry was in a happy and expansive mood. Turning to the conductor of the show, whom he had been treating courteously but not warmly up to that moment, Harry threw his arms around him and exclaimed with feeling:

"I've meant to tell you what a great job you've been doing. Tonight, I somehow feel that you have really become one of us. I welcome you as a member of the Belafonte family."

People who have been associated with Harry have said: "Working with Belafonte is like choosing sides. Competence is not enough, and you can't just work for him. You have to become a follower and share his thoughts. You have to dedicate yourself and believe in him. He has to make a friend of you, make you part of himself. Otherwise, you don't last." The reaction of the conductor to Harry's gesture of acceptance was not what Harry anticipated.

"By what right," he demanded, "do you set yourself up as a judge of other men and their motivations. I'm an arranger and a conductor, Harry. I've proved myself in these fields. What else do I have to prove? And why do I have to prove it to you? You're a very arrogant man, Harry. And sometimes, you almost sound like a Negro chauvinist—which I know you're not."

Harry does not take criticism lightly. He worries it. When the crowd in the hotel room had thinned out, leaving only the conductor, Kennedy, and a few 'members of the Belafonte family,' Harry brought up the conductor's comment. Striding up and down the room, he tried to explain how the edge of his thinking and feeling about race prejudice had become so sharp. He talked of the hardships of his childhood and youth. He told of how his color had made him feel an outcast, not only in the white communities where he lived, but at times even in his own home and among his own relatives. He went on to describe the many embarrassments he had suffered, the cutting indignities, and the deep hurt.

As he continued telling one incident of discrimination after another, Kennedy became visibly more and more upset. After one particularly harrowing tale, his eyes filled with tears.

Finally, he was unable to restrain himself. He stood up dramatically and exclaimed:

"I've made a lot of money. I've been a millionaire several times over. But so long as such things as Harry is telling us continue to happen in this country, I'm a poor and impoverished man."

In the original deal, consummated while Jack Rollins was still technically his manager, Harry agreed to pay Kennedy ten percent of his gross earnings or $7,000 a year, whichever was greater, for serving as "fiduciary manager and financial adviser." This percentage was subsequently revised upward several times. That the scope of the relationship was to be broader than advice on financial matters is suggested by the fact that Kennedy was given power of attorney to transact bond, commodity, banking and something described as "business operating" transactions.

Kennedy went after the big spots for Harry and before long succeeded in swinging certain big deals. Both the Waldorf and the extremely favorable contract with the Riviera in Las Vegas are Kennedy-wrapped packages. Although finances may have been Kennedy's forte, his activities reached into every phase of Harry's artistic endeavors. A number of people, including show-biz observer Maurice Zolotow, credit him, his wife, or both, with adding sex to Belafonte's balladry. This may sound like a strange claim.

The truth is that Harry is not, and never was, a sexy singer. A dramatic singer, yes. A magician at evoking certain moods and emotions, yes. Listen to his voice without looking at him, and it is clear that his sound is not a sexy one, as the sound of Sinatra, of Nat Cole, and even of Billy Daniels, are sexy. Harry's great powers as a singer are in other areas: in projecting hurt, tenderness, excitement, tension, longing, love, hostility.

What Harry sounds like and what he looks like are not the same thing. Kennedy apparently went to work on Harry's dress and manner. In this period Harry deserted the casual slacks and loose denims he had been wearing from Village days and donned tight, black mohair pants that emphasized every move he made. In place of the casual open shirt, Harry began wearing tailored silk shirts with a plunging neckline that almost exposed his navel. Accompanying the change in costume was a parallel emphasis in stance, gesture, and movement that could not fail to arouse the female libido. Harry might deny that this was conscious.

That the effect was there, regardless of the intention, is indicated by many things, among them this comment by a female reporter: "When Belafonte's on stage, with shirt collar open, he moves his body in a tantalizing manner that makes women feel like doing crazy things."

On top of redesigning his clothes, Kennedy worked with Harry on the pacing of his act and, quite extensively, on the lighting. Such colors as lavender, light blue and pink, were used to emphasize sex, rather than drama.

"Millionaire Steers Folk Singer to Fame" was one of the captions in an *Ebony* article that appeared in March 1956, at the height of the collaboration between Harry and Kennedy. The accompanying text stated that "opportunity's third knock," that of Jay Richard Kennedy, was the clincher in Harry's upward climb. Kennedy was described as one of America's most remarkable businessmen, a millionaire financier, also a gifted writer and composer. "When they joined forces," *Ebony* commented, "Belafonte shot close to the top of the entertainment world."

Kennedy is quoted as saying: "All Belafonte needed was a few breaks!" (Parenthetically, it might be added that some of these occurred before his appearance.)

And Harry was quoted as saying: "Kennedy is a genius."

Perhaps that is what Harry thought at the time. Perhaps this was what *Ebony* thought that Harry thought. In any event, Harry's thinking underwent a fairly rapid change. Dateline of the *Ebony* story was March 1956. Six months later, and almost two years before the expiration of their contract, Harry discharged Kennedy—and lawsuits were in the making.

In studying any conflict, historians distinguish between underlying causes and immediate causes. Unquestionably,

Sing, Man, Sing was one of the things that laid the ground-work for Harry's precipitate action of September 29th. *Sing, Man, Sing* never reached Broadway, but several performances were given at the Academy of Music in Brooklyn during April 1956. Some time before these performances, Kennedy tried to persuade RCA Victor to make an original cast album of the "Musical Odyssey as Big as Life."

Decision on this matter was in the hands of E. O. Welker, an RCA Victor executive who supervised most of Harry's recordings from 1954 through 1958. Welker recalls being invited by Kennedy, whom he described as "a dynamic little man with a million ideas," to lunch at a swank apartment on New York's East Side.

Welker remembers a tall room, furnished expensively but in fine taste. This was the room to which they repaired for a light lunch, during which Kennedy, "a sawed-off man with a crewcut," turned on all his charm. Not until afterward did Kennedy launch into what was to be, as Welker discovered all too late, a one-man performance of the odyssey, "big as life."

Kennedy narrated the story, a saga in words and music of man's age-old search for happiness. He read chunks of dialogue from each scene. He drew word pictures of the costumes. He described the lighting in meticulous detail. With no voice at all, he sang most of the songs, which, by the way, included one of Harry's most beautiful calypso ballads *Eden Was Like This,* written by Kennedy and Lord Burgess. It was a full-scale production.

There was only one drawback. Welker thought it was dull, pretentious. Given to straight talking, he gloved his reaction only slightly. He avoided commenting on the material and simply stated that he did not see a successful record album in the production.

"To say that Kennedy was surprised," Welker has said, "is an understatement. He was like a man who has just displayed a million dollar cache of precious gems and offered them to you for a dollar. Words failed him. His feeling was one of the utmost disdain—and his face showed it. He was just not going to be bothered talking to anyone with so little judgment as me. The funny thing is that, until that moment, we seemed to get along quite well. But my one little 'no' brought him to an uncontrolled boil."

Welker laughed dryly under a boyish face and neat crewcut. "I don't want to rub it in. But I'm afraid the public, which loved Harry but not the show, shared my boredom, not Mr. Kennedy's enthusiasm."

Harry ultimately recorded three of the selections from the production. In February of '56 he cut *The Blues Is Man*, written by himself and Kennedy, as a two-sided record. In July he sliced *Once Was*, a song by Kennedy and Will Lorin, at this time, the conductor of Harry's record sessions. Neither of these amounted to anything, although the latter is to be found in the LP titled *An Evening with Belafonte*.

The most important song to come out of the ill-fated show was, of course, the ballad *Eden Was Like This*. The words, by Kennedy, were given a rich musical setting by Lord Burgess. Despite his difficulties with Kennedy, this is one of Harry's favorite and most effective songs—and he has recorded it on three different occasions in an effort to get the best rendition and interpretation. It is also to be heard in the *Evening* album.

Actually, *Sing, Man, Sing* did business wherever it played—in Chicago, Cleveland, Detroit. But this was a testimonial to the box-office power of the Belafonte name, not to the material in the production. In describing man's search for happiness, *Sing, Man, Sing* took Belafonte, who played Man, from the Garden of Eden up to modern times. It was a long trip in time—and that's just about the way audiences felt about it. A full orchestra, a choir of singers, a chorus of dancers, eighteen songs—nothing helped. *Sing, Man, Sing* was a "bomb," despite Harry Belafonte and the talented people in it.

Doubtless, the most positive thing to come out of the production was Harry's association with Phil Stein, the MCA executive who has, since Kennedy's departure, served as Harry's general factotum. Retained by Kennedy to light *Sing, Man, Sing*, Stein has been responsible for the effective lighting of most of Harry's shows. He has also functioned in other business and creative capacities, among them, as producer of Harry's TV programs and associate producer of his most recent film *Odds Against Tomorrow*. Despite his manifold duties, which approximate, if they do not exceed, the functions of a personal and general manager, Stein has never been given the title. Recalling his bitter experiences with Rollins and Kennedy, Harry will not go beyond calling Phil a salaried member of his staff.

"There is nothing amiss in having a flop," Lord Burgess said recently. "All entertainers and writers have them, and frequently people with flops go on together to have hits. But *Sing, Man, Sing* was more than a failure. Its chaos was symptomatic of the chaos around Harry at this time. Its confusion reflected the confusion and the growing gap between Harry and his main collaborator."

Audiences outside of New York seemed no more impressed than Gotham viewers. On tour, Harry ran into the all-too-usual racial problems. In Baltimore, a hotel clerk refused him his room key when he realized that Harry was Negro. According to a newspaper, Harry dashed to a phone and launched a $100,000 suit against the hotel. In Washington, D.C., the Daughters of the American Revolution demanded the deletion of one of the songs on the grounds of immorality. Acceding to this request, Harry was faced with a police ban on one of the interracial dances, lest a riot be caused. Headaches multiplied. In May 1956 an *Amsterdam News* columnist noted: "Seems as though Harry Belafonte is having nothing but trouble with his road production of *Sing, Man, Sing*."

When it came to racial discrimination, Harry knew how to buck it. But how did one fight a flop?

Harry has a tendency to gravitate from one extreme to another. At the time of *Sing, Man, Sing*, his optimism was unbounded. He had gone from triumph to triumph. Each new venture seemed destined to send his star to new heights. He could do no wrong, and nothing could go wrong. The Musical Odyssey proved differently. It was as big a shock as it was

[181]

unexpected. To Harry, it suddenly looked like his zooming rocket was going to crash—not that it had developed temporary trouble. He became depressed, despondent. He discharged Kennedy and dropped Mrs. Kennedy as his analyst.

The lawsuit that Kennedy launched against Belafonte (also Shari Music Corporation, some of whose stock Kennedy held) came to light in April '57, shortly after news of Harry's remarriage hit the papers. Stripped of technicalities, Kennedy accused Harry of diverting, for his own gain, business opportunities and income that rightfully belonged to the corporation. As one instance, he cited Harry's action in taking the title song of *Island in the Sun* and re-copyrighting it in the name of a California corporation, Clara Music, which he contended Harry had organized for the purpose of divesting the Shari company of its properties. He charged also that Harry had hurt this company by making false representations regarding the originality of certain compositions. As a result, Shari Music was threatened with lawsuits on a number of songs, among them *Mary's Boy Child*, *Water Boy*, and *In That Great Gettin' Up Mornin'*.

In his answer, Harry indicated that he had apprised Kennedy of the rights of other persons in these songs. According to Harry, Kennedy had stated that he was not concerned about the claims of third parties and that if such claims were made he would personally handle them. In asking the court to dismiss Kennedy's suit, Harry explained that in May 1954 he had retained Kennedy as his financial adviser for a period of three years. A year later, in May '55, he had been induced to extend the agreement for an additional 15 months and to increase the percentage from ten to fifteen percent, retroactive to January 1, 1955. Just a month later, he had been persuaded again to increase the percentage, this time to 25 percent.

At about the same time, he and Kennedy had come to an agreement, he stated, that a corporation would be formed to prevent others from copying his unique musical arrangements and styling. Originally slated to be called Adrienne Music Corporation, it was named after Harry's younger daughter,

Shari, when it became known that the older girl's name was already being used by an existing corporation and was, therefore, unavailable as a corporation title. All of the capital stock of Shari Music was to belong to Harry and his two daughters. According to Harry, Kennedy had, in violation of this understanding, caused the corporation to issue to himself twenty shares of stock in exchange for $2,000. Harry wanted the court to compel surrender of this stock in return for $2,000.

In July '57 Kennedy's suit was discontinued by agreement. Terms of whatever settlement was reached have never been made public.

People close to Harry and his third manager believe that the final break was prompted by something other than their business and artistic disagreements. To understand this, one must bear in mind that Harry's relation to Kennedy went beyond, far beyond the managerial. If Jack Rollins, Harry's second manager, was like a brother to him, Jay Richard Kennedy, his third, was more like a father. In fact, Harry called Kennedy "Dad," Mrs. Kennedy "Mom"—and they both called him "Son." Margurite Belafonte feels that when Harry went counter to Kennedy's advice, as he did occasionally, he experienced the exultation of the rebellious son. Along with others, Margurite believes that the complete rupture between the two came when Kennedy took a strong position with regard to Harry's interest in dancer Julie Robinson. Apparently, Kennedy, and perhaps, Kennedy's wife, did not approve. Thus Harry was torn between love for his bride-to-be and the disapproval of his "father." That he chose to rip up his agreement with Kennedy is an indication of the depth of his feeling for Julie.

Some people mature naturally, easily. It may be a slow or a quick process. For others, it is a hard struggle. Harry was one for whom the process came hard and painfully. To achieve it, the father image he had created had to be destroyed. And once the son had freed himself and become independent of the father, he had to destroy the mother image. Margurite Belafonte is quite aware of the way Jay Richard Kennedy fitted into this development. Originally, she was not aware of how she figured in it. Since the divorce, she has come to know and to understand.

STEREO

LAS VEGAS TABOOS

When he played Las Vegas in 1952, Harry was not permitted to stay at the hotel or to use any of its facilities. By 1955, the situation had changed so that he had a suite at the hotel and he was allowed to eat in the main dining room. However, the swimming pool and the gambling casino were still out of bounds—the latter, because of a State law; the former, because of sheer prejudice.

At this time, Tony and Fran Scott were traveling with Harry, Tony as his musical conductor and Fran as Harry's personal secretary. One day Tony and Fran got a call from Harry, who asked them to bring their bathing suits to his room.

"We're going to take the pool," he smiled, when they were with him. "Here's the strategy. The three of us walk toward the pool. Tony and I will jump in. Fran, you sit at the edge, dangling your feet in the water. You call to us. After a while, you order some coffee or juice."

The three of them walked slowly from Harry's room into the pool area. Fran seated herself at the edge and dangled her feet. Without warning, Tony and Harry jumped in. Two attendants saw it happen. They made no move to stop Harry. But they looked so startled, it might have been a prehistoric monster in the pool instead of just a man with coffee-colored skin. The swimming instructor looked nonplused and uneasy. After a moment, he beat a hasty retreat.

Meanwhile, Fran was dangling her feet, calling to Harry and Tony and laughing gaily. Within a few minutes, several men appeared on a porch outside the hotel's executive offices. They stood watching the pool, amazement, consternation, and shock written over their faces.

For another suspenseful minute, the whole scene was like a tableau. Except for Harry, Tony, and Fran, the rest of the scene was frozen stiff. Then, an unbelievable thing happened. As if it was prearranged, one woman got up from her sun chair, then another, then a third—and each of them jumped into the pool. Soon Harry was a lone brown face in the water surrounded by a growing cluster of white female faces.

Within a few minutes, all the kids who were lolling around the pool were in the water. And before long, mothers and fathers were asking Harry to pose with their youngsters for pictures.

"Won't you make believe you're teaching Nathaniel to swim, Mr. Belafonte?"

Some years earlier, at another Las Vegas hotel, a well-known Negro pianist had gone into the pool. Afterward, the management had drained out all the water. The following day, the Negro 88'er had gone in again. That evening, the pool was emptied and again refilled with fresh water.

Having cracked the pool, Harry began systematically studying the situation in the gambling casino. The State law did not forbid Negroes walking through it. For several nights, Tony and he kept wandering about the Casino, trying to figure the best maneuver. At one end of the Casino there was a large room—used for private parties—with a piano in it. From this room it was easy to see what was happening at the gambling tables.

One night, at about 3:00 A.M., they decided to make their move. Fran Scott was to act as a buffer. Harry explained carefully what she was to do. The three of them headed for a blackjack table where there was only one player. Tony took a seat. Harry sat himself in the chair next to Tony. Fran stood between the two chairs with a hand casually resting on each.

As soon as the dealer saw Harry, he removed the cards from the table and backed away from it. Then he stood looking at Harry. No one spoke a word. Again, the scene was frozen as in a movie with a stalled projector.

After a tense twenty seconds—it was like an hour to Fran—Tony said: "Come on, man, let's play!"

The dealer did not move a muscle. He stood perfectly still and just stared at Harry.

Tony tried again: "Deal!"

The dealer did not stir. He remained away from the table, the cards in his hands. He was waiting for Harry to make his move. Harry remained motionless, his eyes staring through the dealer's.

Fran asked: "When does the game start?" No one moved.

Then the dealer turned his head. The pit boss caught his eye instantly. Tony glanced toward the pit box. The pit boss's eyes traveled upward. A man they had never seen before on a small balcony overlooking the room caught the glance. For the next two or three minutes, the signal traveled from person to person until it apparently reached the hotel's executive office. Then it traveled back.

The man in the balcony nodded to the pit boss who nodded to the dealer. The cards reappeared on the table and the game was resumed—with Harry in it.

Then a magical thing happened. Word somehow spread around the room that Harry Belafonte was at one of the blackjack tables. Within minutes, the table filled and people came just to watch him play.

Thereafter, the club management was delighted whenever Harry wanted to gamble. People came flocking in after him and joined whatever game he played.

[185]

17. And Triumph

Hoarseness so complete as to deprive him of his singing and speaking voice occasionally assails Harry, sometimes within a matter of hours. This was the case once when Charles Laughton came to hear him at a New York club and again in Miami after a public controversy over his singing the national anthem at a football game.

As far back as any of his friends can recall, Harry has suffered from chronic laryngitis and sinusitis. This could be the result of his singing technique. Harry is not a trained singer. Unlike vocalists who have engaged in years of study, he sings directly from his throat and larynx. Trained singers project from the diaphragm, a mode of vocalizing that reduces the strain on the vocal cords and permits greater flexibility of expression.

Harry regards his throat troubles as psychosomatic and not the result of bad singing technique. "My chronic laryngitis," he once said, "is the organic symptom of subconscious feelings of guilt about my success. I am subconsciously trying to be a failure so I will not feel guilty because some of my friends are still struggling."

Perhaps this was true in the early days of Harry's success. But Margurite Belafonte has another explanation. She says that laryngitis was always an escape device for Harry and that he had it long before he became successful. Whenever things got too tough, whenever he didn't want to make a decision, whenever he wanted to avoid doing something, his throat always came to the rescue.

In May 1956, when it was apparent that *Sing, Man, Sing* could not be saved, could not be brought to Broadway—and when Harry had become despondent about his future—the laryngitis returned. Parenthetically, it should be added that Harry was suffering from other tensions at the time, tensions arising from his domestic situation. These could have been more destructive even than his corrosive feeling about his career. It was one of the worst cases of laryngitis Harry had ever had. And it came on the eve of his spring opening at The Waldorf, scheduled for May 28.

An examination of his throat revealed that Harry had nodes on his vocal cords. They had been there for some time. The doctor felt that they would probably disappear with treatment. He could make no guarantee without surgery. But he saw no need for an operation until nonsurgical treatment proved unsuccessful. Harry is an impatient man. He hates uncertainty. He hates waiting for answers. It is also not unlikely that, in his despondent state of mind, he welcomed something that would provide a focus of sympathy for him.

Harry canceled his opening at The Waldorf. During the first week of June he entered Montefiore Hospital in the Bronx. The removal of nodes is a fairly simple operation, provided no complications develop. Many singers, including Bing Crosby, have had nodes removed surgically. The operation on Harry's throat was without incident. In a few days he was out of the hospital, looking uneasily into the future. Staring him in the face was a solo concert appearance at New York's Lewisohn Stadium.

Ordinarily, an event of this kind would provide no terrors for Harry. But in his tense and depressed state of mind, he saw obstacles that could result only in disaster. The Stadium was huge. It could easily seat 25,000. He had to sing out of doors, under an open sky. He had to rely almost entirely on his voice. This was a concert—and he could not use all the dramatic devices at his command in an intimate night club or hotel room. The Stadium audience came to hear classical and semiclassical music, not folk material. On the same program with him, for the first half, was the Philharmonic Symphony Orchestra. What could one little man with two guitars do to compete? As the twenty-eighth of June approached, Harry continued to magnify the terrors of the Stadium. He became more and more jittery, more and more depressed. It looked as if he was headed for one of the worst attacks of laryngitis of his career, despite the absent nodes.

Finally it was the twenty-eighth. Driving to the Stadium on St. Nicholas Heights, Harry was caught in a traffic jam that held him down to a block a light. Since he was scheduled to appear after the intermission, he was not too worried. But he was mystified—until suddenly it came to him that the cars stalling his progress were all headed for the Stadium. He was actually caught in his own traffic jam.

At the Stadium, the musicians of the Philharmonic Symphony were soon to experience something rare in the annals of concert history. Neglect. Complete and utter neglect. It did not matter what the selection. De Falla's Dances from *The Three Cornered Hat*, Tchaikowsky's *Romeo and Juliet* or Prokofiev's *Classical Symphony*. The audience paid no attention, filling the Stadium with a hum of conversation that made the orchestra inaudible in the softer passages. During the performance of the *Classical Symphony*, a less dynamic work than the De Falla *Dances*, the Stadium management resorted to the desperate device of turning up the amplifiers. It did no good.

The next morning's *Times* was to report that the Philharmonic "made little headway against the continuous roar of excited conversation among listeners who considered the symphonic part of the program an overlong introduction to Mr. Belafonte." In short, Harry's advance uneasiness was totally without foundation. When the Stadium management totaled its receipts for the concert, it found that Harry and his red V-necked silk shirt had brought more people to the huge amphitheatre than had attended any concert in its entire 39-year-old history. "Outside the Stadium," *The Times* reported, "thousands of admirers who came too late to get tickets were

[188]

turned away. But many hundreds lingered, some trying to scale the Stadium walls for a glimpse of the artist, some sitting quietly on the curbstone or in parked cars."

Harry's Stadium concert had made entertainment history.

How the record-breaking crowd taxed the Stadium staff is amusingly told by Margurite Belafonte. Originally, she and daughter Adrienne were scheduled to drive to the Stadium with Harry. But as "curtain time" approached, Harry called Margurite, who was at their Elmhurst home, and suggested that she go directly to the Stadium, instead of picking him up at J. Richard Kennedy's office.

When she reached the Stadium, after traveling through the heavy traffic, she went to the Stadium parking lot, where Harry had indicated there would be space reserved for the car. There was no space. The attendants did not know of any reservation made for Mr. Belafonte's car. And even if it was Mr. Belafonte's car, there just was not an inch of space available.

So Margurite turned the car around and drove with Adrienne to a midtown garage. Then she took a taxi back uptown to the Stadium.

Now a new problem presented itself. When she went to the box office handling seats on the field and asked for two seats left in the name of Mrs. Belafonte, there were no such seats. The attendants had no way of getting in touch with Mr. Belafonte. And even if she was Mrs. Belafonte, as she said she was, there were just no seats available. Not a one.

At this point little Adrienne looked as if all her favorite dolls had been smashed to smithereens by a vindictive playmate. Not to be able to hear her father on this most important occasion! Tears trembled on the young eyelids.

Just about this time, someone entered the box office who seemed to have a little more authority than the several clerks. Margurite Belafonte explained her plight. He took one look at Adrienne, who is the image of Harry, and agreed to do what he could.

"Adrienne was my ticket," Margurite laughed. "If she didn't

[189]

look like her father, we would never have been admitted."

As it was, two folding seats were somehow found and Margurite and Adrienne were seated on the field, a few feet from the stage. Just before the concert was over, Harry sent for them. It took a flying wedge of police to get them out of the Stadium and to clear the area where his manager's car was parked—crawling, like a beehive, with autograph seekers.

After the Stadium, Harry played outstandingly successful engagements at a series of the country's plush hotel rooms. In July it was The Riviera in Las Vegas, where the *Variety* reviewer marveled at his ability to command an audience to a hush, even during the dinner show. In August it was the Palmer House in Chicago, where he had previously smashed the house attendance record and was to do so again. In September it was the Waldorf-Astoria in New York, where the ropes were up for his entire stay. Not the break with Kennedy or even the impending break with Margurite could dim the pleasure of the reception he received here.

For the Waldorf engagement, Harry tried a new drummer. Winslow D. Barrajanos, known to his friends as Danny, came for the date but stayed to become a now-accepted part of Harry's permanent background combo. At the time, Danny was making a living as a take-out order clerk in a restaurant, and his drums were in hock. But his talents as a conga drummer were well-known to Buddy Phillips and Sevilla Fort, the directors of the Phillips-Fort dance studio. It was through Julie Robinson, who was teaching at the studio, that Danny came to Harry's attention. (In 1955 her enthusiasm had led Harry to retain dancer Walter Nicks as choreographer of *Sing, Man, Sing.*)

"Unlike Margurite, Julie was in show business," Fran Scott observed, "and she had the entertainer's sense of excitement about discovering talent. This was a quality which she enjoyed in common with Harry and which led him to turn to her for ideas. It wasn't just a matter of a conga drummer. She could get just as excited about a new record album or book.

"Julie never wanted just to live. She wanted terribly to have

a wonderful life. That almost makes her sound naive, I guess. But it's true and it gave her a kind of animation and vivacity that was catching.

"For all his fantastic energy, Harry also had his moments when he would go bloop. A reserved and indrawn person like Margurite could do little to pull him up at such times. But Julie complimented Harry's energy with her own high-flying spirits."

During '56 Margurite heard the name of Julie Robinson more and more frequently. Not from Harry but from well-meaning friends, who persisted in telling her which restaurants they ate at and which jazz clubs they frequented.

"I was never one to confront unpleasant things," Margurite said recently. "I had the feeling that some people gave me information in the belief—perhaps, hope—that I would go and confront them. That was the last thing in the world I ever thought of doing. I was happy that our paths did not cross and would have gone out of my way not to meet them.

"Perhaps I was at fault. But I never liked to make issues. It's also true that I hoped this was all a bad dream and, like a dream, it would pass away after a time. After all, there had been other bad dreams—and they had passed.

"I guess I did not let Harry know how much I knew. By September of '56 we were really separated and I wanted desperately to make whatever time we spent together pleasant for both of us. But except for the children, about which we were both concerned, we had few points of communication.

"I had never wanted his career although I worked during his years of struggle. Now that he was so successful, he had no reason to turn to me about it. I really had no contact with it."

November was memorable for an incident that moved Harry deeply. He was playing the Town and Country Club in Brooklyn. Backstage to say hello to an old buddy came five guys with whom Harry had grown up in Harlem. What made the visit so unforgettable was that all five were white.

It brought back vividly to Harry the hard days when he and

his brother Dennis were two Negro kids growing up in a white neighborhood. It brought back memories of all the times they both tried to pass and of all their frustrated efforts to belong; of the moments when he did pass and then had to sit and listen with a disinterested air to anti-Negro jokes; and of the many times when he couldn't duck the fact that he was an outsider, a despised outsider.

"That backstage visit was a real flipper to me," Harry said. "I was like the badge of honor for the block . . . I had a responsibility to understand that they had been confused and did not know any better about some of the things they used to do and say, and it was up to me to forgive them . . ."

In December a more public occurrence was once again to bring the Negro question sharply into the foreground of Belafonte's career. The incident was widely reported over the nation's wire services. It originated in Miami, where Harry was playing a personal engagement at one of the super hotels. A local publicity man, Julian Cole, hired by the Shrine to publicize the North-South football game, got the idea of inviting Harry to sing *The Star-Spangled Banner* at the game. Belafonte accepted the invitation. The next he knew, Cole was calling up apologetically to say that there had been a mix-up and the schedule of events for the pre-game program at half-time was so crowded, there would be no time for Harry to sing the national anthem.

Harry refused to back away from the issue. "This is a grave injustice upon me personally," he said, "and upon my race." And he gave the story to the papers. On Christmas morning, the potentate of the Miami Shrine Temple was quoted as saying: "It had nothing to do with the race issue."

Nevertheless, with the eyes of the nation focused on them, officials of the Shrine felt impelled to re-examine their schedule. It turned out that it was all a misunderstanding and, as announced in the following day's papers, "Mr. Belafonte would lead the spectators in singing the national anthem before the kickoff."

After the kickoff, Harry journeyed back to The Eden Roc Hotel, where he was playing the posh Pompeii Room. That

[192]

evening, according to conferencier Harry Tobias, comedian Myron Cohen had to appear in place of the balladeer. Belafonte had a bad case of laryngitis.

STEREO

THE NEGRO ARTIST AS SPOKESMAN

"I never relished the position of spokesman for my people," Harry said recently, "and I neither sought nor asked for the role. It came to me as it comes to almost all Negro artists. A white entertainer can say anything. No one assumes that he is talking for anybody but himself. But as soon as a Negro celebrity says anything, his words are immediately seized as a statement—not for himself but for his people.

"Of course, it is not too difficult to understand why this happens. The Negro people have been suppressed for so long and so few Negro voices have been heard in public that no Negro in the public eye can speak without seeming to speak for the larger group of which he is part.

"This situation does not make things easy for us. I can't say anything about anything without reflecting on how it will reflect, not only on me, but on my people as a whole. This is not a static situation. Young Negroes are today becoming more affirmative about themselves and their rights. As more Negro voices are heard—even in terms of the Negro vote at the ballot box—each of us will stand forth more as an individual, which is as it should be."

[193]

18. "My Closest Friend"

In January 1957 one of the papers ran a dramatic picture of Harry and his wife, Margurite. It showed the two of them at the top of a staircase leading into the cockpit of a plane. In Margurite's face there was stark distress and anguish. In Harry's, a pained plea "to leave us alone." The two were not going on a vacation. Margurite was bound for Nevada to secure a divorce.

When the decree came through on February 28, 1957, their marriage was just scant of being nine years old. In actuality, their marriage had been over for some time, how long it is impossible to say with accuracy. Harry says that he and Margurite agreed to separate early in 1956. A source close to Margurite disputes this assertion, claiming that actual separation did not occur until September 1956, just four months before Margurite left for a Nevada divorce. At this time Margurite went on a tour of the West Indies by herself, and Harry, in a trial move, set up a bachelor apartment on the West Side in Manhattan. Bill Attaway, an intimate friend of the period, tends to support Harry's assertion. According to Attaway, while Harry did not move his clothes out of the Elmhurst house, he did spend many a troubled night at Attaway's or at the homes of other friends in the city.

It has been stated in printed sources that Harry asked for a divorce in September '54 after Margurite discovered letters to Harry from Julie. The claim has been made that the divorce idea was tabled because of opposition by Harry's mother as well as by his wife. Margurite denies that the subject of divorce came up at this time. She admits that Harry was troubled about their relationship, but claims that he was so deeply concerned she had reason to hope that their difficulties could be worked out.

Since Margurite and Harry never entered into a legal separation, except as a formality, the whole question of separation becomes a quibble. What is clear is that from the fall of '54 there was an imbalance and a kind of impasse which had to lead either to a complete rupture or to a renewal of what had once existed. That it no longer existed, regardless of the degree of actual separation, seems undeniable.

It also seems clear that the breakup of the Belafonte ménage was not the result of anybody stealing anybody. Nor was Margurite in a competitive position with the woman who eventually succeeded her. The two represented completely divergent sets of values, one in conflict with Harry's outlook, personality, and needs, the other, harmonious to them. It was not that Harry had changed but that Margurite, who had started at an opposite pole, had not changed in Harry's direction as his course had more and more clearly defined itself. By the time Harry became interested in a new woman, the door to the old relationship had been shut tight for too long.

The lines of cleavage had long been apparent. In a series on Belafonte published in 1957, Harry is quoted as saying: "Margurite had high materialistic values. It kind of kept me under the hammer. Keepin' up with the Joneses one day and then the Smiths and the Browns . . . I was away for long periods touring wherever I could. She felt I wasn't going anywhere. She never understood show business. She still doesn't to this day. She's a perfectly normal person who understands 8 A.M. to 5 P.M. and that's all."

Margurite, who was characterized by the *Post* as "more circumspect in speaking of their difficulties than Harry" was quoted in the following fashion: "Harry felt he couldn't be the family man he wanted to be, what with being on the road so often. He has a guilt complex about that. When he first started on his road trips about three years ago, there was a period of two years when he was at home only a total of six weeks. During holidays, I'd take the kids and meet him on the road.

"It was a difficult climb for Harry. I'm really surprised he made it with all his personality problems. He has always run the gamut of emotions. He had a terrific drive that he 'had to make it' and to do that he had to stay on the road.

"I had to give him the freedom that he needs to give the kind of performance he does give."

Allowing for differences in expression, there would not seem to be much discrepancy between the lines of cleavage singled out by each. What was undeniably different, however, was the perspective of each. Margurite did not look forward to a dissolution of their relationship and hoped, almost to the last moment, that Harry might change his mind. Without looking forward to a divorce, Harry apparently felt for quite a time that the marriage could not be saved. To him, the lines of cleavage ran too deep.

During '56 Harry did at least one thing that offers objective evidence of his possible direction. He organized a new publishing company named Clara Music. Clara was the name of the mother of the girl who became his second wife. Despite this move, there is no question that Harry was undergoing serious internal turmoil during this period.

A suggestion of this disturbance is to be found even in an examination of the covers of his RCA Victor albums. On the *Calypso* LP jacket, he is eager and expectant in a green silk shirt. On the *Caribbean* cover, he appears satisfied and relaxed in a red shirt. An *Evening with Belafonte* presents a close-up of a man who is determined and defiant. On the LP titled *Belafonte,* released in '56, we see the face of an unhappy and troubled human being. Unquestionably, tensions emanating from Harry's domestic situation, as well as the problems posed by the failure of *Sing, Man, Sing* and the rift with manager Jay Richard Kennedy—all contributed to the despondency suffered by Harry at this time.

Central, I think, to this inner crisis, and more responsible for it than any of the foregoing, were Harry's feelings about another person—one of his daughters.

Harry matured faster as an artist than as a man. But he could overcome certain immaturities as an artist—a tendency to pretentiousness and theatricalism—only by maturing as a man. His divorce from Margurite offers insight into his emotional development as it relates to his first wife and his older daughter. But it illumines basically his hard-won fight to achieve maturity.

Among the explanations that Harry has made of the breakup of his marriage is his restlessness, a quality which had its origins in his childhood. "When I lived with my grandparents as a kid in the West Indies," he said, "I was boarded from house to house. The same thing went on back in New York. My mother was a domestic. I never really had any roots. Restless. Always restless."

Another cause, Harry indicated, was the irregularity and rootlessness of the entertainer's life. "When I was trying to get started as an actor, it was twenty-two hours one day and four the next. Never eight. Always you're going off. Day by day the damage is being done and you don't know it and the gulf widens between a man and a woman. By the time you're really aware, it's too late . . ."

Harry's wild popularity with the girls certainly could not have contributed to the stability of his home life. At the Lewisohn Stadium concert at which he smashed attendance records, Mrs. Guggenheimer, the sponsor, came rushing backstage. "Get scarce, kid," she cried, "the guards can't hold back that mob of girls much longer."

What that feeling among women—expressed frequently in as outspoken a way—must have done to Harry's domestic situation is not difficult to surmise. Margurite Byrd is a very sensible, a smart, and a stable woman. She knew what was going on, but believed that Harry had to be given time to mature. To prying reporters, she would say: "Any man in Harry's position will always have rumors involving women spread about him." That the situation posed problems for her, despite her insight and tolerance, is evident. During much of their life together, Margurite busied herself with work of one kind or another, even after her financial assistance was no longer required, as it was during the early years of their marriage.

Actually, the problems in Harry's marriage lay deeper than his uncontrollable restlessness, the zaniness of the performer's life, or Harry's attractiveness to women. The roots of the difficulties go back to the original shape of their relationship. When Harry first met Margurite during his Navy days, he was an unlettered, embittered, immature youngster while she was well educated, worldly, and self-possessed. Jestingly, he would refer to himself as "a retarded child with lots of problems," hoping thereby to arouse sympathy in the advanced student and soon-to-be teacher of child psychology. In a not unimportant sense, Margurite thus became Harry's first teacher. She worried about all his pent-up hostilities, feeling that unless she guided them into constructive channels they might easily explode into delinquent behavior. Even today, in talking of him, she occasionally refers to him as "the kid."

By the time they were married, four years later, Harry had learned a lot as a student at the Drama Workshop in New York. But he was still a callow youth, now with a frustrating ambition to be an actor. Margurite, who was then teaching, provided a home and financial support that gave him a degree of security. But Harry did not work at building a home even then. That his hours were irregular goes without saying. As he shifted to a singing career and began traveling around the country, their relationship became more tenuous. Harry wanted violently to make something of himself, and he took Margurite for granted in the way that any boy takes his home and his mother for granted.

This is not to say that Harry was unkind or without loyalty, or a man who takes responsibility lightly. I have talked with many of the people who knew him at various times and who were part of his entourage at different periods, people who went to dinner with him night after night after his shows.

[198]

Conversation seldom deteriorated to typical man talk about dames. Even after Harry became interested in a new girl, he tried to manage his affairs so that few knew of her existence or of the extent of his relationship with her. Harry had no desire to embarrass Margurite or to make things difficult for her. And she has said that he was quite considerate in the arrangements he made for her and their two children when the break came. Nor has he slighted his responsibilities as a father since the break.

Despite the fact that he tended to take Margurite for granted, it is clear that he himself needed love as the earth needs rain. Lack of it in his childhood and youth had created a void whose depths are hard to sound or believe. "Like certain celebrities, Harry had a massive hunger for love," a friend of his has said. "He could never get enough of it. And it had to be intense, demonstrative. Passive acceptance was not enough. In an important sense, wildly applauding audiences were necessary, but not enough. Friends had to love him. Business associates had to love him. Relatives had to love him. And so on down the line, to children, animals, insects, and, perhaps, even bacteria."

That Margurite gave Harry many things is quite apparent. But it is apparent, too, that she was a rather reserved woman, not given to open displays of her feelings. Early in their relationship, Harry's Village and theatre friends had, in fact, shocked her by their lack of inhibition. There is no indication that, as their marital relation settled into its day-to-day routines, Margurite ever became more demonstrative than her natural reserve would permit.

There is some question as to whether Harry was ever really in love with Margurite. That he admired and respected and liked her is not to be doubted. When he first met her, as an underprivileged and belligerent young man, she represented many of the things he yearned for. It may well be that Harry fell in love, not so much with a person but with an image of what he himself wanted to be—perhaps, the image of what his mother wanted him to be. This resulted in an attachment that was not easy to sever. The loyalty of a son to a mother, or the devotion a man may feel to a mother image, frequently are not less consuming than the love of a man for a woman.

The idea of divorce was distressing to Harry for another reason—more obvious if more delicate. It came out in many different ways and it had to do with his children. More specifically with his daughter Adrienne. Many men go ga-ga over their first-born. Daughters sometimes become an outlet for affective feelings repressed in the relationship between man and wife. Early pictures taken of Harry and Adrienne reveal a depth of feeling, apparent even in the photographs. In some of these, little Adrienne—enchanted by her handsome father—may be seen wearing a belt whose buckle was a miniature of the curtain-ring buckle worn on-stage by Harry.

Fran Scott, who served as Harry's secretary during '55, offers an interesting sidelight on Harry's concern over Adrienne. Some restaurants around the country maintain a gift shop, or a gift counter, as an adjunct. According to Fran, any time they went into a restaurant with such a counter, their meal was certain to be delayed. How long depended on the size of the counter or shop. Harry immediately became absorbed in finding a gift, not for Margurite, but for Adrienne. Likewise, if they went anywhere near a toy shop and Harry was suddenly not in evidence, Fran knew exactly where to find him and what he would be doing.

"The strange thing," Fran observes, "is the thought and the concern that went into each search for a toy. It was not casual —like 'Wrap that up, Miss.' No, he would find one thing that attracted him and consider carefully how Adrienne would like it. Then he would find another item and wonder whether, maybe, she'd like that better. If I was around, he would ask me my opinion in dead earnestness and discuss pros and cons. During the time I traveled with Harry, he did not pass a single toy counter without buying Adrienne some new, carefully chosen toy."

There can be little question that Harry showered little Adrienne with a depth of affection and a degree of attention that seldom was Margurite's. In a remarkably candid statement, Harry himself has said that the best thing he derived from his first marriage was one of the best things he ever got out of life: ". . . the most rewarding relationship . . . I ever had . . . the only person who ever accepted me completely . . . my closest friend."

The reference here is not, as might be anticipated, to his wife Margurite. It is to his first child, Adrienne.

Paramount in Harry's thinking, in fact, as he faced the problem of divorce was the possible adverse effect on Adrienne. Whether his claim that Margurite and he agreed to separate in January 1956 is true or not, the important thing is his assertion: "But in order to avoid upsetting Adrienne, I went home frequently." This statement is only one of three that occurs in an article Harry wrote for *Ebony*, each of which indicates his deep desire to cushion Adrienne against adverse effects.

First, as to separation: "Both of us wanted to avoid an open break that might have serious emotional repercussions on our oldest daughter, Adrienne, who is now eight."

Then, as to the divorce: "I talked to little Adrienne about the divorce and found explaining it just about the hardest thing I ever had to do."

Finally, as to his remarriage: "My only concern was how Adrienne would react to it."

One must conclude that of all the things that distressed Harry during the *Sing, Man, Sing* year, concern over little Adrienne filled him with the greatest anguish.

During September of '56, Margurite Belafonte toured the Caribbean, modeling clothes as part of a group known as the Brandford Goodwill Tour. This was presumably a "make up your mind" period. Several of the outfits modeled by Margurite were allegedly chosen by Harry. A newspaperwoman, who accompanied the tour, reported that Margurite received several letters a week from her husband and that, as they moved from island to island, the letters were always one stop ahead of them.

Nevertheless, on her return to New York in October, it appeared that the possibility of reconciliation had disappeared. Now the discussions were in terms of a divorce.

One immediate effect of the news of the impending divorce of the Belafontes was that the James J. Hoey Award for Interracial Justice, which Harry was to receive from the Catholic Interracial Council, was withdrawn.

On January 12 Margurite took off for Las Vegas, pursued to the cockpit of the plane by a bevy of reporters. Asked about a possible reconciliation, Margurite put on a smile and said: "Miracles never cease to happen."

Shortly after she left, *The Pittsburgh Courier* ran a story headlined " 'Strange' Breakup of the Harry Belafonte's." Six reasons were given for the word "strange":

1. Harry and Margurite say only the nicest things about one another.
2. They saw each other almost daily after reports of the breakup.
3. Harry allegedly persuaded Margurite to delay her trip to Nevada for one week.
4. They dined together near their East Elmhurst home.
5. Harry baby-sits when Margurite has business engagements.
6. Harry gave Margurite a white mink for Christmas.

In an interview about the same time, Margurite was quoted as saying that she had "the greatest admiration for Harry as a personality and as a person. He's really a tremendous personality, like Moses.

"I won't deny that I've been hurt," she added, "but there hasn't been any hostility between us. I've asked myself often just how I would react if I had met with the great success that Harry has. How would I react if this great boom suddenly came and I found people at my feet? How strong would I be?

"He's still attentive and devoted as ever, both to me and the children. I believe he is a victim of circumstances that he can't easily get out of."

Her parting words: "I plan neither to jump off the George Washington Bridge nor to sling mud."

In April, after the divorce, a columnist in *The Amsterdam News* "itemed" that Harry had showered Margurite with parting gifts of a $10,000 diamond and sapphire bracelet, a white mink, and a $2,500 opal and diamond "friendship forever" ring.

"The opal ring," Margurite said recently, "was actually a gift that went back several years. It became part of the parting in a curious way.

"Shortly after we moved to Elmhurst in '53, Harry and I were walking along 57th Street in Manhattan. In the window of a jewelry shop, two rings caught my eye. Both were opals, my birthstone—one priced at $2,500 and the other at $750. Although things were beginning to move for Harry, the more expensive ring seemed out of reach. I expressed a liking for the lower-priced opal.

"At that time we were quite friendly with a Jewish couple in the dress business. It was customary for us to visit them on the holiday of Succoth, while they came to share the joy of Christmas with us. That Christmas, they arrived with their presents—also a large box containing a dress that Harry had ordered for me. When I lifted the dress box from its position under the tree, a small jewelry box tumbled across the carpet. Imagine my excitement when I opened it and found that Harry had bought me the more expensive opal.

"Now, on the way out to Vegas for the divorce, I was dismayed to find that one of the baguette diamonds, set in a circle around the opal, had dropped out. When Harry learned of it, he arranged for a jeweler to reset the whole circle of diamonds in a more attractive setting and to substitute a better grade of stone. The jeweler completed the job as I was completing my six weeks' residence. That's how the opal became part of the parting."

Concerning the last weeks of their marriage and her Las Vegas residence, Margurite added: "The divorce decision was not reached at Christmas time of '56. It was not made until the day before I left for Vegas. I know it's hard to believe. But really the situation was not finally resolved, as I saw it, until the very day I went into court. That's the way it seemed to me then. In retrospect, I am not sure that it really was that way.

"It seemed an uphill climb all the way. It seemed really difficult for both of us. And the last two weeks that I was in Vegas, Harry was there, too. We were all there together— Harry, Adrienne, Shari, the nurse, and myself.

"I went out to Vegas by myself. He was home for my first two weeks in residence. For the next two weeks, he was in California—at the Cocoanut Grove, I believe. He was in Vegas for the last two weeks. That's how the residence went. He took the kids and nurse with him to California and then brought them to Las Vegas, where we were all together for the last two weeks."

Harry was playing the Riviera Hotel and staying at the Riviera.

"But during the whole time, I heard from Harry almost every day. I received flowers. And he issued orders that I was not to want for anything. He saw to it that I was made very comfortable, with a car at my disposal and a comfortable place to stay. He was most considerate down the line, right up to the very end. Even down to the bracelet.

"I got the bracelet on the night I was divorced. Harry spent the day taking pictures with Adrienne and Shari. He tried so hard to cheer Adrienne but if you look at the pictures—they're candids—you can see a very lonely, troubled girl. Shari was, of course, too young to understand."

In its story revealing Harry's remarriage, *The Amsterdam News* reported that, as a divorce settlement, Harry had given Margurite a $75,000 mansion in California, a $10,000 bracelet, a new car, and cash. Also, that the children were to receive all royalties on his recordings. At a later date, *Ebony* Magazine asserted that Harry had set up lifetime funds for both of his daughters and had given Margurite two homes (one in Elmhurst, Long Island, and the other under construction in Pleasantville, New York), the family's Buick convertible, and $100,-000 in cash. These are all guesses. The actual details of the divorce settlement have never been made public.

Margurite completed her six weeks' residence requirement during the last week of February. On the 28th, she presented the necessary papers and, a few hours later, emerged from the courtroom a "free" woman. The custody of the two children, Adrienne and Shari Lynn, was hers.

Harry had succeeded in destroying the mother image.

Before Margurite left for Las Vegas, certain rumors swept through the Negro community regarding Harry's domestic affairs. Reporters went to his Elmhurst home to ask Margurite whether these rumors were true. For two days, in rain, sleet, and snow, they camped on her doorstep, trying to get her to call somebody else's name, to confirm statements they read to her, to confirm a situation.

"I would not do it. I would not reveal it, although I knew the answers," Margurite stated quite recently. "And I caught myself protecting him. Again, it was this matter of protecting this man."

Margurite thought for a moment, her memory racing back from 1959 to the days when Harry was courting her. "At the outset of our relationship, I assumed a protective role. I don't know. Maybe that's another reason for the failure of our marriage. My feeling toward him probably was more of a mother protecting a child—rather than romantic love.

"It's so strange. Once you begin your relationship in that way, there's almost nothing you can do about it. That's what it remains even after you begin to sense that maybe your husband has outgrown it—and needs something else. Even he continues involuntarily to act in such a way as to invite the treatment he himself has outgrown.

"Naturally, he notices that he's two different people. A big man outside the house to others. And still a delinquent inside to you. Then he dislikes himself, and he begins to dislike you.

"It's so sad that you can both see it going on—and yet be powerless to stop it."

On her return to Elmhurst from the Nevada divorce court, the impact of what had happened hit Margurite with full force. Up until then, she had played a role and summoned the strength necessary to carry it off. Now the unhappy reality stared her full in the face. Like a chronic ailment, it would not go away. Suddenly she found herself unable to eat. For days at a time, she had no taste at all for food.

"I knew what was happening," she told me. "But I seemed powerless to prevent it. I felt destroyed and worthless and I was subconsciously trying to destroy myself. But I was also subconsciously trying to identify myself with the girl whom Harry wanted. She was very lean and long-haired. Apparently, that was beauty in Harry's eyes. Well, I could become lean."

As soon as Margurite was able to start eating normally again —"It took a tremendous exercise of will power"—she cut her hair short. Now she was consciously determined to destroy any vestige of identification with the type of woman who appealed to Harry.

"I am the stronger person for the experience," she has said. "I have been able to survive. I wouldn't carry hostility to the point of trying to destroy Harry or myself. I feel that people should lean on each other, but I do not believe in the degree of dependence of one on the other which leads to self-annihilation or destruction of the other.

"It was necessary for me to take a back seat when I was with Harry so that he could occupy the limelight. Now I'm stepping forward myself. Maybe I helped Harry to channel his anger in certain social directions. I think I did. He was a very confused and undirected kid when I met him. The strange thing is that I now must thank him for provoking me to advance into the public eye and to develop certain social drives.

"During most of our married life, I thought of myself as a mother and a housewife. In the early days I resented his career because it compelled me to work and prevented me from being these things primarily. I still regard myself as a mother and homemaker. But I believe that I also have a social responsibility to fulfill—and I'm devoting every free moment to fulfilling it."

Margurite has become one of the leading fund raisers for the NAACP. During 1959, she visited 168 cities, on occasion addressing two and three groups a day. Recently, when Congressman Adam Clayton Powell, of Harlem, was in a hospital and he was asked about possible successors to himself, he named two women among ten people whom he regarded as potentially competent candidates. One of them was Margurite Belafonte.

Act III

JULIE

Or leave a kiss within the cup
And I'll not ask for wine . . .
—Drink to Me Only with Thine Eyes

19. Why I Married Julie

On March 8, 1957 Harry left the environs of the Riviera Hotel in Las Vegas, where he was appearing nightly, and hopped on a plane bound for San Diego.

Awaiting him in the border city were white dancer Julie Robinson, pretty, petite, and pigtailed, together with her parents. Clara and George Robinson, of Los Angeles, were celebrating their fortieth wedding anniversary. But Harry was flying to meet them for another reason.

By car, the happy quartet motored south from San Diego, crossed the border, and drove on to Tecate, Mexico. There, in the office of the mayor and in the presence of the bride's parents, Harry and Julie were married. The ceremony was secret and unpublicized—at the time. They scarcely had time for a wedding luncheon or dinner. Back to San Diego they sped. Harry picked up a plane for Las Vegas. He was at the Riviera in time not to miss a single performance. For five days, while he played nightly to swarming audiences, Harry kept contact with his new wife by phone. Then he flew to Los Angeles, picked her up, and they planed to New York. Quietly she moved into the bachelor apartment on Manhattan's West Side, which Harry had occupied during the preceding year.

No announcement was made of the marriage until a month later—April 9, 1957—and then, as the result of a maneuver by a Harlem newspaper. Not until the 22nd of April, when she accompanied Harry to a "Salute to Belafonte" rally in Harlem, did Julie appear in public as the new Mrs. Belafonte.

During the month of secrecy, gossip columnists worked overtime to link Harry with Julie. Even while Margurite was still in Las Vegas, certain columnists were "sp-iteming" that Belafonte was regularly dating the white dancer. Mike Merrick, Harry's personal press representative, was quoted in *The Pittsburgh Courier* as saying: "Sure he knows her. But then he knows lots of girls. The divorce has nothing to do with Miss Robinson."

A humorous skirmish occurred at the apartment of a movie actress who was a close friend of Julie's. Because of her dark complexion and the long black braids she wore, Julie was described in some quarters as part Indian. A reporter who went to see the actress friend in an effort to smoke out the tie-up between Harry and Julie said provocatively: "We hear that Harry is planning to marry a girl who is half Indian."

"Half Indian?" the actress chortled. "She's as much of an Indian as I am. Don't you know—Julie's Jewish."

On April 13 a columnist in *The Chicago Defender* gossiped: "Only Harry Belafonte isn't positive about his plan to marry beauteous Julie Robinson, the pigtailed brunette." On the other hand, a "Conversation Piece" in *The Amsterdam News* opined: "If dancer Julie Robinson reaches the altar with balladeer Harry Belafonte (whose pretty brown wife Margurite has just returned to her Long Island home with her Nevada divorce papers) she'll find that Harry still carries a smoldering torch for Margurite . . . as evidenced by the nightly long distance phone calls from California to East Elmhurst when Harry kisses Adrienne, Shari, and Margurite 'good night' . . ."

Doubtless, the strangest occurrence of this period was a meeting, reported in several Negro newspapers, held on the very evening before Harry's office released to the press the announcement of his marriage. According to *The Amsterdam News*: "Two prominent Harlemites, one a politician and the other, a musician, stayed with Belafonte until 5 o'clock Monday morning (the day before the story was released) in a vain effort to bring about a reconciliation with his wife. Apparently, all the while they entreated Belafonte to go back to his wife, he did not tell them he was already married to Miss Robinson."

In its issue of April 20, *The Pittsburgh Courier* repeated the story and identified the politician as Congressman Adam Clayton Powell and the musician as jazz saxist Illinois Jacquet.

Later Harry explained that he had kept his marriage secret for only one reason—out of consideration for his daughter Adrienne. "My only concern," he stated, "was not how the public might accept our marriage, but how Adrienne would react to it." Being aware of how unhappy she had been made by the news of the divorce—although he had himself brought it to her—he was afraid that the appearance of a new woman in his life "might confuse the child." Adrienne was scheduled to spend Easter vacation with her father. His plan, worked out with his new wife, was to hold news of the Mexican ceremony until Adrienne was with him. Then, he would tell her slowly in his own way and "help her adjust emotionally to her father's second marriage."

Despite Harry's plans and precautions, the news leaked out. Or rather, it was forced out by the maneuvers of *The Amsterdam News*, according to a boast of the paper in its issue of April 20. "*The New York Amsterdam News* 'broke' the story of Harry's marriage to Julie first," it wrote. "We utilized three writers and several 'stringers.' We kept three telephone lines open to various towns in Mexico. We finally came up with the information we were seeking in Spanish— and published it first in English."

The Amsterdam News also claimed that it sent a reporter to Harry's bachelor apartment. Posing as a census taker, the reporter rang the bell and asked the woman who answered the door if Mrs. Belafonte was at home. The woman allegedly replied: "I am Mrs. Belafonte." Thereupon, the reporter called Harry's personal representative to ask for a confirmation.

Harry disputed this story. In an interview with Barry Gray, reported in *The New York Post,* Harry claimed that he had himself spoken with the census taker, not Julie. He had given him full answers to all the information requested, he said, including the name of his new wife. That night, according to

Harry, the census taker—who was not a plant—told his brother-in-law, who, in turn, notified one of the metropolitan newspapers.

Whichever is the case, on April 9 Harry's office made a formal announcement regarding the Mexican nuptials to all papers. The following day *The New York Times* carried a single paragraph: "Harry Belafonte, the singer, disclosed yesterday that he had married secretly on March 8 Julie Robinson at Tecate, Mexico. The singer was divorced from his first wife on February 28. Marriage is the first for Miss Robinson, who was a dancer with Katherine Dunham's group."

The Amsterdam News regarded the information as rather more newsworthy. It ran the story on the front page under a heavy black head: "BELAFONTE WEDS WHITE DANCER." In two succeeding issues, the Harlem paper printed provocative stories, both of which focused on the interracial issue and took Harry to task for shedding a Negro for a white. For years, Harry had suffered and fought discrimination from whites. Now he was to have problems with his own people as well.

In the issue of April 20, *The News* story bore the caption: "WILL HARRY'S MARRIAGE AFFECT HIS STATUS AS MATINEE IDOL?" The gist of the article: "Many Negroes are wondering why a man who has waved the flag of justice for his race should turn from a Negro wife to a white wife . . ." Writer Betty Granger answered her question with a defense of Harry that did not bank the fire: "Perhaps, if they can understand that many of Harry Belafonte's closest friends are white, it may tend to show that Harry is living in a world that knows no color boundaries . . ."

A week later *The Amsterdam News* pursued the matter into more delicate areas. Miss Granger's article was innocuously titled: "The Harry Belafontes at Home." It described their apartment as a simple three and a half roomer, and it pictured Harry, first, with a piece of African sculpture and, again, with a copy of Langston Hughes' book *A Pictorial History of the Negro in America*. Having established the point that Harry

[214]

was a man with "racial pride," the article turned sharply critical. It harked back to a saying that gained currency in the twenties as a result of prizefighter Jack Johnson's fondness for white women after he became a celebrity.

The saying: "Give a Negro man fame and fortune, and he's got to have a white woman, a Packard car, and a bulldog."

"Maybe that's why," Miss Granger speculated, "Harry Belafonte's popularity within his own race is hanging in the balance at the moment."

There followed a headshaking narrative of how "as Harry rose up the ladder of success, so grew his personal problems —mainly women." Reference was made to Dorothy Dandridge and Joan Fontaine, both of whom had played opposite Harry in motion pictures. "However, the hottest interracial conquest . . . was one between the balladeer and a famed Italian actress. She is alleged to have completely disregarded his wife, Margurite, and would wake him at 4 A.M. and request that he meet her at once . . ."

In the same issue, columnist Dan Burley dealt with the question of intermarriage via a discussion of what he called Penguin clubs. These were social clubs organized in the twenties by people of mixed marriages who, rejected both by whites and Negroes, sought to create a community of their own. The main point of Burley's column seemed to be that whites run and grab up all rich Negroes, while Negroes practically never marry rich whites.

Whether or not *The Amsterdam News* was accurate in suggesting that Harry's popularity within his race was "hanging in the balance," Harry reached a point in his own thinking where he determined to explain his action to his people. It was not an easy thing to do, for he had three strikes against him.

Strike one: Negroes believe in strong family ties.
Strike two: The wife he had divorced was a teacher and highly respected as such in the Negro community.
Strike three: The girl he married was white.

In July 1957 *Ebony* magazine, the Negro equivalent of *Life,* opened its pages to the singer for a first person piece. Harry called his cover story *Why I Married Julie.*

At the outset of his statement, Harry rejected any racial interpretation of his action. He did not marry to prove a point. "I believe in integration," he stated, "and work for it with all my heart and soul. But I did not marry Julie to further the cause of integration. I married her because I was in love with her and she married me because she was in love with me."

To a *Life* reporter, Julie said: "I just fell in love, that's all. Sure we talked about the problems, especially about children. But for me it was easy. The years I spent as the only white dancer in Katherine Dunham's company gave me an insight into Negro culture and I am proud to be part of it."

Featured on the opening pages of Harry's article, nevertheless, were statements from sixteen prominent Negroes on the question: *"Does Interracial Marriage Hinder Integration?"* Many felt that one promoted the other by providing contact between races. Most felt that marriage was a highly personal matter and should not be determined by race.

A few asserted that there was no relation between the two. Typical of these was jazzman Louis Armstrong's comment. "White men marry Negro women," he said, "and we don't squawk. Why should anyone get hot when it happens the other way around? Sex knows no conscience and has nothing to do with the color of people's skins. It's always been that way and always will be. I don't see what interracial marriage has to do with integration. People should be allowed to associate with whomever they please. If left alone, folks will naturally get together."

As detailed in his *Ebony* article, Harry first met the girl who was to become his second wife even before he was married to Margurite. The year was 1947 and he was attending classes at The Dramatic Workshop. To John Gassner's course in "The History of the Theatre and the Dance" came a group of Katherine Dunham dancers for a demonstration. Among them was pig-tailed Julie Robinson, then a teacher at the Dunham School of Dance and Theatre. When the demonstration was over, someone introduced Harry to her. Apart from an exchange of the amenities, nothing memorable occurred. Harry thought her charming and attractive. That was all, he said. Nevertheless, Harry apparently did not forget her or the meeting, casual though it was.

They were not to meet again until seven years later. At that time (1954), Harry was in Hollywood working on a picture while Julie was living there with her folks. Now, on their second meeting, they found that they had much to talk about. Harry's interest in the expressive arts and Julie's career as a dancer gave them an immediate area of common interest. But they also had an area of common concern—the struggle of the Negro for equal rights. Conversation developed in many directions. Since Julie had been in analysis and Harry was just beginning to undergo analysis, they exchanged views about psychiatry. An animated conversationalist, Julie deeply impressed Harry. In his own locution, their second meeting was "purely intellectual" and he "loved every minute of it."

At this time, Harry also met Julie's parents. It happened quite accidentally, as he described it. In the course of their conversations, Julie offered to lend Harry several books on Negro folk songs and folklore. (During his courtship of Margurite, it will be recalled, she too lent Harry books on similar subjects.) When he dropped by Julie's home to pick up the volumes, he was much moved by the cordiality and warmth with which Clara and George Robinson received him.

By that time, as Harry explained, his marriage to Margurite had begun to fall apart. He did not regard himself as blameless. His work as a performer necessitated his staying away from home for extended periods of time. While he could keep in touch with Adrienne, his daughter, during his absences, his relationship with his wife suffered a steady decline. In fact, their relationship had deteriorated to a point where "we knew that we were both quite unhappy."

Nevertheless, the separation that "was the only solution" was postponed for the sake of the children. (Shari, Harry's second daughter, was born in September 1954, shortly after his return from Hollywood and his second meeting with Julie.)

Both Margurite and he were particularly concerned over the possible psychological effect on the older child and tried to work out their differences.

"I love Adrienne very much," Harry stated, "and would do absolutely nothing that would cause her pain."

Even after Margurite and he decided to separate "early in 1956," he continued to go home to Elmhurst frequently to prevent Adrienne from becoming upset over her parents' split-up.

Harry's courtship of Julie, as he described it, was divided between California and New York. At one point, Julie came east to teach at the Phillips-Fort Studio of the Dance in mid-Manhattan. Whenever Harry's working schedule permitted, they went to the theatre or the ballet. They spent many hours visiting the city's jazz clubs, art galleries and museums. Partial to Italian cooking, they searched out every good Italian restaurant they could find.

According to Harry, friendship with Julie "ripened long after the separation" from Margurite took place. Julie and he did not think or talk about getting married until September '56. They became, in his locution, "real tight" only about six months before they were married.

In October of '56, Harry stated, Margurite and he reached an understanding that she would obtain a divorce. Naturally, the responsibility of apprising the children was Harry's. He found explaining the divorce just about the most difficult thing he had ever attempted in his life. Despite the care with which he approached the matter, Adrienne, then seven, "was very unhappy." But because she could see that he and Margurite "continued to have civilized, friendly relations based upon mutual respect," Harry felt that "the impact of the news wasn't traumatic."

In a letter which *Ebony* was to print in a subsequent issue, Margurite questioned this assertion as well as Harry's statement as to when he proposed to Julie.

As Harry described developments, he did not propose until February 28, the day on which Margurite received her divorce decree from a Nevada court. He was then playing an engagement in Las Vegas and he proposed via long distance phone.

[218]

Julie's affirmative answer—also via long distance phone—came through the following day. Thereafter, he met her and her parents in San Diego and they were married in Mexico. In detail, Harry explained that he delayed making a public announcement of his remarriage primarily because of his desire to prepare Adrienne properly for the news.

In the course of his article, Harry presented the facts of Julie's background so that *Ebony* readers would know of her intimate contact with Negro life and her involvement in the struggle for equal rights. When he met her in Hollywood, he was amazed at her knowledge of the problems of Negroes. But then he discovered that she had attended mixed schools in New York and received "a very liberal upbringing" from her parents, who had "resisted injustice all their lives."

Julie herself, he stated with pride, had spent nine years in intimate association with Negroes, three as a teacher in the Dunham School in New York and six as a dancer with the Dunham troupe. During this time, she had chosen to share not only the triumphs of being a Dunham dancer but their humiliations as well. When the Dunham company had first played Las Vegas, the dancers had been forced to live in the segregated Negro sector, a slum area. Julie did not separate herself from the troupe but went with them. There were other instances, Harry asserted, "when she stayed and submitted to Jim Crow rather than leave the company." In Argentina, where the dancers were discriminated against in restaurants and hotels, she refused to desert them and "learned from bitter first-hand experience just what it means to be a Negro."

As he approached the end of his article, Harry stated that Julie had given him an understanding which he had long needed. He admitted frankly that he was subject to "moods and temperament" that made him a "very difficult person to live with." However, coping with a mood, he explained, did not necessarily mean yielding to it. "Julie often challenges my moods and reacts strongly to them."

In an interview which Julie gave about the same time, she confirmed that "Harry is not an easy man to understand. But you have to stop and consider the kind of pressure he's under. At best, show business is abnormal by its very nature."

Of show business' awful pressure, Frank Sinatra has said: "Like a fighter, I've got all the help I need before the bout. But when the bell rings, I go it alone. There's no one I can turn to except myself. Take a fellow in business who makes a product. It works for him. But I'm my product.

"Every time I go on a sound stage for a record session, there's nothing working for me except myself. I get sick? I'm out of business. I cut a few bad records? I'm out of business. I do a bad job in a couple of films? I'm out of business.

"I'm not copping a plea for sympathy. I've got a lot going for me. But I'm human too. I'm afraid sometimes of the unknown; of the thing I may not be prepared for. And after going it alone all day, I have to go it alone afterward. Loneliness is pretty much forced on an entertainer. I can't walk into a restaurant and sit by myself because I'd never finish. People feel I belong to them. So I have dinner in my hotel room or at home."

That this description does not precisely fit Harry is as clear as the fact that he too is his own product and subject to most of the worries Sinatra details.

At the close of his article, Harry turned away from his domestic situation. He indicated that he had just signed a million dollar contract with RCA Victor Records, which guaranteed him $100,000 a year for the next ten years. He had a four-year contract with the Riviera Hotel in Las Vegas, negotiated incidentally by the manager with whom he had broken, under the terms of which he would receive $560,000 for working one month a year. And he was in the process of negotiating a three-picture deal with Twentieth-Century Fox. Later he abandoned this in favor of making his own motion pictures.

"Making money," Harry concluded, "is not all I'm interested in. I want to use my talent to fight for the freedom of my people. I am going to give as much time as I can to helping the NAACP, which I consider the organization doing the most effective work for racial equality in America."

[220]

Harry added: "I'm going to be a very busy man, but with Julie by my side, I know I'm going to be a happy man."

Be that as it may, it is reported that, a few weeks after his secret remarriage, Harry went back into analysis.

The reaction of *Ebony* readers to Harry's explanation of his remarriage was divided. Five letters printed by the magazine in its September issue were favorable. Two were unfavorable. If this ratio reflects the bulk of the mail received by the periodical, then we must assume that Harry's popularity within his own race did not undergo any marked change.

One of the unfavorable letters suggested that the story of Harry Belafonte was "the age-old tale of the successful man who suddenly finds that he is unable to tolerate the woman who stood by him on the way up the ladder of success." The reader concluded that it was the innocent children who would suffer the most and that Harry would need more than Julie by his side "to keep that old sense known as the 'conscience' quiet."

Typical of the favorable letters was one in which the writer indicated that "as a Negro I was a little opposed to their marriage," but that Harry's article had helped her get a clearer view on how love can conquer all.

In addition to these reader letters, there was a tightly worded note from the ex-Mrs. Belafonte. In her letter to the Editor of *Ebony,* she first accused Mr. Belafonte (sic) of reneging on a verbal agreement in writing the article.

Then she added pointedly: "This story is quite different from the one I know and have had to live with. His new-found happiness is a costly one in view of the fact that the eight-year-old daughter he professes so much love for is now receiving psychiatric care. February 28th makes him three months late in proposing marriage with Julie expecting a baby in September."

During the summer of '59 I asked Margurite Belafonte whether she would care to document her *Ebony* letter and explain how Harry's story differed from "the one I know and have had to live with." The following was her reply:

"For me to rehash the story and to reveal what actually happened between Harry and me would be most unfair to his present wife and to their child. At the time that I wrote that letter, I was very hurt and very annoyed and just terribly disappointed.

"We had discussed the situation, the reason for the divorce. I felt that we had handled it as well as two adults could, involving so many people's lives as it did—trying to keep down as much hurt and pain as possible. I had tried to be reasonable and fair. I had kept everything out of the newspapers.

"Then this thing came out in *Ebony*, which is so widely read by Negroes. It was in direct opposition to what I had been through, what I had been told, what I had been faced with.

"I realized that seemingly I was the one who was getting all the hurt and pain. It was like twisting the knife after you jab it in. And I fought back by saying this is not the real story. If Mr. Belafonte wrote this and this is the way he wants to tell it, well fine.

"But I was going through this terrible traumatic situation with Adrienne, who was catching the brunt end of it. For all the love that he professed for his child, for him to tell his side of it, well, I just had to let people know that he had really crucified us both, mainly Adrienne, who was now forced to undergo psychiatric treatment. And yet he calls this love!

"It was my way of fighting back. But he's married now. And out of respect to his present marriage, to his present family, what happened at that time, it's dead now, so just let it stay that way."

Margurite Belafonte has a Ph.D. in Psychology, and she is entitled to call herself Dr. Belafonte. At the time of her *Ebony* postscript, I asked her why she did not do so.

"I guess you might call it a psychological quirk." She smiled at the unintentional play on the word psychological. "When there's a major crisis in your life, all of a sudden you begin to

[222]

feel inferior in many things. Here, I was moving along in a smooth pattern. You think you have the world tied up in a neat ribbon. Then, all of a sudden, bloop! The bottom drops out of everything.

"That's when you suddenly begin to see yourself as inadequate. I mean that I didn't consider that Harry did me wrong. I began to feel that I had more or less let him down somewhere along the line, or this would never have happened. I began to scold myself, to persecute myself, to lay all the blame on myself for the breakup of the home. It was very destructive to me. Working with disturbed children, I was aware that the majority of them came from broken homes. And this was one thing that you say is not going to happen to you. Why, you know all the answers. But overnight, you find yourself in the same identical position. Then the trauma starts. That was the way it was with me.

"I felt very inadequate. I began to feel that I wasn't beautiful. [*She is.* A. S.] I wasn't representative of what a star's wife should be like. [*She is.* A. S.] I wasn't bright. [*She is.* Very. A. S.] You know, intelligent enough to carry on all kinds of conversation. [*She can.* A. S.] Suddenly, all of these inadequacies were mine.

"I think one of the many reasons for my quick recovery—my improved state of mind, is that I was better prepared for many things than I realized at first. Since it happened, I have been a woman's page editor of a newspaper. I had a radio program. Also a bit part in the movies. And with billing yet. You know, in *Night of the Quarter Moon*. Lecture tours. Fund raising for the NAACP. And to find myself a model. I'm not model size nor model proportions. [*I guess I'm no judge.* A. S.] It's been a way of raising money for something I believe in —the NAACP.

"I am pleased to look back and to see the many areas that I have been projected into and into which I have projected myself. I do recognize that these things have played a major role in my recovery. I think that all this activity has kept down a great deal of hostility in my feeling, in my emotions. I just haven't had time to blame others or to feel sorry for myself.

[223]

"Maybe, when I'm fully recovered, I'll start calling myself Dr. Belafonte. For the present, I am quite satisfied so long as I am recognized, not as the former Mrs. Harry Belafonte, but just as Margurite Belafonte."

Whatever fears Harry may have had concerning the waning of his popularity—as a result of his divorce and remarriage—were put to test quickly. As summer approached, he sallied forth on a round of appearances in the theatres of key cities. One of his first stops was at the Syrian Mosque in Pittsburgh.

Typical of the response he was to elicit both from audiences and critics alike was *Variety's* palm-pounding reaction: "The pretentiousness of *Sing, Man, Sing,* the foray into the concert field of last season, is happily gone. This is pure, joyous Belafonte . . .

"Folksinger, balladeer, minnesinger—all these things Belafonte is, stimulated by a catalyst of unknown chemicals reserved one to a generation."

In the course of his career Harry has participated in many activities to promote the advancement of the Negro people, to further the cause of desegregation, to fight discrimination. Along with tens of thousands of other Negroes and whites, celebrities and average citizens, he has taken part in several Youth Marches for Integration to Washington. On many occasions he has spoken in behalf of the NAACP and contributed of his time to help further its program for justice and equal rights. He is the recipient of the Brotherhood Award from the National Conference of Christians and Jews, and he and Margurite jointly received an award for their work with children from Mizrachi, a Jewish welfare organization.

"Harry has the Mizrachi award," Margurite said recently. "It's the one award I would like to have, you know, because of the children's angle. But I've never made an issue about it. The inscription is to Mr. and Mrs. Harry Belafonte so that it's not entirely out of place in his new home, except for the date on it."

Of all these political and humanitarian activities, unquestionably the Prayer Pilgrimage for Integration in 1957 remains as the most memorable. It was made so by an accidental occurrence—one that tried the emotions of those who participated in it as well as of those who watched the dramatic moment.

On the platform of the Pilgrimage to Washington were many celebrities, among them Margurite Belafonte, who was herself active in fund-raising for the NAACP, and Harry, who was accompanied by his new wife.

At one moment in the proceedings, as they moved about the platform, Margurite Belafonte came unavoidably and inescapably face to face with Julie Belafonte, then in her fifth month of pregnancy. It was the first actual meeting of the woman who had been Harry's wife and the woman who had succeeded her. It was, in the eloquent expressiveness of the Spaniards, a moment of truth.

That greater self-possession was demanded of Margurite Belafonte, the vanquished, than of Julie as the victor, is hard to question. But both women carried the accidental confrontation off with a touching dignity and a heart-rending civility. No greeting was exchanged, although each paused momentarily. Then both turned to the cause of integration that had brought each—one white, and the other Negro—to Washington.

STEREO

SAMMY DAVIS, JR.

Recently, when Sammy Davis, Jr., was playing the Copa in New York, he dined at Danny's Hide-a-Way, an East Side midtown restaurant frequented by many entertainers. As he was standing at the hat-check counter, waiting to retrieve his derby, cape, and umbrella, a teen-age girl asked for his autograph. Davis paused to sign a post card for her.

A heavy-set blond man, waiting impatiently to get to the hat-check counter, said: "That's very nice, but why don't you do that in the *street—*"

A car was waiting for Davis. But, as reported in *Esquire,* Sammy stood inconclusively on the sidewalk. He looked through the window into the restaurant, trying to spot the man. Then he got into the car. By the time he arrived at the hotel where he was staying during his Copa engagement, he was deeply hurt, upset, and enraged.

"What a Jackson!" he exclaimed.

"What's a Jackson?" *Esquire* writer Thomas B. Morgan asked.

"A Jackson is some guy who calls a Negro 'Jackson' or 'Bo,' " Davis explained. "I'd like ten seconds with that rat!"

"What can happen to Davis at any time," Morgan observed, "no matter how high he is flying, had happened.

"Davis' early show was, in many subtle ways, below par. His timing was off. He did not kid with the audience. The beat of his songs was slower. It was not a happy show. Afterward, he returned to the dressing room, changed into the terry-cloth robe, and lay on the couch. Mike Silver, the drummer who travels with him, sat in a chair with his sticks in his hands, watching TV. Murphy Bennett straightened the bedroom. Davis was almost as alone as he ever is.

" 'I've never, never tried to be anything but what I am,' he said. 'I am a Negro. I'm not ashamed. The Negro people can mark a cat lousy for that and they won't go to see him perform. Well, we have Negroes here every night. If you go hear a Negro and see some Negroes in the audience, then you know how they stand. They'll ignore a guy who's marked lousy, see? So, I've never been the kind of guy who was ashamed. See, it's a matter of dignity. That's what makes something like that Jackson

[226]

so tough on you. One time I went on in San Francisco and a guy down there in the front row says to another guy, 'I didn't know he was a nigger,' and walked out. It's tough to play against that. In the Army, the first time anybody called me a bad name, I cried—the tears! I had spent all my life with my dad and uncle. I was loved. I was Charlie-protected. But now, this is the thing that is always just around the corner. It's like you can't get into El Morocco because you're colored. See?'

"Davis' second show that night was better than the first, but he still seemed chilled. About four A.M., accompanied by fifteen men and women, he went to a West Side night club. Legally, it was closing time, but the bartender gathered up bottles, mix, ice, and glasses and carried the makings into a large back room. Cecil Young and three fourths of a Canadian jazz quartet were having a last drink before calling it a night. Like the patrons, the fourth member of the quartet—the bass fiddler—had already gone home. Seeing Davis, Cecil Young began telephoning around to find another fiddle player. When the man arrived, sleepy-eyed, the jam session began. Davis, Young, the Canadians, and the new man played wildly and wonderfully for ninety minutes. Davis sat in on drums, blew the trumpet, and sang scat with Cecil Young. When it was over, the hurt was out of his system.

"During a break, Cecil Young had said to me: 'Jazz isn't polite, son. Jazz is, pardon the expression, screw you. If you don't like it, well, that's all. But if you do like it, then I like you, dig? With jazz, you thumb your nose when they don't like you. You get the message out, daddy.' "

20. Reluctant King of Calypso

In 1957, while he was embroiled in lawsuits with his third manager, his nine-year-old marriage was being dissolved in a Nevada law court, and the news of his marriage to a white dancer was subjecting him to calumnies among his own people, Harry awoke one morning to find himself an international singing star.

Previously he had been able to demonstrate again and again —at the Copa, at the Lewisohn Stadium, at the Riviera, at the Greek Theatre, at the Waldorf—that he was the first folk singer in history to command a mass audience. In 1957, however, that audience overflowed national boundaries. The man, soon to be known as the first Negro Matinee Idol, exploded on the international entertainment scene and zoomed into the select circle of the million-dollar performers.

The charge of entertainment dynamite that ignited Harry's career was an ordinary-looking RCA Victor album bearing the title *Harry Belafonte—Calypso*. Cut in the winter of 1955, released in the fall of 1956, it became a best seller in January 1957, just about the time that Margurite Belafonte was leaving for Nevada. Thereafter, it remained on best-seller charts for over a year and a half to become the first Victor LP by a single artist to sell over a million.

During its initial sales period, LPM #1248, the magic number of the *Calypso* album, actually sold over a million and a half copies. That's like selling eighteen million records. And before it left the best-seller charts, it vested Harry with the title King of Calypso, a crown he wore reluctantly despite the fame it brought him. There were a number of reasons for this.

"Listen," he told one reporter, "I'm a singer, period. I sing all types of folk material—English, Irish, Israeli, from every section of the world. I don't believe in being cultish and I don't want to be known as the guy who put the nail in the coffin of rock 'n roll."

About the same time, he informed another interviewer, "My two big records right now aren't calypso at all—even though everybody seems to have hung that tag on them. One is a West Indian ballad. [He was referring to *Jamaica Farewell.*] The other is a West Indian work song." [He meant *Day-O, Banana Boat.*]

The actual origin of the *Calypso* album is a story that somehow has never been told. It goes back to September 1955, when Harry was making plans for a guest appearance on the Colgate Comedy Hour. Fifty-five was a strange year for Harry in that a remarkable photo exhibit, *The Family of Man,* led to a flop show *Sing, Man, Sing,* while a flop TV show "Holiday in Trinidad" led to a smash record album.

Harry's appearance on NBC's Comedy Hour, then bucking the top-rated Ed Sullivan show on CBS, was set for the first week in October. At first he considered devoting his twenty-minute segment to a folk-blues story built around John Henry, the Negro rail splitter. Then, while he was playing Blinstrubs in Boston and discussing his forthcoming TV show with his musical conductor Tony Scott and writer-friend Bill Attaway, the thought suggested itself of a musical with a Caribbean flavor.

Although Belafonte and Attaway had been friends from The Sage days, their collaboration on "Holiday In Trinidad" was a coincidence. Novelist Attaway was then an NBC staff writer, who worked on Dave Garroway's *Wide, Wide World* and other shows, including occasionally the Colgate Comedy Hour. The program of October 2, which included Mel Allen, the Dodgers baseball team, Martha Scott, and Harry Belafonte, was assigned to him, and he was responsible for the script, not only of the interpolated Belafonte segment, but of the rest of the show.

Once the Carib-flavored musical was agreed on, Attaway enlisted the collaboration of a calypso singer-composer, who calls himself Lord Burgess, in the preparation of the score. The Lord's meeting with Harry was a fateful one, for he became the writer or co-writer of eight of the songs in the hit *Calypso* album. He was later to figure in other Belafonte projects, among them, *Sing, Man, Sing* and *Island in the Sun*.

Surprisingly, The Lord was a native of Brooklyn, and had studied voice and theory at the Juilliard School of Music as well as at the Universities of Mexico and Southern California. Born Irving Burgie, he was of West Indian descent. In the year preceding his meeting with Belafonte, Burgie had traveled around the country with a group known as Lord Burgess and his Calypso Serenaders. A student of folk music, he had become a songwriter out of a self-discovered need to shape and create fresh material for himself.

The precise form of a musical trip around the Caribbean, which became "Holiday in Trinidad," was apparently Lord Burgess'. Jack Carson, emcee of the Colgate Comedy Hour, was cast in the role of a tourist out on an island-hopping jaunt. Interpolated in the Attaway script were such calypso tunes as *Hosanna, Come Back Liza,* and *The Jack-Ass Song,* on which Attaway collaborated with Burgess. Also heard for the first time by American audiences was the now-famous *Banana Boat Song* or *Day-O,* as it was then known. Burgess, Attaway, and Belafonte are named as the writers. Despite the writer credit, Harry does not accept any portion of the song's writer earnings. This seems to be the case with other folk tunes which he has helped rewrite.

According to Lord Burgess, he worked mainly behind the scenes of the Colgate show. "I wasn't yet in the clique," he explains. "It was only after Colgate that Harry and I became thick as fleas."

Up to the present, Lord Burgess has had almost twenty-five songs recorded by Belafonte. He has supplied Harry not only with his most successful song, *Day-O,* but with at least four other outstanding compositions. Among these, the tender ballads *Jamaica Farewell* and *Lucy's Door* are by Burgess alone. *Lead Man Holler,* a work song, is credited to Belafonte and

[230]

Burgess, while the beautiful ballad *Eden Was Like This* is by Burgess and Kennedy.

Both Attaway and Burgess have participated in the preparation of calypso or Caribbean song anthologies. Attaway is the informative author of a thin, attractive tome called *Calypso Song Book* (1957) while Burgess is responsible for the descriptive notes to a soft-cover collection known as *Folk Songs of the Caribbean* (1958).

Both agree that calypso is historically the exclusive product of one particular island in the West Indies—Trinidad, off the coast of Venezuela. Sung first in African and later in French patois, the type of tune spread eventually to the other islands of the West Indies and came into English around the turn of the century.

Not unlike American blues, calypso seems to have had its origin in the work song. During the eighteenth century, when slaves first arrived in Trinidad, the Spanish overseers forbade conversation in the sugar fields but allowed singing. They found that the rhythm of song increased productivity. The African slaves found that they could converse, spread gossip, voice their grievances, or plot revolt, since the overseers did not understand their language.

When slavery was abolished in Trinidad in 1838, the tradition of story-singing—by then practiced in French patois as a result of emigrations from the French slave colony of Haiti —was taken over by the work gang leaders. Known as *chantwelle*, they employed a falsetto voice, not unlike that heard in the American field "holler," also a precursor of the blues. The gangs apparently responded to the *chantwelle*, giving us the beginnings of the verse-chorus, question-answer form. Eventually, the *chantwelle*, who traveled from one plantation to another and extemporized in song about topical items and his experiences, began competing with each other at carnival time. Here we have the origin of something that has become an integral part of the calypso tradition.

Today, in Trinidad, there exists a group known as The Old

Brigade. It is composed of professional calypso singers of ten years' standing. Although it does not call itself a union, it actually functions like one. Each year, at carnival time, it considers the applications of new calypsonians to a group known as The Young Brigade. Each applicant sets himself up in a tent, usually supplied by a promoter who handles the gate receipts, and tries to establish his prowess as an extemporizer. After acceptance into The Young Brigade, the new calypsonian may work anywhere. To be accepted, he must be a native Trinidadian and prove his ability to invent lyrics on the spot about any subject. They must be funny. They must rhyme. No one worries about accents. .

As The Gorilla has written:

"Calypso is a thing I'm telling you,
  When you are singing, you must learn to impromptu.
    Never mind your English, but mind your rhymes,
  When you get the gist of it, just sing in time,
    For veteran calypsonians are known to be
  Men who can sing on anything instantaneously."

Calypsonians all adopt colorful and regal-sounding names like the Mighty Panther, King Radio, Lord Invader, Duke of Iron, and Lord Flea.

One of the high points of the two-day carnival at Port-au-Spain is the "Calypso War," a battle of slanderous repartee in which calypsonians vie for the august title of King of Calypso. The singer who, in the opinion of a carnival judging committee, most wittily and most sarcastically insults his competitors reigns for an entire year. No holds are barred, so that the magnificent slurs may include reflections on a competitor's physique, mental ability, parenthood, or even sexual limitations.

In some ways, these planned Calypso Wars remind one of the cutting contest that presumably occurred spontaneously in New Orleans at the turn of the century when one Dixieland jazz band encountered another. The wheels of the wagons on which they rode would be tied together—to prevent the horses from bolting—and each band would try to outplay the other.

In its origin unaccompanied, calypso singing acquired instrumental backing when it moved away from the work field. Naturally, the first accompanying instruments were drums. When drumming was banned around the middle of the nineteenth century because of its role allegedly in fomenting revolt, the natives began using bamboo poles to accompany themselves. These were simply struck against the ground. Poles of different lengths and widths produced different timbres and pitches, and the bands were known as "tamboo" bands.

But in the 1920's "tamboo" instruments, too, were banned, because they were used in gang wars and as instruments of crime. Now the inventiveness of the Trinidadians took a new turn. During World War II and the lend-lease era, Trinidad, along with other West Indian islands, was the recipient of thousands of drums of petroleum. At first these were simply used as percussion instruments. But then a native—one, Winston (Spree) Simon—discovered that different notes could be produced by cutting a drum down, marking the head off into different, petal-like segments, and tempering each segment separately with fire and a sledge hammer. Hung from the neck and struck with a soft mallet, these cut drumheads produced a muted, bell-like tone. This was the beginning of the "steel bands," which today are articulated into soprano, tenor, and bass "ping-pongs" and "harmony pans."

There is no agreement as to the origin of the word "calypso," although most authorities feel that it is the Anglicized version of some earlier word. Candidates include the French words *calisseaux* and *carrouse,* meaning "to carouse." Also the African word *Kai-so,* meaning *bravo.* Also, the Spanish word *carrizo,* meaning "reed" or "cane" and used as a term of applause. The great Attila the Hun, author of *Victory Calypsos, 1944,* and now a member of the Legislative Council of Trinidad and Tobago under his own name, Raymond Quevedo, picks the Spanish word as the most likely source. Choice of the word now in vogue, interestingly enough, is attributed to American record companies who ostensibly were casting about in the 1930's for a term to describe the humorous, crazily accented, and frequently bawdy type of song.

[233]

At the height of the calypso rage, Harry told off a reporter who suggested that the songs are dirty.

"Sure they contain blue material," Harry said, "but so does every form of music. If you go looking for such material, you will find it in Shakespeare.

"I think that when people object to dirty lyrics, what they're really objecting to is the debasement of the original material —the same thing I don't like.

"One thing I want to make clear. I'm going to go on singing true calypso as I see it—just as I intend to go on singing every other kind of music that carries truth in it.

"And even if phony, synthetic, cliché calypso material floods the market—and it looks like it might—they're not going to get me to sing it or pose with one of those straw hats."

Why Harry felt called on to make this statement is hard to surmise, since pictures in *Down Beat* and other publications show him in a typical calypso outfit—hat included.

Before Belafonte helped make a rage of it, calypso was not unknown to American audiences. Wilmuth Houdini, who still sings today, made calypso recordings before World War I and had a smash in a song called *Stone Cold Dead in the Market*. In 1944 a calypso entitled *Rum and Coca-Cola*, brought back by comedian Morey Amsterdam from Jamaica, swept the country. The work of the Lord Invader, whose authorship was established after a drawn-out suit, *Rum and Coca-Cola* was made into a million-copy record by the then popular Andrews Sisters.

What causes a given song or record or style to smash at one time and "to bomb" at another is one of the enigmas of music business.

The fact is that the "Reluctant King of Calypso," as one publication called Harry, recorded calypso or Caribbean songs on his earliest dates for RCA Victor. *Matilda, Matilda,* virtually his theme tune, was cut in the spring of '53, while *Man Smart* was waxed even earlier. In 1954 Harry recorded several calypso numbers, among them, *Man Piaba* and *Hold 'Em Joe*. Apparently the country and the world were not ready for them then. Yet by the fall of 1956 an album containing similar songs

[234]

was on its way to becoming one of RCA Victor's first sensational million-copy albums.

Of course, Harry's contact with calypso material goes back even farther—to his youth when, as a lonely boy being reared by relatives, he roamed the streets and beaches of Kingston.

"Jamaica had no means of mass communication then," Harry said recently. "The people saw few movies. Thus they never lost the power to communicate and to relate to each other through song. It became a part of me before I was in my teens."

Within days of his October '55 appearance on NBC-TV in "Holiday in Trinidad," Harry was in the studios of RCA Victor recording two of the songs in his *Calypso* album, *Hosanna* and *Will His Love Be Like His Rum*. The following day, on October 20, Harry cut the most successful number in the album *Day-O*, which became known as *The Banana Boat Song*, also *Star-O* and *The Jack-Ass Song*. Tony Scott, whose orchestra accompanied Harry, arranged and conducted the double session on the twentieth, but not the final one on November 9, 1955.

According to Victor exec Edward O. Welker, who supervised the date, it was a difficult one. Harry had just completed an extremely successful and tiring return engagement at The Waldorf. He was beat, somewhat hoarse, and suffering, as he put it, from "a collection of psychosomatic ailments." Moreover, he had to leave almost immediately for an engagement out of New York.

The historic double session began at 2:00 P.M., and Harry completed only one song during the first three hours, a period in which, according to the rules of the Musicians Union, he could have cut four tunes. When the clock stood at five and the first half of the double date was at an end, Harry still had four tunes to do in order to complete the *Calypso* album.

At Welker's suggestion, he stretched out on the floor of the control room. He was asleep before his head touched the rubber tile. Forty-five minutes later Welker aroused him and ordered some hot tea. As the hands of the clock touched 6:00 P.M., the small complement of musicians—two bass play-

[235]

ers, a drummer, and three guitarists—filtered back into the studio.

Lord Burgess, one of the guitarists, had written two songs almost overnight for the session: *I Do Adore Her* and *Dolly Dawn*. He was represented on the double date by a third composition, the tender and haunting ballad *Jamaica Farewell*, which, like *Day-O*, made its way on the hit lists as a single. *Farewell* was adapted by Burgess from a Caribbean folk tune "Iron Bar," whose melody he had slowed down and used as the basis for a new lyric. Still another tune, *Come Back Liza*, was the result of a collaboration by Burgess and Bill Attaway, responsible for the liner notes on the album.

In the course of this "double date," Harry's sense of humor came into play at least once. The first session was, of course, not going as easily as some dates do. After several takes, Harry came back into the engineer's booth to listen to a playback. He was calm, but he was tired in a way that made him plop down in a chair. As he listened to the playback, he toyed with a grease pencil, used by the engineers to write on metal reference disks. Directly in front of Harry on the engineer's control board, and jutting up like a headstone, was a time clock about a foot in diameter. As Harry rose wearily to go back into the studio for another take, he paused and scribbled on the glass face: "Here lies Harry Belafonte. He done ticked out!"

There was some controversy, at the height of the calypso craze, as to whether Harry sang authentic calypso—a claim which he never made. Tony Scott, whose orchestra backstopped Harry on his calypso date, had this to say: "It's not authentic because the real calypso is so pure; it's got that syncopation and is really too deep-rooted . . . Harry has been like Glenn Miller, who used to take a jazz piece and do it very simply. Harry takes this authentic material and works on it until it's ready for American consumption."

Harry himself told music critic Jay S. Harrison of *The New York Herald Tribune*: "Well, of course, it's not pure. I never put it on the market as genuine. Calypso is a kind of music that comes from the West Indies. It is any artist's right to interpret the subject matter as he sees fit. So long as he adds a new dimension to it, it's valid.

[236]

"Listen, if I wanted to sing pure calypso, I could have. I spent part of my youth in the West Indies. And I could also fake it in all the conventional ways, too. You know, use only *double-entendre* Trinidad stuff. But that kind of material does not reflect the dignity of the people and the calypso I sing, even in my own version, does show the people. The tender side, the human side. That's what's important: reflecting the people."

To put the overnight vogue of the calypso craze in perspective, Harry's triggering of it was most immediately preceded by the work of a singing group known as The Tarriers. Two of The Tarriers play banjo, while the third plays guitar. Associated with a small, independent record label (owned, incidentally, by Phil Rose, co-producer of the Sidney Poitier success *Raisin in the Sun*), The Tarriers made a hit, first, of a folk ballad, *Cindy, Oh Cindy,* to which they added a distinctly Caribbean flavor. This occurred just about the time that RCA Victor was releasing Harry's now-famous *Calypso* album.

The Tarriers also played a part in making a number one tune of *Banana Boat Song*. Although their version of the Trinidad work song came out after Belafonte's album, it was their disk that first aroused popular interest in the song. Harry's rendition, originally in his *Calypso* album, was released as a single disk only after The Tarriers' recording on the Glory label began "making noise," as music biz jargon would have it. Eventually Harry's record outsold theirs by a wide margin, not only in the U.S.A., but throughout the world. (My path crossed Harry's for the second time in four years in that I purchased the publishing rights to the Tarriers' version of *Banana Boat Song*.)

Harry had a follow-up hit in a song called *Mama Look-A BuBu*, written by Fitzroy Alexander, who uses the name Lord Melody. About the same time, Rosemary Clooney had her last mild noisemaker on Columbia in a Tin Pan Alley written calypso called *Mangoes, Papaya*. There was a rash of lesser known imitators, of course, who tried to capitalize on the trend. But except for Terry Gilkyson and *Marianne,* no one succeeded in launching a new calypso hit—and even Gilkyson achieved no identification as an interpreter of calypso.

Harry's fear of being typed was obviously well advised. Although his LP of *Caribbean* songs sold well, it never approached the sales figures racked up by the first album. Moreover, less than a year after it reached its peak point—when many of the larger American cities had Calypso night clubs and rooms, and youngsters were doing a dance known as the Calypso, later The Cha-lypso—the craze was, to adapt a phrase from an earlier calypso hit, "stone cold dead in the market."

STEREO

EARTHA KITT

"Sinatra and scores of other white entertainers," Eartha Kitt said recently, during a booking at the Apollo Theatre in Harlem "do not need to fight the battle of the good life as virtually every Negro performer must and should. No matter how big any of us gets, we still remain Negroes—and subject, as time goes on, to the headaches and heartaches and problems of the rest of our people.

"For this reason, it is important that we do not lose contact with our people or give them the feeling that we're deserting them. After all, they do have so few of us, and their needs, despite some progress, are still so great.

"I believe that Harry's second marriage was good for him and good for Julie Robinson, whom I love and admire from the days when we were in the Dunham dance group together. But I cannot help saying that I had a great fear that the Negro people would misunderstand Harry's action in divorcing a Negress and marrying a white girl. It had to look as if he were deserting them—and after they had come to look upon him as one of their militant spokesmen. I am not sure that Harry has completely healed the breach. There are too many whose feelings toward him are still 'anti,' whether it has hurt his career or not.

"This is something that no Negro performer can afford. It has to play havoc with him inside and perhaps, after a time, create problems for him outside. I know this—from personal experience.

"Some years ago, I received very adverse publicity in the Negro press. Your own people can hate you because they think you reflect badly on them—as well as because they may think you are deserting them.

"I wanted very much to correct this feeling, or at least to cope with it. Why, I was even uneasy in this period about coming to Harlem. I just didn't know what might happen.

"Then, along came an opportunity for me to play in Harlem—at the Apollo. At first I was afraid. I had visions of my own people driving me off the stage. But I decided that, perhaps, this was just the opportunity I needed to straighten things out.

"I'll never forget the reception I got at show after show. The very fact that I was there told them more than almost anything I could say. But I did usually make a curtain speech in which I would say:

" 'I know what you've been reading about me in your own papers. I didn't know whether you would believe material that editors printed merely to sell papers and with no concern for the truth. I didn't know whether you would receive me as a friend or just shut me out. But now that I see your faces and hear your applause, I don't even have to ask whether I am welcome—although I greatly feared that I was not.'

"The applause after that was always ear-shattering and so heart-warming.

"A man like Harry Belafonte should come to Harlem and play the Apollo. It won't mean anything financially to him and it can't advance his career in any way. But it would mean something to his people.

"There are still many Negroes who won't go to a downtown theatre in New York, even if they can afford the prices. They have not yet overcome —strange as it may seem—fears that go back centuries. These people can't see Harry Belafonte unless he comes to them. And I don't mean just the Apollo Theatre in New York. There are theatres in Negro communities all over the United States.

"It's an important thing that Harry Belafonte, as a Negro, can have a one-man show at the Palace Theatre. But it is not enough for us to charge into the white man's world and win a place there. We must also maintain contact with our own people. For the problem between our races cannot

[239]

be solved by the white people alone. Our own people have to be educated as to their responsibilities and role.

"And this can be accomplished only if we keep contact with them, if we keep their faith and confidence and trust so that we can influence them. As spokesmen, we have a responsibility not to go too far away from the people we are representing."

Eartha Kitt furrowed her brows momentarily and then immediately opened her eyes wide, as her face lighted up with a smile.

"But I have a great intimation," she added, "that Julie is aware of this problem and that she, more than anyone else, can, and perhaps will, help Harry solve it."

Sharp disagreement with Eartha Kitt's position was voiced by one of Harry's close friends—white, not Negro.

"Why should he play Harlem?" the friend asked. "Does Sinatra play Mulberry Street? Does Eddie Fisher make a point of playing the Bronx? Why then should Harry be made constantly to feel guilty about not playing Harlem?"

To which Eartha replied: "To be a Negro is to be Negro-conscious in a way that no white person can be white-conscious and no other minority in America is minority-conscious. This is not a choice. It is a condition forced upon all Negroes by the world in which we live. It creates burdens which are special to the Negro and which saddle him with special responsibilities to himself and his community. That's why Harlem is a problem to the Negro entertainer in a way that Mulberry Street is not to an Italian and the Bronx is not to a Jew."

On which Harry's friend commented as follows: "What is important is Harry's international, not his Negro, following. That's the measure of how much the world has changed and is changing. It may well be that Harry no longer is a Negro artist, that he now has only a limited Negro following. It may be that the more he is accepted in a white world, the more he is rejected by some sections of the Negro community. But this is the personal price he has to pay. He should not be made to feel guilty about it, considering the social progress his acceptance represents."

In a lighter vein, another friend of Harry's told the story of how an indigent Negro painter came to Harry and tried to sell him some of his paintings. After looking over the canvases, Harry made a suggestion to the painter.

"You paint Harlem," he said, "and I'll buy it."

To which the painter is supposed to have responded: "You play Harlem, and I'll paint it."

21. Hollywood and Vinegar

Some time before Harry found himself the center of controversy among his own people over his marriage to a white girl, he completed making a movie in which he had to cope with the same problem on the screen. In *Island in the Sun,* playing a role natural to himself—that of a belligerent fighter for Negro rights—Harry and the aristocratic girl decide against the mixed marriage. One of the reasons: "A girl like you would only mean snubs and misery. Besides, the girl would forget herself one day and call me a nigger."

Shot in the spring of '56, *Island* (to follow the music biz custom of abbreviating all titles to one word) was released in June '57. Although it was the third picture in which Harry starred, it represented an important first in movie making. *The Bright Road* and *Carmen Jones,* Harry's two previous films, were both played by all-Negro casts. (The former actually included one white actor.) *Island* not only had a mixed cast, but Harry became the first American Negro to play a romantic role in a feature film opposite a major white actress. His vis-à-vis was blonde film star Joan Fontaine.

Although Harry was not entirely satisfied with his role, he felt that the theme of the movie was much too important for him to pass up. Based on Alec Waugh's best-selling novel of the same name, *Island* deals with the problem of intermarriage on two levels: the white man who loves a Negro girl and the Negro who loves a white girl. An additional development, representing a rather daring innovation for Hollywood, is that Harry plays a trade union leader who beats a white man in a hard-fought political battle. The discovery by Maxwell Fleury, acted by James Mason, that there is "Negro blood" in his aristocratic family background, shock though it was to him, was hardly a fresh concept for Hollywood.

Set on an imaginary island (Santa Marta) in the West Indies, the *Island* story develops out of the unrest currently rocking many colonial areas. Rich British planters, who have lived in luxury for generations, are compelled to face the challenge of intelligent natives who refuse to continue in inferior positions, politically and socially. The star-studded cast included, in addition to Belafonte, Joan Fontaine and James Mason, Dorothy Dandridge, Joan Collins, and Michael Rennie.

In his two previous films, Harry had been confined to acting. The West Indian setting provided an opportunity no smart producer could pass up—of having Harry sing several Caribbean songs. Harry collaborated with Lord Burgess on two calypso-gaited melodies, both of which may be heard in his album *Belafonte Sings of the Caribbean*. The title tune, *Island in the Sun*, is descriptive and elegaic. *Lead Man Holler*, a work song of the sugar cane cutters, is Belafonte in the rousing, throbbing tradition of *Jump Down, Spin Around*.

As in most films, the music was dubbed in after shooting was completed. Harry pantomimed the singing while the film was being shot. Then he and a vocal group had to synchronize their voices with the lip movements as shown on the screen. This is not too simple a process. But it becomes even more difficult when the tempo at which a song is originally mimicked and photographed turns out to be erratic. This was the case, according to Lord Burgess, with the up tempo work song *Lead Man Holler*. It took many hours of rehearsal and many takes before the singers could deliver the song so that the sound seemed to come from the lip movements on the screen.

At the beginning of the film, David Boyeur (Belafonte) and Margaret Seaton (Dorothy Dandridge) are lovers. Soon, however, each falls in love with, and in turn, is loved by, a white: Dandridge, the shop girl, by the Governor's aide-de-camp (John Justin) and Belafonte, the union leader, by Mavis Norman, the wealthy colonial played by Joan Fontaine. The Dandridge-Justin affair ends happily when the two leave the imaginary island of Santa Marta to settle in England. Not so, the love affair between the characters played by Fontaine and Belafonte.

In a colorful picture story, *Ebony* observed: "Strangely, shortly after the movie was finished, Belafonte did marry a white woman." In fact, the *Ebony* story on *Island* ran coincidentally in the same issue (July 1957) with Harry's by-line explanation of why he married Julie.

The crucial problem faced by Hollywood in the making of *Island* was, of course, whether a Negro would be permitted to kiss a white on the screen—and vice versa. "To Kiss or Not to Kiss," was the way *Ebony* headlined the matter. It is not difficult to surmise that neither pair of lovers was permitted to touch lips in the film. Belafonte told newsmen: "I definitely think that the movie industry has a policy which prohibits love-making and kissing between interracial couples. In this movie, where the normal sequence of events would have led to romantic situations between myself and Joan Fontaine, they were played down."

Miss Fontaine was quoted as saying: "At least I made them agree that Harry and I can drink out of the same cocoanut together in a scene. But they insist on no kissing—and that we give one another up at the end of the picture."

In a whimsical vein, Harry observed that the greatest proximity he and Joan were permitted in the film was a touching of elbows: "There's a scene showing us drinking from a cocoanut. But the day we filmed that, I caught cold. I guess that's what happens in these interracial situations."

Darryl Zanuck, who independently produced *Island* as a British film, denied that there had been any pressure either from possible markets or Hollywood censors. "There is no scene that calls for kissing," he said. "There was no conscious effort to avoid it."

The movie was shot largely in Grenada, on the island of Barbados, and completed in England. To the inhabitants of Grenada, Belafonte became known as Uncle Harry. They would follow the company around and after the shooting was over, they would re-enact his part. One night Harry participated in a native hoe-down on a wharf. At one point he started dancing with a 250-pound woman. He was so graceful and exciting as a dancer that he created a sensation among the natives.

RCA Victor executive Ed Welker has observed: "Any one who has ever worked with Belafonte discovers that if he had not made it as a singer, he could have been an equally great dancer."

During the filming of *Island,* Joan Fontaine received hate letters. The Defense Department was showered with demands that the film not be shown to the Armed Forces. A bill was even introduced in the South Carolina Legislature, levying a $5,000 fine on any theatre that exhibited the picture. Darryl F. Zanuck, the producer, immediately announced that he would pay the fine for any exhibitor so persecuted.

State Representative John Hart, who urged the banning, was reported in *The Pittsburgh Courier* as saying: "This is a sickening, repulsive, indecent spectacle to which no one in South Carolina should be exposed or subjected." Similar sentiments were voiced by the head of an Arlington, Virginia, group that called itself the Defenders of Sovereignty and Individual Liberties. In a letter to Defense Secretary Wilson requesting that the film be banned from all Armed Forces bases, the committee's spokesman characterized the picture as "revolting to the sensibilities of an overwhelming majority of our citizens," and warned that it "could lead to civil disturbances."

During the filming, relationships within the mixed cast were as pleasant and relaxed as anyone could desire. Candid pictures appearing in various publications reveal a camaraderie that cut completely across race lines. Whatever friction developed—and no working group is ever devoid of it—emanated from personal and craft considerations, not color.

Harry himself indulged in a harmless type of posturing and fibbing at which he was eventually caught. Irked by something which Joan Fontaine had done, Harry added several years to his age, invented a sister who was teaching at Vassar, and boasted of a brother on *Time* Magazine. Actually, his younger brother Dennis was just out of the Army. A half brother and half sister, living with his mother in a West Los Angeles home he had bought for them, were both teen-agers. What had annoyed Harry were airs which Miss Fontaine had allegedly put on during the first days of the shooting to establish her dominant position as the film's leading lady.

The same motivation was clearly at work in Harry's calculated use of polysyllabic words and his constant references at mealtime to scholarly books he had read. One evening at dinner Harry was carrying on about the ethnic contributions of this and that racial group and of the ethnic significance of different things. Just about the time some of the company were beginning to be ethnically bored, Joan turned to Harry and asked him "to please pass the ethnic butter." Harry broke up with the rest of the cast.

After the picture was completed, Twentieth-Century Fox allegedly requested Harry to refrain from referring to Joan Fontaine in any public statement. It appears that the movie company was fearful that such statements would play into the hands of those who were trying to promote a mixed off-stage affair between Harry and Joan. "Here I am," Harry is reported to have said, "one of the stars in the picture—trying to do a little publicity the way all stars are expected to do. And they tell me to keep quiet."

As to Harry's role in the film, Robert Rossen, the director, had this to say: "Belafonte possesses a remarkable combination of violence and sensitivity and knows how to put them to use. On top of that, he has the powerful ability to communicate and reach an audience."

In one scene Harry speaks steadily for five minutes on the social and economic problems of the natives. "He lived that scene," Rossen said. "He meant what he was saying. To look for complete technical proficiency in it would have been a mistake. The content created its own technique. We shot and printed it after only one take. In this business, that's really remarkable."

When Harry had finished his stint in *Island in the Sun*—it

was the early summer of '56—he felt for the first time that he had realized his original goal. He had completed his apprenticeship as an actor.

On its release in June '57, *Island* met a barrage of critical bullets. Nor did Harry escape being hit by most of the firing squad.

"Actually, the picture is lacking a precise and confident theme," wrote Bosley Crowther in *The New York Times.* "It pretends to be scanning racial conflict, but its viewpoint is vague, its observations are fuzzy and no conclusion is reached." Referring back to *Pinky,* an earlier Zanuck race film, Crowther added: "As was the case with his production of *Pinky,* Mr. Zanuck has really not compelled a frank, unembarrassed and conclusive grappling with the subject of race."

Harry's acting fared no better at Crowther's typewriter than the film's treatment of the racial theme. "Harry Belafonte is aggressive," Crowther wrote, "without persuasiveness or purpose . . ."

Post reviewer Archer Winsten, who shared Crowther's conviction regarding the film's lack of courage, said this about Harry: "As for Belafonte, his singing and looks need no praise from this quarter. As an actor, he tends to become an heroic bronze with a wonderful white smile, in short, a reigning personality. Whether his talents include versatility in characterization, this picture does not indicate."

William K. Zinsser of *The Herald Tribune* was a minority of almost one in feeling that the film dealt "candidly with the color issue." But he was with the majority regarding Harry's contribution: "Belafonte as a Negro agitator seems to wish he were asleep instead of acting and sometimes he almost is."

All reviewers agreed on one thing. The real star of *Island* was the scenery of the West Indies.

In July '57, while he was playing an SRO engagement at the San Francisco Opera House, a *Variety* reporter caught Harry off guard. Still smarting from the stings of the reviewers' fusillade, he could not prevent the full force of his hostility from boiling to the surface. The resulting story, in which "he clawed at Hollywood and Madison Avenue," as *Variety* put it, was headlined: "Harry Belafonte a Tough Critic." Among the barbs attributed to him were the following:

"Take the stinking quality of my last picture—of all three pictures.

"The first picture, called *Bright Road,* was a nice, bland Lassie-like thing based on a story in the *Ladies' Home Journal.* Then *Carmen Jones*—bootleg Bizet. Now *Island in the Sun,* a terrible picture based on a terrible best-selling book.

"But we had to prove in *Carmen Jones* that an all-Negro cast could gross fat profits. Now *Island* is going great, just great, and—wonder of wonders—I get to best James Mason."

He added: "They call me the 'King of Calypso,' the man who almost bumped off Elvis Presley at the jukebox . . . I was catapulted out of drama school into a series of compromises like these pictures. And into monstrous competition among performers. And into a vicious scramble for TV ratings —stupid IBM tallies.

"I hate Madison Avenue and Hollywood and the clichés of American culture, which is efficient in form but makes content secondary."

That content was not secondary to Harry—in a film script as in the lyrics of a song—was emphasized by his treatment of a later offer to star in the film version of *Porgy and Bess.* Despite his intense interest in acting, he rejected the Goldwyn bid. It was not an easy decision, considering the surrounding cast of topnotch performers, the seven-million-dollar budget, and the world-wide popularity of the George Gershwin score.

Harry's fears were well grounded. In spite of the over-all excellence of the production and praiseworthy performances by Sidney Poitier, Dorothy Dandridge, Sammy Davis, Jr., Pearl Bailey, and the rest of an all-Negro cast, *Porgy and Bess* encountered considerable criticism in the Negro community. *Ebony* reflected the prevailing attitude in a lead article titled: "Why Negroes Don't Like Porgy and Bess."

In an interview with Paul Werth of KRHM of Los Angeles,

Harry explained his own attitude: *"Porgy and Bess* represents an important step in the development of the musical American theatre. But in this period of our social development, I doubt that it is healthy to expose certain images of the Negro. In a period of calm, perhaps this picture could be viewed historically. But skins are still too thin and emotions still too sensitive for a lot of Uncle Tom in *Porgy and Bess* to be shown now."

At a later date, Harry added: "I am not opposed to showing the Negro as being impoverished or anything like that. But when Dubose Heyward made the leading lady a prostitute, a leading male character a peddler of narcotics, another a man of lust and sex and wouldn't even let the hero stand on his own feet, I've had it up to here."

At about this time the Scotts learned that a pianist friend was giving up his apartment. Since Belafonte was looking for a place, they asked their friend about his letting Harry have it. He indicated that he would be delighted to do so but that he would check with his landlord, as a matter of form. Accordingly, the pianist invited the landlord for a drink.

After the atmosphere had been warmed by martinis, the pianist told the owner of the house what he wanted to do.

The landlord sipped his drink pleasantly. "This man's a friend of yours?" he asked.

The musician nodded.

"What's the problem? If you like him—he can have it."

The pianist was pleased. Conversation returned to the casual.

As he was preparing to leave, the landlord said: "Thanks for the drink. But I'm not sure that I understand why you asked me to your apartment."

"Well," the pianist said, "I just wanted to be sure. And so I thought I'd just ask you outright."

"All right. So ask me."

"I did."

"Oh," he said, "you mean about your friend."

"I didn't know whether you'd be willing," the pianist continued, "to let me give the apartment to Belafonte. I didn't know if you'd permit a Negro in the building."

"But I still don't understand why you had to send for me," the landlord announced.

"That's nice," the eighty-eighter said. "I'm glad that you don't mind having a Negro in the building."

The landlord opened his eyes wide, as if he had just heard something for the first time. "Who's a Negro?" he demanded. "What are you talking about?"

The pianist did a double-take. "Belafonte is a Negro," he said. "I thought you knew."

"Colored!" the landlord exclaimed. "Not in my building. Nothing doing."

"But he's a celebrity," the pianist tried, "and he's quite a wonderful guy."

The landlord was firm. "I don't have nothing against them. But I don't want them—no matter how wonderful they are. That's final."

That terminated the conversation.

But the following day, the pianist received a call from his landlord. *Could he come over?*

When he arrived, the musician was courteous but not cordial.

"Your friend," the landlord began awkwardly. "Harry Belafonte."

The pianist made no attempt to ease the situation.

"I'm sorry if I was abrupt yesterday. I've thought things over. I'd like your friend to have the apartment."

The pianist opened his eyes wide in amazement. "But why the overnight change?" he asked.

"Well, to tell you the truth," the landlord said, "I don't think I was listening too carefully yesterday. I was kinda tired and that drink—"

"I still don't get it," the pianist said. "His color didn't change overnight."

The landlord looked uncomfortable. "I guess I didn't make myself too clear. Yesterday I just didn't realize who your friend

[249]

was. But at the dinner table last night, when I mentioned his name, my wife and daughters went out of their minds. I had to promise that I would talk to you the first thing this morning."

"It's too late," the pianist said.

"Look, I'm sure he didn't find an apartment overnight. Call him now and tell him he can have the apartment."

"It's no use."

"But why?"

"It would take too long to explain," the pianist said.

"But he's welcome. I didn't say anything against him. I want him to have the apartment."

"It won't work."

"I don't understand."

"Would you take any colored family?" the pianist asked. "Would you take him if he weren't Belafonte?"

"But he is."

"Yes, he is," the musician said. "And he knows that you turned him down."

"But I didn't turn him down. I turned down—" The landlord paused and took a deep breath.

"That's just it," the pianist said quietly. "He knows what you turned down. So do I. And, now, probably, you do too."

STEREO

NAT (KING) COLE

At the Municipal Auditorium in Birmingham, Alabama, in April 1956, Nat (King) Cole was singing to an all-white audience of four thousand. He had just launched into a lilting second chorus of *Little Girl* when a wolf whistle sounded through the quiet of the auditorium. Down the aisles bounded five men. Dashing headlong toward an amazed Cole, they leaped the four-foot stage. One swung at the Negro singer and knocked him over the piano bench, which cracked under him. Another grabbed Cole's feet as he fell and began twisting them.

Police, who had been tipped of a possible demonstration, were caught off guard. They had expected the demonstrators to come up the steps at each side of the stage. But they quickly surrounded the five fanatics and marched them out of the hall while English bandleader Ted Heath led the orchestra through *America*. Outside, police found a sixth man in a car loaded with a blackjack, brass knuckles, and two rifles.

When emcee Gary Morton came out to explain that Cole could not continue, several listeners shouted: "Ask him to come back so we can apologize."

Flanked by police, a distraught Cole reappeared on-stage for a five-minute ovation.

After resting, he hurried through a second performance for Negroes alone.

While the six men rested in jail, Birmingham police discovered that the attack had been planned at a gas station in a town sixty miles from Birmingham. A mob of 150, led by an officer of the North Alabama Citizens Council, was to have invaded the auditorium and kidnaped Cole. Only six white supremacists showed up.

When the six appeared in the court of Judge Ralph E. Parker eight days after the attack, four were given a maximum jail sentence of six months (for the misdemeanor of preventing a man from carrying on his lawful pursuits) and fined a hundred dollars each. The other two were held for the grand jury on the more serious charge of intent-to-murder.

While Judge Parker commended Cole for his conduct, Negro newspapers blasted him for singing to a segregated audience. Also for his rejection of an invitation from the NAACP to join its ranks.

"I'm an entertainer," Cole is said to have said, "not a politician."

Later, however, he made a $500 contribution and became a life member of the NAACP.

22. First Negro Matinee Idol

Watching Tab Hunter on a movie set recently, curvaceous dancer Gwen Verdon, the star of *Redhead*, could not resist exclaiming: "That man has no bad angles! You can photograph the back of his head and he'll look attractive. Why, he's a white Belafonte!"

In somewhat more analytical terms, and without knowing of the redhead's remark, Negro novelist Bill Attaway, a long-time friend of Belafonte, had this to say:

"At the present stage of the struggle for human freedom, the need is for a bridge Negro—one who serves to connect white and Negro. Harry fills that need remarkably. Although he is brown-skinned and unmistakably Negro, his handsomeness is acceptable in terms of white standards of beauty. Brown up Tab Hunter, and you could hardly tell him from Harry Belafonte."

In explanation of his comment, Attaway went on to add: "The timidity of the American integration movement has created a need for an interim Negro. This explains in part Harry's phenomenal rise and his widespread acceptance as a matinee idol. It does not in any way detract from his greatness as an artist.

"But the fact is that we are at an interim stage in humanity's fight for racial equality. First, we had movies like *Pinky* and that film about the New England Negro doctor who looked white as white. At this stage, you could get acceptance only of the Negro who did not seem to be Negro. That's how you could communicate the idea that the differences were really superficial—simply a matter of skin pigmentation.

[252]

"The present level of public taste—a higher one—is one of accepting the Negro as a Negro, provided his physical appeal is that of a white person. That's Harry's unmistakable achievement.

"The third stage is Sidney Poitier, who is less handsome in Caucasian terms but beautiful on a Negro level. It is a testimonial to the work of the good people who have been conducting the fight for freedom that Sidney's acceptance is so rapid. We are moving."

1957 was the year in which Harry became big news to the big circulation magazines—the year in which he became a celebrity as distinguished from a celebrated artist.

This is a special stage in the career of any entertainer. Scandal and gossip contribute to it. When a singer breaks as fast as Elvis Presley did—and is as controversial as Presley was—the gap between his acceptance as a performer and as a personality is diminished. With most entertainers there is a lag—as there was with Belafonte.

Except for occasional stories, it was not until 1957 that Harry began receiving top coverage in the nation's periodicals. In April, a long story, *Belafonte Gives It All He's Got*, appeared in *The Saturday Evening Post*. In the same month, *The New York Post* ran a week-long serial on Harry's life and career. In May, *Life* devoted a picture spread to him, its title taken ironically from Harry's current favorite: *I Wonder Why Nobody Don't Like Me—Or Is It a Fact That I'm Ugly*. In June, *Look* ran a long feature story, *The Storm Over Belafonte*. In July, *Time* devoted its music section to an article, *Wild About Harry*.

In all of these, there was spelled recognition of the fact—a fact for some time—that Harry had achieved the remarkable status of being America's first Negro matinee idol. Indicative of Harry's appeal was the comment of a female newspaper columnist: "He's as handsome as sin and blessed with sufficient West Indian tradition to remind women of romance under the sun."

Look keyed its story: "Singer-actor Harry Belafonte, one of the most acclaimed entertainers in America today, has also become the first Negro matinee idol in our entertainment history. This has raised a storm over him equaled only the storm raging within him over the issues his position has highlighted."

When *Life* queried Harry on how Harry felt about his attractiveness to American women, he replied: "The idea that I may be the first Negro matinee idol isn't half so flattering as it is a reflection of the change that's come over American life. What else can we be but optimistic? For me, it's a great responsibility. Even if I wanted to, I couldn't live in a vacuum. I'm always on trial."

Much as he disliked the King of Calypso crown, Harry was even more upset by the Matinee Idol monicker. He seldom heard it without expressing his distaste for it.

In several interviews Harry told reporters: "I don't pitch to women especially." But one male heckler, watching his wife's growing excitement during a performance, shouted angrily: "Do I have to pay to watch you steal my wife?" In the course of a Las Vegas engagement at The Riviera, the management had to replace a large picture of him displayed in the lobby no less than thirteen times within a week. Almost as soon as a new picture was placed on display, another adoring female would make off with it.

That Harry is very conscious of his physical appeal to women is well-known to his friends. That he plays up to it is likewise not easy to deny.

"This has nothing to do with his being a playboy," one of his friends has said. "It goes deeper. It has to do with Harry's tremendous need for love. If he pitches constantly and if he works at being a charmer—and he does both—it's almost compulsive. He's still reacting to the world of his youth when he seemed to have no place and nobody seemed to like him. Subconsciously, he's always trying to meet that challenge and elicit a show of positive feeling."

Among the singers and actors who have climbed to the top rungs of their professions, there have been only a few who have also become sex symbols and love gods to American women. One thinks of silent screen star Rudolph Valentino, his smoldering eyes, and the fantastic funeral which drove females to a frenzy and gave birth to a Valentino cult that still exists. Rudy Vallee, The Vagabond Lover, and his megaphone had a brief vogue. Also Clark Gable, he-man of the big ears, fragile Frank Sinatra and his little-boy-lost look, James Dean and his premature death, Elvis Presley and his wriggling pelvis. What makes any man so appealing to the nation's women (or youngsters) that they swoon over him, sigh and squeal over him, rave and pant over him, is partly an enigma. But, as the saying goes, you have it or you don't. Harry Belafonte does.

The components of Harry's appeal include several old-fashioned elements and at least one that is new. He has the good looks that go with love gods, the dynamic bearing, and on a night club floor, the catlike movements that arouse the female libido. But in a sense all these seem less important than another element—his hostility.

"Most recent matinee idols seem to share this quality," Pete Kameron, a manager-publisher friend of Harry's has observed. "Marlon Brando has it. James Dean had it. It's the newest wrinkle in feminine abnormal psychology. But what makes it so remarkable in Harry is that, whether he intends it so or not, his hostility has racial overtones. Certainly, his initial hostility was that of the proud Negro reacting to white prejudice. And strange as it may seem, it was just that quality that appealed to white women."

By the time movie publicists had taken up the title and the country's periodicals had helped fix it on him, Harry had had substantial evidence of his appeal to the females. But it is not without its significance that he became known as the first Negro matinee idol in the very period in which some Negro newspapers cried that his popularity hung in the balance.

The truth is that in 1957 Harry's career still continued its unbelievable upward curve. In February, before the news of his remarriage became known, his stand at The Cocoanut Grove brought the biggest crowds he had ever attracted at the Hollywood nitery. So tremendous was the demand for reservations that The Grove was compelled to hire an extra girl just to inform callers that the place was completely sold out for the two-week Belafonte stand.

In July, Harry played the Greek Theatre, also in Hollywood. An open-air amphitheatre, it seats 4,400. According to *Variety*, Harry set a new Greek Theatre record "with a walloping $84,500" during the first week of his appearance. This was after the tale of his remarriage had been given a thorough combing by the nation's press.

In its same issue, *Variety* carried a separate story headlined

BELAFONTE RIDING WAX AND P.A.'s INTO $1,000,000 CIRCLE

P.A.'s is show biz slanguage for "personal appearances." This was an increase of nearly $300,000 over the previous year's gross.

Harry disclosed that up through July, he had earned $780,000 in signed contract P.A.'s and from album and single sales. His tour, which had opened June 5 and would end September 1, alone would bring him over $400,000, most of his deals involving a guarantee plus a percentage as high as 70 per cent. Of the anticipated million-dollar gross, Harry would be left with a net personal income of around $150,000, the rest of it going to the Government.

Scarcely a month after the appearance of this tale of accelerated progress, Harry ran into a siege of unexpected trouble —medical, not domestic or business. The source of the difficulty, threatening to mar the facial appearance that helped him earn the accolade "First Negro Matinee Idol," could be traced to a boyhood injury. The immediate cause of the crisis was an appearance on a TV show.

Jazz-pop singer Nat (King) Cole—he of the soft velvety voice and the crystalline diction—had a show on television, which was a first for that medium. It was actually the only regular show on the TV screen that starred and was titled after

[256]

a Negro artist. To many, Cole represented to TV what Jackie Robinson had once meant to baseball. Unfortunately for the future of Negro performers on TV, Nat's show was unable to find a sponsor, despite its high audience ratings.

"The men in the gray flannel suits," Nat said, "are afraid of the dark."

When it appeared likely that the network would drop the show as a sustainer after its contract period was over, Harry was one of a group of entertainers—white and Negro—who pitched in, disregarding the show's limited budget for talent, to try to save the show. Harry's appearance and the appearance of other entertainers eventually failed in their purpose. The NBC sales staffs in New York and Los Angeles were unable to find a national sponsor—fear of antagonizing Southern markets was the presumed reason—and the show was dropped after a year of telecasts. Ironically, it was Harry's gesture that brought misfortune to him.

During rehearsals, it is reported, a piece of scenery accidentally fell and struck him. It was a serious blow, but Harry paid no attention to it after he got over the initial shock. While it did him no real external damage, it apparently aggravated an internal condition which had been with Harry from his youth. As a boy, Harry had sustained an eye injury from a pair of scissors that pierced his eyeball. Nervous tension over a period of time stretched weakened membranes. The blow from the falling scenery caused a retinal detachment—a condition in which the screen or retina of the eye moves so far away from the lens that images become blurred or are thrown off screen.

The full impact of the blow he had suffered did not become apparent at once. But as Harry continued on a tour of personal appearances, he noticed that his right eye had increasing areas of blackness. Two days before he was to open in Washington, D.C., he finally became so uneasy that he consulted an eye specialist. The doctor gave him no choice. He had to go to a hospital immediately or chance losing complete sight in the eye.

On August 21 Harry entered New York Hospital. In the first stage of his ordeal, Harry was required to lie perfectly still, in one position, for eight hours. Purpose: to allow gravity to settle the floating elements of the eye. Then he had to lie still for eight hours in another position. This was repeated for an additional sixteen hours. In all, Harry was flat on his back or side for thirty-two hours. The average individual would doubtless find this enforced immobility difficult to take. For a man who frequently went without sleep and had to be on the move all the time, it was sheer torture.

The operation to correct detachment of the retina is an extremely delicate one, as is all surgery within the cranial cavity. Three days after his arrival at the hospital, Harry was on the operating table for four and a half hours. The operation went off without incident, but it took two weeks before the result was known.

During that period Harry was forced to live in utter darkness —both eyes were bandaged—and he was virtually immobilized. A sharp turn of the head, a fast upward or downward motion of the body, etc.—any of these could destroy the surgeon's work and reinstate the detachment. It was an extremely depressing and enervating time for Harry, full of fears and uncertainties. But when the bandages were finally removed, vision was restored to the bad eye.

On Tuesday, September 11, Julie, who was then pregnant, came to call for Harry and took him home. A widely circulated UP photo, taken of the two as they were leaving the hospital, shows Harry in a strange pair of glasses that were to become a regular part of his wardrobe for many months. Completely opaque to keep out light—with a pinhole opening in the center of each lens—they gave Harry such a grotesque, owl-like appearance that he tried not to appear in public with them.

At the time the Belafontes were still occupying the three and a half room apartment, which had served as Harry's bachelor quarters in the Seventies off Central Park West. As *Time* magazine pointed out, this was living "in relative austerity" for a man whose earnings hovered around the million mark a year. It did not indicate that, when Harry went to rent an apartment, landlords seemed to forget that he was a great performer and a matinee idol, and remembered only that he was a Negro. A friend of Harry's said: "Belafonte is the only millionaire in America who goes down to the cellar to empty his own garbage."

The three and a half room apartment was a palace after the weeks of tension and worry in the hospital, even though Harry could not do anything so strenuous as emptying his own garbage. Eating home-cooked meals, instead of hospital food, was something Harry had anticipated with great relish. Julie had become expert at making some of the West Indian dishes Harry enjoyed. A devoted basketball fan, Harry was looking forward to the up and coming games of the Knickerbockers, his rooting team.

The excitement of settling back into the contentment and relaxation of being at home was short-lived. Harry had been home only a day or two when vision in the right eye became clouded. He tried to pretend that it was a temporary aberration —the result of his excitement at being back home. But after forty-eight hours of pretending, with the fear inside him growing like a malignant tumor, Harry sank into a mood of deep depression. Julie had sensed what was going on. But she too had tried to pretend that everything was all right. Except that on several occasions, she had unobtrusively spotted Harry placing his hand over his left eye (the sound one) to determine what he could see out of the other. It was clear that he was upset by the results.

When a mood of quiet desperation settled over Harry—succeeding the air of coiled-spring tension with which he had moved around the apartment, Julie decided it was time to act.

"Let's call Dr. Norton," she suggested.

"What for?" Harry demanded. "I've got an appointment to see him on Friday."

She studied Harry's face. "Don't you think it would be better to find out instead of living with this uncertain fear?"

"Find out what—" Harry started to say. He sighed. "I'm sorry, Julie." He was silent for a troubled moment. "I guess so," he admitted in a whisper.

The examination by Harry's physician confirmed their worst

fears. Harry had to return to the hospital. Another operation? The surgeon was not sure. Healing was proceeding, but it looked as if there might have been a recurrence of the detachment. Why couldn't he stay home until they were certain? Because he needed absolute quiet and rest, and because they could conduct additional tests to determine what was causing the renewed blurring of sight.

So Harry, who had left New York Hospital on Tuesday, September 11, returned on Saturday, September 15, for observation. The following day he underwent a second operation to correct "a partial recurrence of a retinal detachment of his right eye."

This operation was successful. It eliminated the detachment and the worry of several difficult months seemed over. Thereafter, Harry had his eyes under wraps—bandaged, in short—for twenty-eight terrible days. "I nearly went crazy," Harry has said. "I would imagine all kinds of things—that there were strangers in the room, that I was really going blind. Since the muscles of the eyes had been cut through twice, they had to be given time to heal. The eyes are the only part of the body that do not move independently of each other. So both eyes, the good as well as the problem one, had to be bandaged."

When the healing was over and the worry of several months seemed over, a new problem appeared. Movement of the eye is controlled by a series of tiny muscles. When one of these is too long or too short, too tight or too elastic, in relation to the others, the eyeball goes off-center. This is what happened to Harry after the second operation.

In an attempt to avoid a third operation, the doctors gave Harry special glasses. Naturally, he could not wear these when he was performing. He could not actually allow his public to know he was wearing them at all. Matinee idols did not go with eyeglasses. Thus, whenever Harry was not in the public eye during the fall of '57 and the winter of '58, he wore corrective spectacles—designed to center the eyeballs—a procedure which, ultimately, did not eliminate the need for a third operation.

Harry had been away from the hospital for only nine days

after the second operation when a new but short-lived crisis developed. This one involved Julie. Labor pains, which at first had been regarded as "false" and a reaction to her concern over Harry, became quite pronounced. On September 23 Julie entered Mt. Sinai Hospital in Manhattan. The following day she gave birth to a boy. Their first child—and Harry's third— the infant was named David Michael Belafonte. The choice had been delegated by Harry to his daughter Adrienne, who had selected the name of one of her favorite uncles—Margurite's brother David.

Harry's recuperation from his second operation was gladdened by Julie's convalescence from the birth of their first child.

At Christmas '57 Harry decided that the time had come for rejoicing. It had been a hard year, filled with the worry and tension of lawsuits, unpleasant publicity, and a series of difficult operations. The eye problem was still with him. He wore dark glasses to conceal—and correct—the off-center position of the eye. And there was still the possibility that America's first Negro matinee idol might be cross-eyed. But Harry wanted a party—and he rented a large, private dining room at The Waldorf to celebrate with his staff and friends.

The high point of the party's proceedings was a Noah-like call-and-response number which he and Tony Scott improvised and which, before it was finished, involved virtually everybody at the party. It came after Harry's choral group had sung a series of delightful, but oh-so-stiff, Christmas carols and madrigals. These were obviously keyed too low to invite participation or to stir the diners. As if they were down at The Sage in the Village, after the one-armed restaurant had closed for the night, Harry and Tony could not resist the challenge. Suddenly they were in the center of the floor—the high-spirited preachers at a Southern revival meet.

"Who built the ark?" Harry chanted.

"Noah!" Tony shouted.

"Who built the ark?" Harry cried.

"Noah!" was Tony's response.

Soon others added their voices to the responses. A circle began to form around them. As the chanting continued, Harry and Tony began to lead the line around the room. The chanting grew louder. Excitement mounted. Almost everybody was now drawn into the mock revival meet. The line of gospel singers wove around the room. Now, people were beginning to gesticulate and to flail the air with outstretched arms.

At the peak of the proceedings, Tony and Harry glanced around and suddenly realized that the doors of their private dining room were ajar and a group of spectators were standing outside, staring in amazement at the spectacle of what looked like a group of well-dressed people gone berserk. Among the celebrities the surprised spectators saw in the weaving line of mock revivalists were dramatic actor Frederic March and his wife Florence Eldridge, both of whom were then appearing on Broadway in Eugene O'Neill's somber tragic drama *Long Day's Journey into Night*.

Sitting in a corner of the room as a nonparticipant was Julie Belafonte, with an expression that Harry's old friends found difficult to interpret. Whether it was that she was concerned about Harry's boyish conduct as it related to his eye condition or that she felt that he had outgrown this kind of exhibitionism, Julie was obviously not sympathetic to the proceedings. Friends who had known her as Julie Robinson of The Dunham Dance Company suddenly saw a transformation that bewildered them. The Julie they had once known was an uninhibited, high-spirited girl, with a love of gay parties, unconventional clothes and excitement. But here was a sedate woman dressed in a black taffeta hostess dress, trying to play the role of the dignified matron, and acting protective about her husband's festive antics. Alas, the Bohemian had gone bourgeois.

Tony said: "When she got up to dance with me, even before we cut up, I couldn't help saying: 'Relax, kid. What's bugging you?' Fran and I sat at the main table with Harry and the Marches. I don't think Julie was pleased at the way Harry and I were rehashing the past for the Marches. They got quite a charge out of hearing about the crazy things we did in the

[262]

Village days. But Julie kept trying to switch the conversation away from the cut-ups of the past."

Fran Scott had overheard Florence Eldridge say to Julie: "You seem tired, child. Are you well?"

To both Tony and Fran, Julie's behavior recalled the way Margurite had once sat in a corner at a party in their Greenwich Village loft and watched the crazy proceedings with a faintly amused air . . .

Fran Scott's most vivid memory of the party is of something that happened just as dinner was finishing and before people began cutting up. Harry had been engaged in animated conversation with Tony and with Florence and Frederic March. As the conversation lulled to a temporary halt, Harry turned full face to Fran and slowly removed his dark glasses. He said nothing but just sat wordlessly facing her, allowing her to study his face.

"There was this handsome, young face," Fran recalls, "with one eye off to a side. A moment previous, he looked like a well-possessed Adonis, despite the glasses. Now, in an instant, he was a sad little boy with a cross-eye, looking so hopeless and forlorn you felt like taking him in your arms and coddling him. It took all the control I could muster to hold the tears back."

STEREO

MILES DAVIS

On Tuesday, August 25, 1959, jazz trumpeter Miles Davis, who was playing at Birdland with his sextet, went upstairs for a breath of fresh air. He had just finished making a twenty-seven minute recording for the Armed Services in connection with a bond-selling campaign.

As he stood smoking a cigarette in the hot, muggy, summer night, a policeman came along and said: "Off the sidewalk!" Miles indicated that he just wanted a breath of air and that he would go inside the club in a minute.

The cop said: "Are you a wise guy or something?"

Miles replied: "No, I just want a breath of fresh air."

"You know, I'll arrest you," the cop said.

"Well, arrest me," Miles said, wondering what he could be arrested for.

"Okay," the cop said. "I'm going to take you in." And he reached for his club.

The next Miles knew, a detective in plain clothes came up behind him and began beating him on the head with a blackjack.

Five stitches were required in two head wounds that spattered blood all over his band uniform.

The policeman and the detective excused their brutality on the ground that Davis refused to move when ordered and allegedly grabbed the patrolman's night stick.

"If I had taken his club from him," Davis asked, "would I have these two head wounds?"

23. Belafonte Sings the Blues

When Harry entered the Victor recording studios early in February 1958, Ed Welker, who was supervising the date, sensed something strange in the way he walked. Harry seemed in good spirits, and he made a joke of taking off the dark glasses he wore out of doors and putting on a pair of special reading glasses.

It was now more than five months since Harry's troubles with his eyes had begun. They had been five bad months. With his activities severely circumscribed, he had tried to occupy himself by making plans for several movies he wanted to produce through his own company, Harbel. But here it was February and there was no indication as to when he could begin shooting or return to his routine of personal appearances.

The February recording session was the first of several designed to produce a new album, *Belafonte Sings the Blues*. After kidding briefly with Welker, Harry went into the studio and began warming up under conductor Alan Greene, an old friend.

"After a while, we tried a take," Welker recalled. "It was good. Hell, perfect—if it wasn't Belafonte. It had the polish and the finish. But it had no life. Well, we tried a second take. Then a third. They were all good. But not one had the cutting edge that Harry gets into his best records."

Welker was set to go for a fourth take when Harry stuck up his hand and came out of the isolation booth. This is an upright wooden crate that looks very much like a phone booth. It permits separation of the sound of the singer and the orchestra accompanying him, and thereby allows for a better balance, also greater clarity. Actually, the orchestra, except for the conductor, does not hear the singer. And the conductor himself listens to the singer through a pair of earphones. Likewise, the singer hears the orchestra either through earphones or a speaker inside the booth.

When Harry came out of the booth, Welker could tell from the facial expression that the balladeer wanted more than a sip of water or a breather.

"What's up, Harry?"

"They're all going to sound like this," Harry grumbled. "Today's not the day. I've got the blues, but I'm not singing them. Let's send them home." Harry pointed to the musicians.

Once they appear for a date, musicians are paid full union rates even if the date is called off. Although the recording company advances the cost, it is charged against the royalties of the singer.

So the musicians were sent home, without the date being completed. Welker did not learn until almost two months later that Harry was then under sedation. While his doctor was relying on the glasses to correct the eye position, he wanted Harry to remain cool and relaxed.

"Can you imagine Belafonte relaxed?" Welker asked. "It was like a coke without fizz."

Harry's February visit to his eye doctor brought unpleasant tidings, although he had then been wearing corrective glasses for five months. The doctor was dissatisfied with the results. Reluctantly, he admitted to Harry that it looked as if a new operation would be necessary. He was willing to try the glasses for another month, but if improvement was not manifest then, only surgery would work.

Harry had no difficulty making a decision. As long as he wore glasses, or was required to wear them, he could make no public appearances. Nor could he go into movie production as he wished to do. He was just marking time. If surgery was necessary, the sooner the better.

The problem presented by an operation was that, in trying to correct the position of the eye, the retina might well become detached again. This could mean the loss of sight. Before Harry's doctor would agree to the operation, he wanted him to consult a Boston surgeon. It was a good move. The surgeon recommended the startling procedure of tackling one eye through the other. This would reduce the possibility of a new and dangerous retinal detachment.

On February 17 Harry entered New York Hospital again. This was to be his third operation since the preceding August. Apparently, the procedure recommended by the Boston surgeon was followed. Harry remained in the hospital for four days. This time surgery did the trick. When the healing was complete, the position of the eye was on-center.

The following month, on March 29, Harry returned to the RCA Victor studios.

"He came in wearing dark glasses," Welker said. "But there was something in that loping walk of his that made me feel that things were all right. I sat down in the engineer's booth and looked through the heavy soundproof glass that separates the booth from the recording studio. As soon as Harry saw my face through the glass, he pulled his glasses off and flipped them jauntily on a music stand. It was his way of letting me know that things were okay with his eye. It was a honey of a date and Harry sang with all the conviction and intensity that are his special mark."

At this session, Harry recorded only two songs, *The Way I Feel* and *Fare Thee Well,* used in *The Blues* album. The remaining numbers were not cut until after Harry had finished shooting his first independent picture around New York and had settled in Hollywood for his annual appearance at the Greek Theatre. Two sessions, one on June 5 and the other on June 7, both under the baton of Dennis Farnon, were required to cut eight additional sides and to complete the album.

"This is the area—the blues," Harry has said, "with which I have the strongest identification. Blues and spirituals contain without doubt the most powerful songs in terms of lyric content in the American tradition. That's why people, no matter what their walks of life, always respond to them."

Harry's love for the blues is based on another consideration. "Here I can just step out," he says, "and sing wholly the way I feel. Of course, when I started singing, I was involved with an environment that emphasized the modern school of jazz. It was difficult for me to adapt the way I felt to the requirements of that kind of singing. But that was what I was exposed to at the time. I've always had a feeling for the basic blues. But it took several years of removing myself from the predominantly modern jazz environment and finding myself and my *own* set of values before I had the courage to attempt an album like this."

This is tantamount to a statement that he felt unable to tackle the music that is the unique creation of his own people until he had attained a certain level of maturity. Harry actually makes this point in another way. He names among the singers who have influenced him and whom he admires: Big Bill Broonzy, Memphis Slim, Mahalia Jackson, and Billie Holiday. What is it that these have in common?

"These are people," Harry says, "who continually go back to the source of their music, who relate to their environment, who know who they are."

On another occasion, Harry credited two other Negro blues-folk singers with inspiring him. One was Leadbelly, whose murderous temper twice landed him in jail for life and whose twelve-string guitar and songs twice got him out. Like Mahalia Jackson, the great contemporary gospel singer, Leadbelly impressed on Harry "the enormous quantity of material that still exists in Negro life and culture, much of which is yet to be uncovered and artistically interpreted."

The other and more recent influence was a young contemporary contralto and folk singer who goes under the name of Odetta. Born in Birmingham, Alabama, in 1933, operatic-trained, and built like a giantess, Odetta Felious currently may be heard on three albums released by small record companies. Harry was so impressed by her singing that he himself annotated her most recent LP and introduced her to a nationwide audience on his CBS television spectacular of December 10, 1959. Until then, Odetta's biggest single audience had been at the 1959 Newport Folk Festival, with most of her bookings running to far-out night spots like the hungry i in San Francisco and Chicago's Gate of Horn (the title of one of her albums).

Since 1953 Odetta has addressed her capacious talents, despite her operatic training, exclusively to the folk-blues field. Her three record albums are, in fact, composed entirely of blues, spirituals, and folk songs, most of them known in versions made familiar by earlier folk artists. Her range is startling. There are songs in which she sounds like a young, exuberant Leadbelly. Others, where her rich, deep, swelling voice reminds one of another Negro contralto, the great Marian Anderson.

In an introductory note to her third album, *My Eyes Have Seen,* Harry clearly defines his debt to Odetta: "There are many singers with fine voices, great range, and superb technique," he writes. "Few, however, possess that fine understanding of a song's inner meaning, which transforms it from a melody into a dramatic experience. Odetta, who has influenced me greatly in this area of dramatic interpretation, is just such an artist." Harry adds: "I have been impelled by her artistry to approach my repertoire with a keener sense of its meaning and a more searching study of its lyrical content."

Of course, anyone familiar with Belafonte knows that "lyrical content" has been Harry's concern from his earliest days as a singer. Monte Kay, his first manager, found that this was what distinguished Harry from most of the jazz and pop singers of 1949. As recently as January of '59, I personally had the experience of watching Harry turn down a song for recording because the writers could not come up with a lyric which he considered probing enough. Although he liked the melody and the basic idea—and an arrangement had been made by his conductor Robert Corman—he rejected rewrite after rewrite on the ground that there was no fresh penetration of experience.

"I like to feel that each new song I record represents growth," he told me. "I can make it meaningful to the listener only if it gives me new insight and provokes deep feeling within me."

In addition to her concern with meaning, Harry finds an-

[269]

other quality in Odetta, which he admires in other singers and which he has long sought.

"Those of us who call ourselves artists," he writes, "can learn much from her strength, simplicity, warmth, humor, and complete humanity."

The initial word in this group is one that recurs frequently in Harry's comments on the songs in Odetta's albums. "Strength" is at times elaborated to a "granite-like fortitude," or used in connection with another word of great significance to Harry: "defiant strength." Harry touches this same concept in another way in a collection of songs he has himself published. In referring to Leadbelly, Mahalia Jackson, and Odetta, he states: "All of these performers have given me pride and confidence in the material and therefore in myself."

If jazz is the original creation of the Negro in the instrumental field, the blues are his unique contribution to vocal music. "People are always pestering me to become a blues singer," Mahalia Jackson, the great gospel singer, has said. "They'd tell me, 'Girl, you could be a blues singer.' I'd answer, 'What Negro couldn't be a blues singer!'"

"Like the spirituals," said W. C. Handy, writer of the famous *St. Louis Blues,* "the blues began with the Negro, it involves our history, where we came from, and what we experienced. The blues came from the man farthest down. The blues came from nothingness, from want, from desire. And when a man sang or played the blues, a small part of the want was satisfied from the music."

"Go any place where there's a group of Negroes," said T-Bone Walker, guitar accompanist of Ma Rainey and other blues singers, "and you'll hear them singing blues you never heard of—wonderful blues."

A style and a tradition, the blues are also a touchstone. Among Negro jazz musicians, the primary and basic test, in fact, of any sideman is what he can do with the blues. Thus it seems more than an accident that, when Belafonte's marriage to a white girl brought accusations from the Negro community of his crossing into the "ofay" world, Harry should have turned to the blues. No other material could have served so forcefully as a statement of identification and of his consciousness of his heritage.

It was in connection with this album, too, that Harry called Billie Holiday's blues *God Bless the Child*—"the greatest song in the world." Its harsh and well-known message: "whatever mommy and poppy may have, that's theirs—God bless the child that has its own"—is probably the strongest and most cynical declaration of filial independence to be found in song literature. Is it reading too much into Harry's fulsome comment on this number—the longest in the *Blues* album—to contend that this was his musical declaration of freedom from insecurities that had haunted him from his youth. He had in life asserted his independence. Now he was doing so in song.

From both a psychological and musical standpoint, it is difficult to exaggerate the importance of the *Blues* album in Harry's development.

What does mystify is his choice of material. Instead of going back to the rich repository of great old blues, Harry turned his attention to blues of very recent vintage. No less than five of the eleven selections are songs that were either written by a contemporary of Harry's or recorded by him. In fact, these five numbers are all to be found in one album by Ray Charles, a rather remarkable Negro singer, writer, saxophonist, pianist, and arranger, still in his twenties who, as a singer-writer, has had a succession of big recent hits. The other six blues are also contemporary and include only two songs that might be regarded as standards: *God Bless the Child,* already mentioned, and *One for My Baby,* the well-known torch blues by Johnny Mercer and Harold Arlen.

Harry's interest in the work of Southerner Ray Charles, as with his interest in Odetta, is a testimonial to his feeling for new talent. Born in Albany, Georgia, Charles grew up in Greenfield, Florida, and, after an illness at the age of six had left him totally blind, in Augustine, Florida. Here, at a school for blind children, he became interested in music. By the time he was seventeen, he had his own instrumental trio, which played jazz in the vein of the early King Cole Trio. Since then he has traveled a musical road in which he has fused early gospel influences with a feeling for the blues and modern jazz. Today he is simultaneously accepted by the rock 'n' roll set, who have made best sellers of his new songs, and by the Newport Jazz crowd, where he has appeared as jazz pianist and saxist. The Atlantic album which so impressed Harry was not only a R 'n' R best seller; it also won the Grand Prix of the French Academy of Recorded Music as best in its class.

Of Charles, Harry has said: "Ray is one of the very few contemporary artists to know and appreciate and take advantage of his folk heritage in order to expand and develop his own identity . . . What Ray writes are folk songs in almost the traditional sense of spontaneous material that comes out of a people's needs."

Since Harry offers his own interpretation of five songs previously recorded by Charles, comparison of the two is inevitable—also informative. There is virtually no similarity in tone, style, or mood. Charles's tone is raw and biting, while Harry's is tender, delicate, polished. Charles's style, stemming from a country, gospel tradition, relies for expressiveness on vocal scoops and rhythmic variation. Harry, with an urban, theatrical background, relies on dynamic shading. Charles's mood is one of self-possessed pride and defiance while Harry's, surprisingly, is one of self-analysis and self-pity. Ray Charles declares; Harry Belafonte introspects.

In a sense, the contrast here is between two great traditions of the blues—folk and modern. Ray Charles goes back, despite the modernity of his material, to the early, hard, declamatory "shout" style of the Ma Raineys, the Bessie Smiths, and the Leadbellys, while Harry goes forward to the smoother, the more musical, and the more polished approach of a Joe Williams, Billie Holiday, or Ella Fitzgerald. The blues have been urbanized. They have come North. And they are being sung in a world with the atom bomb.

Harry's search for his own identity, and identity with his own people, might have fared better had he returned to the folk blues as he did in his earlier peregrinations. As an album, the *Blues* LP is disappointing not only in its choice of material but in its lack of pace and variety. There is a sameness of mood (self-pity), of dynamics (soft), and of tempo (slow), which give the album a surprising monotony for a Belafonte album. As a friendly critic has said: "One number erases the next." Except in *Sinner's Prayer, Cotton Fields,* and *God Bless the Child,* which seems too long, Harry is unable to achieve the dramatic tension, the excitement, and the emotional freedom which are his special mark.

Whatever its aesthetic shortcomings, the *Blues* album, nevertheless, represents a vital stage in Harry's evolution as an artist and person. For all its shortcomings, it is a declaration of identity and an affirmation of his growing maturity.

S T E R E O

CHUCK BERRY

In August '59 hit rock 'n' roll singer Chuck Berry performed at an all-white high school fraternity dance in Meridian, Mississippi. Before the evening was over, Berry was in the local jail. He was being held without bail on the charge of a white girl who had attended the dance.

The charge—he had tried to date her.

24. The Australian Penny

Harry's first "invasion" of Europe came during the summer of 1958. It confirmed his stature as an international star. But events abroad and on his return to his native land once again reminded him that, with all his widespread popularity, he was still nothing but a black man to many, including many in a cosmopolitan northern city like New York.

Harry departed for the continent on the *Île de France* shortly after completing his *Blues* album. It was June, and with Julie and young David, then not yet a year old, he was set for a four-week romp around Europe. After that, beginning with an August 3 presentation at the Brussels World's Fair, he was to give concerts in England, Paris, Berlin, Frankfurt, and Munich. The singing tour would finish with the Scandinavian countries and Rome.

Interviewed by *Variety* on the eve of sailing regarding foreign picture offers, Harry indicated that he was primarily concerned about the racial angle in suggested parts.

"The colored people are being accepted throughout the world," he said, "on a level as never before. There is a much broader avenue of expression open to them. But we must be careful not to use our art in the negative interest of our people." Queried as to whether he would accept a part as a villain, he stated that he would, "but only if such a part did not imply that all Negroes were villains."

In England, Harry appeared under the aegis of J. Arthur Rank. Eight concerts were scheduled for August 10 to 16 at the Gaumont State Theatre in Milburn. Like the Greek Theatre in Los Angeles, the Gaumont accommodated over four thousand. But this was London, not Los Angeles. If Harry had any doubts as to how his first appearance would be received, they were erased even before his arrival. Immediately after tickets went on sale in July, the British trade papers reported in alliterative syllables: BELAFONTE TRIGGERS OFF BIG BOOM AT BOX OFFICE.

Of course, Harry was not unknown to British audiences, although he had never played the Isles. And, strangely enough, his popularity was not based solely on the popularity of his *Calypso* album. Harry actually had had a hit record in England that had not started in his native land, and that had racked up unbelievable sales within a remarkably short period.

Included in his album *An Evening with Belafonte,* released in Britain during the fall of '57, was a pop-religious song—"religioso" in Tin Pan Alley slang—entitled *Mary's Boy Child.* One of the few areas where English record buyers do not follow American trends is in the religious field. The British Broadcasting Company takes literally the injunction against using the name of the Lord in vain. BBC censors will frequently not clear songs for public performance where there is the slightest hint that God is being exploited for profit. Accordingly, British music publishers who scramble over each other to buy English rights to American hit songs will generally pass up "religiosos" like *It Is No Secret (What God Can Do).*

The point of all this is that, during Christmas 1957, English record buyers suddenly found *Mary's Boy Child* as sung by Harry in the album *An Evening with Belafonte.* The making of a hit is a completely unpredictable development. But what happened with *Mary's Boy Child* bordered on the fantastic. The population of England is less than one third of the United States. The biggest American hits were, in 1957, known to cross the million mark in sales. But for England, a million record seller was almost like sending a man to the moon. With all these odds, Harry's recording of *Mary's Boy Child* hit the astronomical million mark—in a matter of six weeks. In English pop music circles it became known as "the fastest-ever million" in the entire history of the British record business.

Harry's two-hour concerts at The Gaumont were naturally

billed as "An Evening with Belafonte." For the eight appearances, Harry had with him his own group of musicians, including Millard Thomas (guitar), Vic Messer (guitar), Danny Barrajanos (bongos), and Norman Keenan (bass). In addition, he was backed by a twenty-four-piece orchestra, specially formed for the occasion by British bandleader Geraldo and conducted by Harry's own musical director, Robert Corman. The eight concerts were not only a sellout in advance. But evening after evening, after offering 120 minutes of song, Harry had to beg off amid enthusiastic cheering and whistling.

On the same night that Harry made his debut at the 4,000 seat Gaumont, Paul Robeson sang his first English concert in nine years at Royal Albert Hall (capacity 8,000), some three miles away. *The New York Journal-American* headlined: "Belafonte Lauded; Robeson Decried." *The News Chronicle* critic wrote: "Belafonte's racial awareness is as keen as Robeson's but it has an added quality the great bass lacks—humor."

Interviewed later by Art Buchwald, *The Herald Tribune's* Paris correspondent, Harry commented: "I've got a social consciousness about my people, but I'm less bitter about our problems than someone like Paul Robeson is. Robeson is of the old school. I'm of the new. But, perhaps, if Robeson hadn't been so bitter, I wouldn't have the opportunity to be less bitter."

Before the first of the Gaumont concerts, Ed Welker, then Harry's recording supervisor at RCA Victor, visited him at The Dorchester where he was staying. When he arrived at the suite, Welker was surprised to learn from Julie that Harry was rehearsing. Since Belafonte does not add new selections to his repertoire too readily, Welker assumed that Harry must have found a new number that he wanted to introduce to English audiences. He discovered quickly that he was mistaken.

In the room of the Dorchester suite where Harry was rehearsing, Welker found the recording star hard at work with the four-piece combo that accompanies him. To his amazement, Norman Keenan, who plays string bass, stood plucking his instrument on top of a sofa. Norman was in his stockinged feet but the bulbous instrument was also perched on the expensive sofa with him.

Harry saw the look of surprise in Welker's face. "Norm's up there," Harry chuckled, "because the management had complaints about all the rehearsing we're doing. Seems that the bass was booming all over the place. Up there, the floor can't act as a resonator and broadcast the plucking through the other suites."

"Rehearsing some new numbers, Harry?" Welker asked.

"No, Ed. We're going over the old," Harry replied. "All of us have been relaxing a bit since my last P.A. (personal appearance). So we're trying to get back into top form. I don't want to get in front of these new audiences and give the impression that I've got it made."

When Welker appeared the following day at Harry's suite to introduce a British representative of RCA Victor, he again found Harry deeply immersed in a rehearsal that went on for several hours.

"It's what makes the difference," Welker observed. "There are few artists as dedicated as Belafonte. Each new performance is a challenge to him. It has to be the best he can possibly give. He has the most persistent drive toward perfection I've ever encountered in any artist."

From London, Harry embarked on a tour of the top Continental concert halls, presenting a program arranged in three parts: *Moods of the American Negro, Songs of the Caribbean* and *Around the World.* His European appearances were rousing repeats of his reception in England.

In Paris, impresario Bruno Coquatrix showed a timidity which he was later to regret. Although he himself was the director of the Olympia Music Hall, a cavernous theatre that played host to the biggest American acts, he decided to book Harry into the smaller Palais de Chaillot, which seats only 2,000. Coquatrix had a number of reasons for what turned out to be a mistaken decision. For one thing, some American headliners had not lived up to expectations, drawing only limited crowds despite their popularity on records. For another, because of Harry's folk, spiritual, calypso repertoire, Coquatrix felt that he would fare better with "specialized exposure." Then, again, this was Harry's initial appearance in Paris.

After the first concert in Harry's four-day stand at the Palais, Coquatrix was ready to admit that he had made a bu-bu. He had felt that Paris reviewers, who sometimes can be quite murderous, would probably be receptive to Harry. But he had never anticipated that they would wax purple-prosed about the balladeer. They did. In two of the papers, *Paris-Presse* and *France-Soir,* Harry's presentation was likened to "rites in a temple or Notre Dame." The high-priced seven-dollar seats were a complete sellout while empties showed only in the very low-priced section. By the time Harry was leaving Paris for his next stop, Coquatrix stated that Harry could pack the Palais for a month.

Incidentally, Harry's entry into Paris was not without its ludicrous side. A French newsman printed the curious report: "On arrival, Belafonte carried his child in one hand and a bottle of Scotch in the other." Since Harry is widely known as a light drinker and smoker, it is difficult to surmise what this reporter actually saw. However, the item arrived on American shores via a cable from a French correspondent to New York's picture newspaper *The News,* who described the reporter as "sharp-eyed." A more accurate word would probably have been "imaginative" or "inventive."

Of his invasion of the Continent, Harry had this interesting observation to make:

"Rock 'n' roll especially has spread," Harry said, "because the teen-agers of England and Europe are conditioned to the same kind of fears and insecurities as teen-agers in America. Rock 'n' roll enables youth anywhere to express their rebellion against certain things. I know from having talked with teen-agers while in England that their needs are the same as those of their American counterparts. This is true from the gates of East Berlin to the Golden Gate Bridge of San Francisco."

In this connection, Harry produced an unusually moving letter from a girl in East Berlin who had seen him perform in Germany:

"Dear Mr. Belafonte: You will hardly remember that girl

from the Soviet Zone whom you made so happy by allowing her to come into your dressing room at the Berlin Theatre and to speak to you.

"You were so kind but you can't imagine what it really means to me. I have to thank you for the most delightful moments in my life—this dull and hopeless life here in the atmosphere of eternal fear, which you can never fancy, living at the end of the rainbow."

Enclosed in the envelope with the note was a "talisman," an Australian penny, which a friend had brought her from the Olympic Games. And there was this postscript: "I had written this letter three months ago, but I couldn't make up my mind to take my penny from off my neck. But now it's off! Good luck!"

In his appearance on the Continent, Harry found to his great satisfaction that he was able "to communicate" to audiences unable to understand his language. In Milan, in Rome, he played to wildly receptive crowds.

"On the tour through Europe," he said, "I sang in many countries where I'm positive the content of what I was singing wasn't wholly understood. And yet all these societies are becoming more and more related to each other in their art forms and techniques. European audiences were as enthusiastic—I am happy to report—as American ones."

Returning to New York in October, Harry ran head-on into a housing problem. Julie and he liked a number of midtown apartments located on Manhattan's East Side. Renting them was another matter entirely. Once again he was a star only onstage. Off-stage, he was just another man with a black skin. His money and his renown did not help. When the newspapers reported the plight of the Belafontes, Mrs. Franklin Delano Roosevelt got in touch with Harry and offered to buy a building with him.

"But I'm not looking for the easy way out," Harry said. He thereupon settled his family in a ten-room apartment offered to him by the landlord of a building on the West Side of Manhattan, considered the less desirable section of town.

Two weeks after his return, Harry went to Washington to

participate in a demonstration for Negro rights. Along with Jackie Robinson, Mrs. Martin Luther King, and other prominent Negroes, he led a procession of several hundred white and Negro students down Constitution Avenue to the Lincoln Memorial. Thereafter, he served as spokesman of a group of twelve that went to the White House to present a petition. They were not permitted to enter the grounds, allegedly because they did not have a confirmed appointment with the President.

On November 9 Harry made a rare appearance on TV, singing a medley of folk ballads, spirituals, and calypsos on the Steve Allen Show. Shortly before his face was seen on the television screen, station WSFA in Montgomery, Alabama, was knocked off the air. A Negro-hater had placed a small chain across a power cable at the station's transmitter. Although he had turned down an Ed Sullivan offer earlier in the year because performing on the medium meant giving oneself "to the mediocrity of many TV people," he accepted the Steve Allen assignment. Two considerations figured in the change of heart. He was given a twenty-minute segment, which allowed for changes of pace he considered necessary to a successful performance. He produced the segment himself without interference.

At Thanksgiving, Harry made one of his semiannual appearances at The Waldorf in New York. Night after night he played to a packed room with turnaways. Night after night, "they loved him, tried to beg him back with sustained applause, and the room buzzed with laudatory comments for some time before returning to normal." (*Billboard*)

One Saturday evening the number of reservations rose to such a flood and the hordes of disappointed turnaways threatened to become so large that the management of the Empire Room decided, as the day wore on, to close the room. Instead, they commandeered the Grand Ball Room, which happened to be available, for Belafonte's performance. There Harry presented his program before 1,200 enraptured diners, perhaps the largest audience that had ever spontaneously appeared at a supper club for one performance by an artist. Certainly it was the first time in the Waldorf's history that it was compelled to close the Empire Room because of the flood of reservations. So electric was the atmosphere and so excited were the viewers that the management later reported an unbelievable number of waiter mishaps.

Thus, within two months of his return to his native land, Harry Belafonte once again had run the gamut of exalted acceptance as an artist and utter rejection as a Negro citizen.

While he was concertizing in London, the Rank organization would not permit Harry to appear on TV. They felt that it might hurt his grosses at the box office. Afterward he gave a one-hour program on the BBC, which is said to have received the highest rating of any show next to the Coronation.

1958 ended in a blaze of glory for Harry when the BBC sent booker Tim Holland-Bennett to the United States to negotiate a five-year deal with him. By Christmas week the papers were signed and *Variety* announced that the BBC had "shelled out the highest individual fee paid to one performer in its history." Reports have it that the fee is around $70,000. For this, Harry is to make seven appearances on the BBC, each thirty minutes long with a possible ten minutes extra on some airings.

Queried as to why he had chosen the BBC for his first TV series when he had turned down huge sums of money offered for a series of programs on American TV, Harry commented:

"For one thing, there are no Southern markets in England to deter or to deny my artistic efforts. I can do whatever I want to do. I chose the BBC because I won't run into panic there on the basis of what the sponsor thinks or what the rating reports would show.

"In England there won't be people between me and the audience I want to reach.

"My experience at the BBC before I signed was that I had greater freedom there as an artist and a human being. Everything concerning the artistic content of the BBC shows will be determined by me and my staff. We will, of course, be bound by the ground rules of the BBC. But what counts is that when I'm at the BBC and I want to sing a song or say something, so long as it's not immoral, nobody will run up to

[281]

me and say: 'The sponsor won't like that!' There isn't any censorship within the framework of civilized, honest behavior."

During his engagement at the Greek Theatre in '56, Harry cut sides for his *Evening with Belafonte* album. One of the songs that interested him was a calypso Christmas tune about "Mary's Little Boy Child." Harry felt that it needed rewriting. He wanted the chorus to have a strong, affirmative message as to the meaning of Christmas. When Lord Burgess, who worked with Harry, effected a rewrite that Harry liked, an arrangement was made overnight by Will Lorin and recorded the following July day.

Belafonte and his associates apparently proceeded on the assumption that *Mary's Little Boy Child* was in public domain and that they were, therefore, free to create their own version. But the fact is that the song was copyright by Walter Schumann Music Corporation before Harry recorded the Lorin-Burgess version. Named as writer was Jester Hairston, for many years an assistant conductor of the Hall Johnson Choir and a well-known choral arranger who had worked with Harry in *Three for Tonight*.

Regardless of whether the song was of folk origin or not, unless a copy could be produced that antedated the Hairston version, its priority and status as a copyright would have to be recognized. This is precisely what happened. On the initial record release, Lorin received credit as the writer of the moving song. With threats of a lawsuit hovering in the air, against Harry's Shari Music, which claimed the Lorin version, label credit was changed, first, to "Lorin-Jester Hairston" and eventually to Jester Hairston alone. All this explains why the chorus as sung by Harry is not the same as the chorus that appears in the printed copy.

Just about the time Harry was signing the BBC contracts for TV appearances, a British musical journal paid tribute to Harry's popularity in England. The headline set the frame:

"CAN BELAFONTE'S *MARY'S BOY CHILD* BECOME ANOTHER YULETIDE CLASSIC LIKE BING'S *WHITE CHRISTMAS?*"

[282]

It pointed out that in Christmas 1958, as in Christmas 1957, Harry's "enchantingly wistful" record of *Mary's Boy Child* was again headed for fantastic sales. Since in 1957 the disk had sold the "fastest-million" copies in the entire history of English record business, *The Melody Maker* found its renewed popularity in '58 difficult to understand.

"Based upon these figures," the paper observed with bewilderment, "it would appear that everyone in Britain possessing a record-player has a copy of Belafonte's *Mary's Boy Child*."

In the interview with Art Buchwald mentioned earlier, Harry had this to say of Little Rock—a subject that Europeans kept asking him about wherever he went. "I feel as an American and a Negro and an artist I have a great responsibility when I'm traveling abroad.

"When they ask me about Little Rock, I admit it's horrible and there is much to decry. But there's something wonderful about it, too. You can't view Little Rock as anything but a sign of progress.

"If the Supreme Court hadn't ordered integration, there would be no trouble in Little Rock. There would be no problem. But in the history of the world, there has never been progress without conflict.

"It would be wonderful if integration could take place without the need of troops. But if Justice with her smile can't enforce right, then Justice with her sword must do it."

STEREO

MAHALIA JACKSON

In 1959 Mahalia Jackson, the great gospel singer, toured the south, giving concerts from Virginia to Florida. Since her program consisted wholly of religious music, she took the position that it would be un-christian to sing to segregated audiences or to permit segregation in the halls where she sang. Neither the local authorities nor the white people who attended her concerts made an issue. In fact, many whites came backstage to praise Miss Jackson for her inspirational singing.

But to her dismay, as soon as she left the concert hall, she was faced with the same embarrassing and painful experiences as had been endured before her by Negro performers like Roy Eldridge, Duke Ellington, Billie Holiday, Harry Belafonte and others. Travelling in her car with her Negro accompanist and a young cousin who acted as her chauffeur, she found that restaurants along the highway would not serve them. Even at drive-ins, car-hops would ignore them as soon as they discovered that the occupants of the car were Negro. Gasoline stations would not permit them to use rest-room facilities and some declined to sell them gas and oil. In desperation, Miss Jackson and her associates bought bags of fruit and lived on these by day while they drove in fear through the night.

Nor did Chicago, where she had a very popular gospel program on TV, treat her with greater decency when she wanted to purchase a home in a quiet suburb. Accustomed to adulation from white people in her audiences, she was disturbed to find that they still would have none of her as a neigh-bor. Houses with "For Sale" prominently displayed on their lawns would invariably turn out just to have been sold. Other owners would decline to show their premises on the ground that they had changed their mind about selling.

When she finally found a surgeon who was willing to sell his home to her, serious trouble stared her in the face. She received threatening phone calls, warning her that the house would be blown up if she ever dared to move in. When she refused to back away and did move in, bullets were fired through her windows. For the better part of a year, police remained posted outside the house. As time went on, the white people around her began

[284]

putting up their homes for sale. Real estate agents quickly discovered that they could not find white buyers. Today, the entire suburb is colored as it once was white.

One of the reasons ostensibly given by the whites for moving out was that the Negroes would turn the neighborhood into a slum. But Mahalia points out that the lawns are well-kept and the children, mostly the sons and daughters of professional and business people, are as well-behaved as they ever were.

"On Sunday mornings," Mahalia has said, in a story by Evan McLeod Wylie in the *Saturday Evening Post,* "when I sit in my garden, it's so quiet all you hear is the birds singing. The same birds are in the trees. I guess it didn't occur to them to leave just because we moved in."

25. The Integrated Story

During the filming of *Odds Against Tomorrow,* Harry's first fully independent movie, released in the fall of '59, the company went on location at Hudson, New York. As a publicity stunt, the girls of nearby Vassar College were invited to watch the shooting of some of the scenes. At the outset, the trip apparently had the blessings of the Vassar public relations office. The day of the visit proved something of a disappointment. Weather conditions forced the company, which included movie star Robert Ryan and Ed Begley, to indoor shooting. A scene shot inside a bus barely accommodated the actors, camera, and lighting equipment. The girls had only a limited and distant view of movie making. Afterward, however, the *Odds Against Tomorrow* company played host to the co-eds at a light lunch. A special photographer shot candids of Harry and the girls, including a series of pictures in which the balladeer-actor made mock love to some of the co-eds.

"What a way to die!" Harry exclaimed, as he stood surrounded by a bevy of Vassar pretties.

When Gene Cook, former *Life* staffer and now a free-lance photographer, forwarded the candids to the Vassar public relations office, he was amazed to receive in reply an angry, threatening letter. Vassar did not want the photographs used anywhere in print.

Some days later Harry inquired of Gene about the pictures. Cook told Harry of the letter.

"Do you think it's the usual thing?" Harry asked.

Cook thought for a while. "It looks that way to me," he said. "I called the public relations office after I got the letter. They were very apologetic about it. Sorry they sent it. But apparently somebody in the higher administrative circles felt that Vassar and Belafonte didn't mix."

Harry was silent. A troubled look passed over his face, then gave way to a smile.

"The hell with Little Rock!" he exclaimed with animation. "Let's march on Vassar."

Harry's plan for moving into independent movie making took shape in the summer of 1957, after his domestic situation had been cleared up. In August of that year he formed Harbel Productions, a name concocted out of the first two syllables of his own name.

In a later press statement, Harry explained his move as follows: "I view the position of the Negro actor in the movies with a cautious eye. I don't want to be a spokesman for my race. I'm not prepared to take the world by the horns. I grew up without any idea of being a leader or a follower. But I do want to make pictures.

"It's kind of like Jackie Robinson. All he wanted to do was play ball for the Dodgers. When he did he became a symbol in the eyes of the nation. He had no choice. Circumstances forced it.

"I haven't wanted to become a symbol, but I have. And since I want to work, I at least want to do pictures I consider worth-while and the film industry is not really geared to . . . That's the reason for forming my own company."

The first production of Harbel was to be a film called *The Brothers,* an original screenplay by John O. Killens, a Negro writer. The following month Harbel made an alliance with veteran film producer Sol C. Siegel to shoot a picture then called *The End of the World* for Metro-Goldwyn-Mayer. Under a revised title, this became Harry's first independent starring production.

However, in October of '57, after his second eye operation and the birth of his first child with Julie, Harry announced a new distribution tie-up, this time with United Artists. Along with this announcement came tidings of two new film projects. One: a movie version of his own night club act. The second:

a bio of the Rev. Martin Luther King, Jr., the courageous Negro minister who became nationally known for his leadership of the Negro boycott of Alabama buses and who later made news when he was stabbed by a berserk woman in Harlem. It was indicated that United Artists had advanced Harbel the funds necessary for the research and writing.

Despite the several announcements and the ambitious plans, the year ended without Harbel going into production. Not until the spring of the following year, when Harry's doctors were successful in eliminating his eye troubles was he able to start moving. By April, the cameras were rolling on *The End of the World,* a gloomy title later lengthened to the more provocative *The World, The Flesh and The Devil.*

Starring Harry, Mel Ferrer, and Inger Stevens, the film was based on a strangely prophetic novel, *The Purple Cloud,* published in 1902. The particular cloud referred to was to become known to the world less for its color than its shape—that of a giant mushroom. It was, of course, the fearful cloud that fills the sky after an atomic explosion. *The World, The Flesh and The Devil* probes the consequence of such a disaster, not so much in terms of science fiction as of the social frictions that persist even in a decimated universe.

Harry plays one of three people, who are the sole survivors left in the world after an atomic holocaust. He is a Pennsylvania coal miner who finds his way out of a sealed shaft (which saved his life), apparently to find himself alone on the earth. In the eerie and completely deserted streets of New York, he encounters a second survivor, played by Inger Stevens, who escaped the bombs by being in a decompression chamber.

Even though they are the only two survivors in the entire world, the question of intermarriage ironically becomes an issue. As in *Island in the Sun,* they are kept apart largely by his fears that latent prejudice may rise to the surface and destroy their relationship. After a time, a third survivor appears—a white man played by Mel Ferrer—and the issue of mixed marriage is complicated by a love triangle.

Developed as a suspense melodrama, *The World, The Flesh*

[288]

and The Devil presents no easy solution to the problem of prejudice. Eventually the three reach a point of understanding that, to survive, they must function together. But the love triangle remains unresolved at the close of the film.

Released in April 1959, Harry's first independent production received mixed notices. Insofar as his own acting was concerned, the picture marked a rising improvement. Where *Island in the Sun* had netted him poor notices that criticized him as static and unconvincing, this film attracted favorable comment. *Variety* noted that he contributed "pace often by the subtle play of his moods alone." Hollis Alpert of *The Saturday Review*, who criticized the film's handling of the race problem, praised Harry for the versatility and persuasiveness of his work.

The first twenty minutes of the film, Alpert noted, "are the best . . . and Mr. Belafonte has a variety of reactions to show his mounting bewilderment, fear, and panic, along with an awesome sense of loneliness."

During the filming, writer-director Ranald MacDougall expressed amazement at Harry's ability to sense and project the emotional basis of any scene he played. MacDougall told reporters of how at one point the script required that Belafonte go into a wrecked church, sit down in a pew, and break into tears.

"I gave him no direction on this scene," MacDougall stated. "I simply told him that he was to go into the church and sink down into a pew. But, without any hint on my part, he broke spontaneously into tears. He really cried. Oh, God, how he cried."

MacDougall feels that the physical magnetism which has made Harry the star he is on a night club floor is now carrying over onto the screen. "People will recognize Harry," MacDougall said, "even when he's walking across an eighty-foot screen and looking about an inch and a half tall."

In addition to Harry's acting, the critics liked other things in *The World, The Flesh and The Devil*. They praised Ranald MacDougall's script and direction, Miklos Rosza's score, and the camera work of Harold J. Marzorati. All reviewers were enthralled by Marzorati's skill in projecting visually the eerie and terrifying sense of New York deserted.

It was on the racial issue—of such basic concern to Harry—that *The World, The Flesh and The Devil* came a critical cropper. Reactions varied from *Playboy*'s comment that the film was "over-preachy" to *The Saturday Review*'s assertion that it evaded the issue it had raised. To *The Review,* the ending was the stumblingblock—where the white man and the Negro, their differences over the girl settled "in some unexplained way," are last seen walking hand in hand with her down empty Rector Street.

"Are we to assume," *The Review* asks, "that some sort of polygamous arrangement has been worked out, or will the three henceforth lead entirely sexless lives, thus dooming both white and colored races to extinction? No answer being given, we must assume that the color issue was injected into the story more as a gimmick than out of real seriousness."

In October '59, just before the release of *Odds*, Harry gave a press party in England, where one British editor said: "Lots of us felt that your last film *The World, The Flesh and The Devil* failed because it shied away from the more delicate aspects of racial relations. Would you agree?"

Harry's reply—a strange one considering that he was a co-producer—was: "Not only do I agree, but I said as much to Sol Siegel while we were making the film. And the protests of Inger Stevens and Mel Ferrer were even stronger than mine. But it didn't do any good. They [*sic!*] had a wonderful basis for a film there, but it didn't happen."

Actually, the producer(s) of *The World, The Flesh and The Devil* could have ended the picture in one of three different ways. The girl could have favored the white man over the Negro, which would have pleased the segregationists and the white supremacists. She might have chosen the Negro over the white man, thereby cutting off a potential block of bookings and opening the film to boycotts, etc. As the film ended, the girl chose neither, and the viewer was left with a generalized concept concerning the need for all people, white and Negro, to work together.

When Harry made *Island in the Sun,* playing the lead opposite Joan Fontaine, he accused Hollywood of having a code that forbade intimacies, such as kissing, between mixed couples.

Since Harry and white actress Inger Stevens are in love in *The World, The Flesh and The Devil,* it is not irrelevant to ask: Do they kiss?

The answer is: They do not. Harry cuts her hair in one delicately humorous scene, he touches her chin affectionately in another, and as the picture closes, there is a close-up of his hand clasping hers.

Perhaps Harry Belafonte as co-producer would make the same comment as Darryl Zanuck, the producer of *Island in the Sun,* when he said: "There is no scene that calls for kissing. There was no conscious effort to avoid it."

Harry and Inger were just in love—and since when do lovers kiss?

Of course, it should be added that the various compromises and even such limited contact as the picture permits, did not prevent it from becoming controversial in the South—a showing was halted in Georgia—as well as among Northern audiences.

"Philosophically," Harry said in a recent radio interview, "we tried to point out that if man does not overcome inhumanity to man, the world will become a very lonely and a very tragic place in which to live."

Clearly, this is the point stressed in the very last frames of the movie when, as the three principals walk off hand in hand, the words that flash over them and grow in size on the screen are, not *"The End"* as in all movies, but *"THE BEGINNING."*

In *The World, The Flesh and The Devil* Harry sang a tender love ballad *Fifteen,* the work of Alan Greene, one of Harry's musical conductors, and Robert Nemeroff, a writer of the hit song *Cindy, Oh Cindy. Fifteen* may be heard in a recent Belafonte album called *Love Is a Gentle Thing.*

Recorded during January and May of '58, the album is

deeply expressive, even in its very title, of the inner Belafonte.

"Despite his outward air," Margurite Belafonte has said, "the inner core of Harry is soft, sensitive, and fragile. This was true even in the days when hostility was his most marked characteristic, in the days when he was outwardly defiant and at times belligerent. This man needed love like breathing things need air."

The truth is that in the range of Harry's recordings there are boisterous folk ballads, powerful songs of protest, angry blues, hilariously humorous calypsos. But the overwhelming number of songs recorded by Harry are tender and gentle and mournful and haunting love ballads.

Unsatisfactory though the ending may be to *The World, The Flesh and The Devil,* there can be little question regarding Harry's seriousness in using the film medium to contribute insight into the racial problem. From what he has said, as well as what he has done through Harbel Productions to date, there is every indication that his position as a Negro is central to his thinking concerning future productions.

In a press interview, Harry has stated that Harbel Productions would seek "to create avenues for Negro artists to perform and to function in their profession.

"I will go outside the United States to find subjects, if necessary. We'll make pictures, employing Negroes, and maybe about Negroes, but not necessarily in the context of race conflict.

"Producers in Hollywood today generally are reluctant to go into the area of the Negro without the race conflict theme. I plan to do the story of Pushkin, which has virtually nothing to do with the fact that he was a Negro. Nobody in Hollywood has as yet stepped out on what you might call an integrated story level."

Just before he began shooting his second independent film *Odds Against Tomorrow,* all these matters were aired on a TV discussion program in which his friend, actor Sidney Poitier, also participated. The program was David Susskind's *Open End* on WNTA-TV. There was no script, no story, no songs, and only incidental comedy. But the discussion proved so engrossing that it held an unbelievably large audience glued to their TV screens from 10:30 P.M. until 2:00 A.M. The four-cornered discussion, expertly moderated by Susskind, involved Shelley Winters (who was to co-star in *Odds*), her husband, actor Anthony Franciosa, Sidney Poitier (headed for Broadway stardom in *A Raisin in the Sun*), and Harry. It was largely the interplay between the two men whose lives have crossed and been paralleled in a number of ways, and their searching exploration of the problems of the Negro performer, that made the discussion stimulating and even stirring.

"This was Poitier's and Belafonte's show," wrote *Variety*. "Both are highly articulate men and under the expert prodding of Susskind, many of the things they said provided a fascinating insight into the contemporary problems of the Negro performer, conscious of his responsibilities to the audience generally and to the people of his race specifically."

At one point Poitier movingly echoed Harry's own statement about an integrated story line. "My dream," he said, "is to be able to function as an artist first. As things are now, I rarely can play the part of just a human being caught in conflict. There is great narrowness in our work."

While Harry was on location with *Odds Against Tomorrow*, Actors Equity put on a show provocatively called *The Integrated Showcase*. Its purpose was to demonstrate that Negro actors could be cast in white roles without altering the intent of the author or the integrity of the production.

In a review, *Variety* took a negative position, contending that this was impossible of achievement at the present stage of our social development. It felt that audiences can never forget that an actor on-stage is a Negro and therefore cannot be cast in a white part without distortion.

Comedian Orson Bean came forward with a vigorous letter of rebuttal. "I have seen Negroes in several productions," he wrote, "playing friends and even relatives of white characters, with no mention of color. For five minutes or so, I was aware that they were Negroes. But after that, the consciousness of

[293]

race difference diminished as the story became more interesting. Since no one on-stage paid any attention to it and since there was a plot to become involved in, I ceased to be aware of it.

"The reason the South is adamant," Bean added, "about even token integration of a single colored kid into a classroom is that they know that if no one else pays any attention to it, in about ten minutes the other kids in the class won't either."

Impelled to defend its position, *Variety* granted that such racial consciousness was unfortunate and undoubtedly diminishing. However, it argued that "so long as complete, free racial integration remains a social issue, with powerful emotional overtones, it was not likely that the average *theatregoer* could accept a Negro in a white role without irrelevant feelings intruding into playgoer's reactions.

"Hopefully, the day of integrated casting may come sooner," *Variety* wrote, "than now seems likely. Possibly the presentation of mixed cast shows such as *Integrated Showcase* may hasten the day, as did even the cautiously staged scenes between Paul Robeson and Uta Hagen in the Theatre Guild revival of *Othello* some years ago."

Singled out for mention of another mixed-cast production was *The Winner* of several seasons ago, in which author-director Elmer Rice used a Negro actor, Frederick O'Neal, as a Domestic Court judge adjudicating the divorce of a white couple. Also the recent musical *Jamaica,* in which Lena Horne and Ricardo Montalban "played fairly torrid love scenes together without precipitating a Dixieland filibuster in the United States Senate."

In September '59, at a drive-in theatre in Fayetteville, Georgia, a showing of *The World, The Flesh and The Devil* was halted abruptly when the sheriff's office warned the operator that trouble was brewing.

The film was being run in a theatre, with separate sections for Negro and white. About four to five hundred persons, mostly Negroes, were in attendance. According to the sheriff, a group of white persons became riled at the conduct of Negroes in the drive-in theatre.

What that conduct consisted of was not specified. Nor was there a report of specific misconduct on the part of anyone.

Sheriff Stinchcombe was able, after the abrupt stoppage of the showing, to assure the good white people of Fayetteville that the operator had agreed to spare them the provocation of any future running of the film.

STEREO

INTERRACIAL RECORDING DATES

"The appearance of a Negro musician with a white band," jazz critic Leonard Feather has observed, "even in the seclusion of a recording studio, was a rarity until as late as 1933, a commonplace among small jazz combos by 1937, still an exception among large studio orchestras through the 1940's. The participation of a white musician in a Negro record date was rarer."

After combing the archives of the thousands of jazz recordings made between 1917 and 1932, Feather could find only about a dozen instances of interracial recording dates

Today in 1960, by contrast, the interracial session is not an infrequent occurrence in the limited area of jazz as well as in the more general field of popular music. Largely as a result of the rise of rock 'n' roll, with its emphasis on the big beat, opportunities for Negro vocalists and musicians have grown by leaps and bounds.

How far integration has proceeded in the recording field is suggested by the make-up of the orchestra and staff at a recent Dinah Washington date. The choral group and string section were white while the four-man rhythm section was Negro. The engineer was white. But both the conductor of the orchestra and the A & R supervisor of the session were Negro.

Many sessions at Mercury Records have the same interracial composition. For the first time in the history of the business a Negro is at the helm of the pop A & R department of a major recording company.

[295]

26. No Private Mistakes

"He's got millions of admirers but only a handful of friends." That was one sentence of a notice in *The New York Journal-American* advertising a forthcoming Sunday article on Belafonte. "Famous writer Maurice Zolotow rips the mask off Harry Belafonte and candidly reveals the inside story of the singer's ingratitude to those who helped him get started . . . his behavior which shocked his own people . . . the ups and downs of his fabulous career and his mixed-up life and loves."

As surely as panegyric heralds the entertainer who is arriving, "the knock" is a sign of the entertainer who has arrived. It was not until May 1959 that Harry was treated to his first full-fledged going-over. Maurice Zolotow, who wielded the scalpel, is widely known for his acute pen portraits of entertainment personalities. His caustic piece appeared in *The American Weekly* on May 10.

Zolotow had many positive things to say about Harry. He described his "unique contribution" to the art of folk balladry as "the blending of the sex drive into it." He praised Harry for giving "himself up to his audience" as only two other performers have, Al Jolson and Judy Garland. He acknowledged that Harry was wonderful company, gay, witty, charming, and clever, a good storyteller and a good listener. He conceded that "whatever personal qualities of egocentricity and selfishness Belafonte has, he has always given generously of his time and talent to any charity, especially the NAACP." He granted that "when it seemed impossible, Harry had, by the sheer magic of his personality and his courage, overcome a classic combination of personal and professional disasters."

But Zolotow was not interested in praising Caesar. He was writing an exposé. He accused Harry of being the most ego-centric of entertainers, of thinking that he is the first star of his race, of being pretentious, of being basically insecure and alternating between states of high exhilaration and deep depression, of not being a "genuine folk singer," of callously firing the manager who helped him get started, of wanting to be white, and of divorcing the Negro wife who supported him through his early struggles in order to marry a white woman.

After he read the article, Jackie Robinson phoned Harry, who was then making his annual appearance at The Riviera in Las Vegas. Jackie wanted to express "my disgust over a hostile and unwarranted article."

Harry's comment over the long distance phone: "It's pretty cruel, isn't it, Jack?"

Four days later Jackie Robinson spoke out against the attack in his three-a-week column in *The New York Post*. He suggested that Zolotow's "snide and intemperate" remarks stemmed from Harry's refusal to permit him to write an article in Harry's name two years before.

Robinson raised two basic points. One was Zolotow's contention that Harry, not being a "pure Negro," could never identify himself with other Negroes.

Robinson questioned Zolotow's use of the term "pure Negro," pointing out that an anthropologist had recently found Negro ancestry is as high as 65 per cent of all so-called "white Americans." Conversely, as a result of the cruelties of slavery, white genes are to be found in many Negroes. However, he rejected the whole "blood" approach.

Robinson was more upset by Zolotow's charge that Harry "wants to be white." In rebuttal, he noted that Harry had participated in two Youth Marches for Integration to Washington; that he had spoken publicly and privately on behalf of Negro causes and benefits; and that he had taken "particular pains to make public at all times his identification with the NAACP." Since a great deal of Harry's song material "springs from Negro life and folklore, both here and in the West

Indies," Robinson felt that Harry "certainly picks a strange way of going about" his alleged desire to be white.

Robinson felt that any Negro who shows "the kind of militant, uncompromising attitude Harry does in basic human rights" lets himself in for charges such as those leveled against him.

"There are many prices a man pays for fame and fortune," Robinson concluded. "And I guess the jealousy and hostility of some people is one of them. But no matter what anyone says to me and millions of others, Harry Belafonte is not only one of the greatest artists in his field America has produced. He is also an intelligent, dedicated, and positive human being."

To Margurite Belafonte, Zolotow attributed the following statement: "I think that what Harry really wants is to be white. I think that is his real problem. I think that is why he is so unhappy. He's never been able to accept as an everyday fact that he is a Negro and always will be."

According to Margurite Belafonte, Zolotow misunderstood her. She did not say that Harry wanted "to be white" but that he wanted "to be accepted as white." There is more than a difference of wording here.

"What I am getting at," Margurite explains, "is the desire of most Negroes to be accepted *as Negroes* in a white world. You can hear Negroes telling their friends that they were at a dinner where there were more whites than Negroes, that they buy at a certain store which obviously caters to a white trade, that they stayed at a hotel whose name they emphasize because it is a white hotel.

"Harry does this thing in another way: by surrounding himself with white people. His secretary is white, his publicity man is white, his conductor is white, his psychoanalyst is white, his managers have always been white. So have his lawyers.

"I think this is strange considering that, when he was young and struggling, he constantly cried out against the lack of job opportunities for Negroes.

"Of course, someone might interpret his employment of

whites as a kind of Emperor Jones complex. Now that he has attained a position of wealth and power, he may enjoy having whites in subservient positions, in a position where they have to do his bidding and where he can throw them out if they don't. This may be a form of revenge for all the indignities and humiliations he has suffered.

"On the other hand, one might say that he surrounds himself with whites because he has achieved control of all his early hostilities. He is as much at ease among whites as he is among Negroes, and he selects people to employ purely on the basis of ability without regard to color.

"Whichever view one takes, my point is that Harry wants —not to be white—but to be accepted as white. He wants, as a Negro, to move without restriction and with ease in white circles. Once, exclusion from the white world angered him. Now, when it happens, it angers and surprises and baffles him. He cannot accept the fact that, despite his popularity and success and wealth, he is still not welcome everywhere, he is still not as free as white people are, and he is still not acceptable to all whites. With all his money, he couldn't rent an apartment on New York's East Side. That's what I meant when I said that he's never been able to accept as an everyday fact that he is a Negro and always will be."

Of his son David, born to him and his second wife, Harry has said: "He will have to have some of the experience I had as a Negro and that his mother had as a Jew. I don't necessarily want to save him from it."

Among those who do not question Harry's employment of white people is entertainer Eartha Kitt. She feels that it is a necessary phase of his—and any Negro's—effort to cope with a white world.

"When one country wants to do business with another, it chooses as representatives people who speak the language of the other country and appeal to folks in the other country.

"Most of the people with whom Harry must do business are white. All Negroes face a handicap in dealing with whites. Regardless of their competence, they tend to overplay or underplay their hands. In other words, this is not a question of giving employment to Negroes, nor of whether Harry is surrounded by whites."

One of Harry's associates favors a broader policy. "Competence, not color," he asserts, "should be the sole criterion. Harry should employ people without regard to racial considerations at all. He should get the best man for the job. To do anything else is to fall into one of two pitfalls. To hire Negroes because they're black, is to be guilty of chauvinism. To hire people because they're white, is the approach of the racist. Ability and talent should be the sole considerations in any employment policy. Harry's or anyone else's."

Considering the discrimination practiced even today against Negroes and the difficulties Negroes still encounter in finding jobs, this approach impresses another associate of Harry's as being rather removed from the realities of the moment. "If there are two equally competent men available for a given job," this associate states, "the Negro should be favored."

While Harry has himself not enunciated any general employment policy, he has made it amply clear that he plans, through his movie production company, to give employment to Negro actors and talented Negroes in the allied creative fields of writing, designing, etc. Among Negroes retained by Harry are Ike Jones, until recently a key executive in his film-producing company, and Charles Colman, production stage manager of *Belafonte at the Palace,* whose association with Harry dates back to pre-Sage days.

Concerning Harry's activities in behalf of his people, Margurite recently said: "Years ago, when Harry was scrawling derisive comments on subway posters, he was full of an undirected kind of hostility. Because he was so frustrated, there was a danger, as with those who become delinquents, that he would strike out against anything and anybody. I used to hope for the day when he would be strong enough and important enough to be heard.

"Now that he's in such a position, I'm a little disappointed that he doesn't give out with some of the hostility he exhibited in days back. Although he occasionally participates in NAACP activities, he's not a member and he refuses to join.

"I will say that it was my relationship with him that ultimately led me to involve myself, as I have been doing recently, in the work of the NAACP. I feel that this is the organization that is making strides in improving the position of the Negro in America. Certainly, somebody's got to do the work.

"Of the degree to which Harry is actively contributing, I have not heard much.

"And so I'm devoting myself to what I fear he's no longer doing."

In February, three months before the Zolotow analysis appeared, *Variety* reported:

BELAFONTE FOUNDATION
HELPS SNUBBED TEXAN

The accompanying story told of how Barbara Smith, a Negro student, had been booted in 1957 from the lead role in a University of Texas production of the opera *Dido and Aeneas* when East Texas legislators had complained to university officials. At the time, Harry had sent a sympathetic wire advising her that there were "people in her corner."

Now, in February '59, Barbara Smith, a candidate for Bachelor of Music in voice, was leaving the university to study drama, dance, languages, and voice at the studio of the Metropolitan Opera's Maestro Danise.

Funds for her living expenses were being solicited by the campus Baptist Church, one of the first to integrate in the South some ten years earlier. Her tuition was being paid by the Belafonte Foundation, which had also provided a scholarship in dancing at the Phillips-Fort Studio where Julie Belafonte had taught prior to her marriage to Harry.

Harry's favorite show place, The Greek Theatre, was only one of many where he was able to demonstrate in the summer of '59 that his power to draw crowds was undiminished—in fact, was at an all-time peak point. While Harry was appearing at the 4,000 seater, Judy Garland held forth at the neighboring Shrine Auditorium. Pictures of such extreme contrast were provided by the respective attendance records that *Variety* felt impelled to comment: "Miss Garland at the Shrine grossed a losing $43,000 for five performances. On the other hand, Belafonte finished a three-weeker at the Greek Theatre with a mighty $252,000.

Thereafter, at the Red Rocks Theatre in Denver (12,500 capacity), at the Forum in Vancouver (6,000), and elsewhere, Harry toppled long-standing attendance records. In *Variety*ese, "Belafonte Hits Smash Takes in Western Tour."

Equally stimulating—and, in some ways, more satisfying—was *Variety*'s observation that Harry's performance showed unmistakable growth. The review of his appearance at Balboa Park Bowl in San Diego bulged with phrases such as, "he matures in concept and style," his approach is "increasingly subtle," his manner "more compact and restrained." The critique concluded: "If there's been a noticeable diminution of external fire, there is deeper emotion expressed along with a more complete absorption into mood and character. With this subtlety has come, moreover, a more intense warmth."

While Harry was playing The Greek Theatre, he arranged for daughters Adrienne and Shari to come out to California for a visit with him. The children were then enjoying the summer at Sag Harbor with their mother but were anxious to see their father too.

When Margurite was getting the children ready for the trip, Adrienne, the older girl, exclaimed: "You and Daddy must think we're doll babies to play with. You play with us for a while. Then Daddy has us to play with for a while. We're just doll babies."

In March '59 The Friars gave a testimonial dinner to TV celebrity Steve Allen. Harry was invited to sit on the dais. What contributed an unexpected bit of hilarity, if not electricity, was that Belgian actress Monique Van Vooren sat one chair away, separated from Harry only by the slender, tender figure of dead-pan comedian Joey Bishop. That same week a letter had appeared in *Time* Magazine from Van Vooren asking whether the tape machine described in the cover story on Belafonte was the machine she had lent him in 1954 when he was too poor to purchase one. An editor's note said that Belafonte denied ever borrowing the machine. A rebuttal note by the Belgian Bulge said that he had "borrowed" it from her and that she would like it returned, even if it was five years late.

Harry's volatile temper is widely known among his friends and a matter of uneasiness among his associates. That it had not yet come fully under control as recently as the summer of '59 was evident during his appearance in August at The Carter Barron Amphitheatre in Washington, D.C.

During the show, a free-lance photographer went about snapping pictures. Invited to meet Harry in his dressing room, Al Muto went backstage in pleased anticipation. Once there, he suddenly found himself confronted by an angry Belafonte who grabbed his camera and tore out the film on which he had just been shooting. A heated argument ensued.

According to *Jet*, it terminated when Harry voluntarily paid 250 dollars for possible damage to the camera and, after mutual apologies, invited the bewildered photographer to return and take pictures any time he wishes.

On August 23, despite his heavy ten-week schedule of concerts, Harry took time out to appear on an NBC-TV panel program "Youth Wants to Know." A mixed panel of students from Washington, D.C., where the program originated, peppered Harry with questions ranging from rock 'n' roll to racial discrimination. Reviewers found his answers "refreshingly frank."

Harry had previously attacked rock 'n' roll. "Certain people have found that there's tremendous profits," he said, "to be made with this musical rot, and have therefore taken steps to force it on the American public."

[303]

One of the girls on the panel pointed out that the vogue of rock 'n' roll went beyond the confines of the United States, and that its popularity in sections of Europe indicated that it had a more universal appeal.

It was a difficult position to combat, and Harry agreed in part. But still, adhering to his concept of enforced acceptance, he added: "If America had a more worth-while musical form that was popular with young Americans, then it, too, would find great favor in London, Paris, Vienna, Berlin, etc. The structure of rock 'n' roll is moronic and sending abroad this kind of musical trash isn't the best way of putting our best foot forward in cultural exchanges with European countries."

"He had obviously failed to cope with the all-important question," a trade paper editor observed, "as to why what he called 'musical trash' was popular with young Americans. As one who had once created an international vogue for calypso material, he surely must have known that just as people didn't buy calypso until it filled some musical need, so he was unable to sustain the vogue beyond a certain point.

"What is, perhaps, even more surprising," the editor added, "is his cavalier dismissal of the entire structure of rock 'n' roll as 'moronic.' He has himself put out an album of songs in which he imitates the great, blind rock 'n' roll singer Ray Charles. In fact, he sings some of Ray's rock 'n' roll songs. That should have been enough to warn him against a wholesale rejection of what is, in fact, the musical language of the teen-age generation. Even more inexplicable is Harry's disregard of the two folk traditions—country and blues—out of which rock 'n' roll has evolved and the degree to which rock 'n' roll represents a white man's aceptance of a musical language once enjoying a limited and restricted vogue among Negroes.

"How Harry reconciles his attack on rock 'n' roll with an earlier statement that regeneration of the arts would come as the contribution of the Negro is brought more and more into the different arts is difficult to surmise. There can be little question that the rise of rock 'n' roll has advanced the careers, and is due to the creative efforts, of a large number of new

[304]

Negro recording artists, new Negro writers, new Negro musicians and arrangers."

"Not even the presence of a small, rarely used orchestra," wrote *The New York Herald Tribune*, "or the intrusion of some garish lighting were able to deflect the instant rapport that Mr. Belafonte is able to effect between himself and an audience."

The particular audience to which *The Trib* was referring was not in a night club, not in a theatre, or in a swank hotel. It was at New York's stately Carnegie Hall. Harry had appeared there once, just at the start of his career in 1949, and, while he had sung, he was just one of a group of artists who had received awards from a Negro newspaper. For his "second" appearance at Carnegie, on April 19 and 20, 1959, Harry gave a one-man show.

Both concerts were benefit performances, the former in behalf of the Lincoln School (attended by Adrienne and Shari), the latter in behalf of the Wiltwyck School (which works with emotionally disturbed boys). Belafonte's balladry contributed $58,000 to the Wiltwyck School alone. The program was the same for both evenings. But seldom have packed houses responded more affectionately and enthusiastically to Harry's spontaneous sorcery.

While the orchestra under the direction of Robert Corman played the overture, Harry stood at the huge curtain with an old friend, Buddy Phillips, the dancer and co-director of the Phillips-Fort dance studios. As he stared out of a peephole at the huge audience, tears suddenly welled up in Harry's eyes. At first Buddy pretended not to notice. But as the trickle of liquid down Harry's bronze cheeks increased, Phillips, without knowing why, found himself crying along with Harry. At that moment Phil Stein, Belafonte's chief of staff, came by. Stein began asking a question, noticed the silent play of lachrymose feeling, and cut his query as Harry embraced him spontaneously, still crying uncontrollably.

Of Frank Sinatra, a friend has said: "Even when he's with

several people, he occasionally breaks into tears. It's hard to tell what will set him off—a song he's listening to, the memory of some unhappy experience, or just the violent emotional pressures within him."

Appearing in his traditional V-cut silk shirt and tight black pants, Harry divided his Carnegie Hall programs into three parts: Act I. *Moods of the American Negro,* Act II. *In the Caribbean,* and Act III. *Around the World.*

Of the six folk ballads describing American Negro moods, four were work, chain gang, and protest songs. After *Darlin' Cora* came *Sylvie,* the Leadbelly favorite, with its contrasting dynamics, *Cotton Fields,* a more recent addition to the Belafonte repertory, and *John Henry,* with its chugging train-rhythm accompaniment. A spiritual, *Take My Mother Home,* offered a change of pace. Then Harry came to the high point of this portion of the program: *The Marching Saints,* which, like *Take My Mother Home,* goes back to *Three for Tonight.*

"In American folklore, we find a great deal of the European," Harry said, "and ofttimes I've wondered what would happen if songs which are truly indigenous to America had, in fact, gotten their start somewhere else.

"To illustrate the point, we've chosen *When the Saints Go Marching In.* Now, if this had originated in England, it could have sounded like an old English madrigal."

Harry began: "Oh, when the saints . . ."

And the orchestra, under Robert Corman, came in behind him with a typical madrigal arrangement.

Harry added the "tra-le-la-la-la-lis" and exaggerated the "nuh-huh-uh-huh-umbers"—and ended with an appropriate "Good show!" which brought a roar from the audience.

"But *The Saints* wasn't meant to be a madrigal," he said, when the applause died down. "It was meant to be exactly what it was, a historical opportunity for a group of Negro musicians down in New Orleans to play and to celebrate on some festive occasion.

"And at the time that this song came about, what could

[306]

have been more festive, during that period, than a funeral!"
The guitarists punctuated the word.

As he picked up the opening words, "Oh, when the saints . . .," bassist Norman Keenan, who has been with Harry for years, came walking in behind him. The rest of the rhythm section followed. Then came the chorus and the handclapping —for a rousing rendition of a great New Orleans standard.

In the middle of the Caribbean group of numbers, Harry worked himself into a slight impasse. This proved a spontaneous test of his showmanship. He had opened the group with the now-famous *Day-O*, which had brought the house down, after which he had sung the beautiful and tender *Jamaica Farewell* of Lord Burgess. Then he started to introduce his third number, the charming calypso novelty *Man Piaba*.

"As a small boy," he said, "I spent many, many years down in the West Indies . . ."

He paused and thought for a moment. "I already said that." The audience laughed. He had said exactly that in introducing *Jamaica Farewell.*

"Well, I'll tell ya, ah . . ." he tried. Then, he half cackled to himself. The audience began laughing, and broke into spontaneous applause.

"I wasn't always a small boy in the West Indies," he said. And this time, the audience laughed with him.

"I was a small boy in New York City first. But my parents are from the West Indies. And they wanted to go back to pay a visit.

"At the age of seven, it is very difficult to exert your individuality. No one ever wants your opinion about anything, on any subject, at any time—about NUTTIN'!"

The audience roared.

"Consequently," he continued, "I went to the West Indies." The audience chuckled. "My father was a seaman. He used to go drifting every now and then." Harry laughed huskily. "As a matter of fact, we used to call him Old Drifter."

The audience chuckled.

"And I'll never forget one day down there in sunny Jamaica. Old Drifter and I were drifting along the beach together. And I turned to him and I said." Harry paused deliberately.

"Father," Harry laughed dryly. "I always called him father." The audience laughed.

"Father. Tell me the story about man and wo-man, man to man." Harry chuckled audibly. "I was seven."

The audience chuckled.

"He got that glazed look over his eyes and I realized then and there—I had to rephrase the question."

Laughter ran through the audience.

"So I turned back to him and I said. 'Fa-Father.' " More laughter. "Same feller." The audience roared. "Tell me the story of the birds and the beeze—if you pleeze."

As he chuckled, the audience topped him. The guitarists punctuated the laughter and Harry was into the number.

After *Man Piaba,* Harry sang the West Indian lullaby *Hush, Little Baby,* his hit song *Mama, Look A Boo Boo,* the tender *Come Back Liza,* and closed this segment with the calypso novelty *Man Smart.*

In the concluding group of songs Harry displayed his versatility in handling the folk tunes of several lands in their native tongues. He sang in Hebrew (*Hava Nageela*), in the French patois dialect of Haiti (*Merci Bon Dieu*) and in Spanish (*Cu Cu Ru Cu Cu Paloma*).

The climax of the enthralling evening came with the final selection—the inescapable *Matilda,* where Harry evinced his remarkable ability to mesmerize an audience and make it do his bidding. Although it seems inconceivable, Harry took a traditionally difficult "benefit" crowd and had it singing as if they sat around a campfire.

It was a well-planned attack in which Harry started with his own musicians and chorus—and slowly worked around and out to the audience. First it was "just the trio," then Danny, the conga player, then the group, then one section, then another section.

When Harry got to "de conductor," Robert Corman, he

began improvising. With a whistle, as if he were summoning a cab on a street, he stopped the band.

"Good heavens, Bob," he said, in his best Oxonian accent, "we've been together a good long time, man! You can't do that! You must learn! You can't turn your back on the masses, man! Turn about! Face them!"

Carnegie rocked with applause as Corman turned his balding head to them.

"Splendid! Now, sing! *One,* two, three, four!"

Corman got a round of applause for his off-key rendition.

Then Harry brought a rush of laughter, as he called: "Now, the whole mah-shpooch-a now!" (A Yiddish word meaning family.)

After several choruses, Harry swung off-stage and asked for:

"Just the audience!"

The response was mild.

"A little louder," Harry called. As a few more added their voices, he announced: "Ah, it's delicious!"

Now Harry sang some of the verses himself and urged his listeners to come in for each of the choruses. The audience was responding without realizing it.

"All de big spenders" got a big laugh and applause. Then Harry called, "The whole ground floor!" Now the audience was beginning to respond with enthusiasm. "People in the tiers now!" The magic had worked.

When he called "Those people on scholarship!" laughter and applause burst spontaneously from the audience.

Again Harry whistled as if he were hailing a cab. When the orchestra cut, Harry said, "Bob, how many times have I asked you not to do that?" The chiding tone was bathed in Oxonian accents. "You must wait for the masses, man!" He waited for the laughter to subside. "Scholarship section, bless you. Now, you wait for those people because if you don't, and they catch up with you, they'll trample you to death." Laughter. "Group, fear not! Big Brother is watching! Altogether now, scholarship section after four. *One,* two, three, four!"

"Mah-til-da! Mah-til-da!"

"And there they are," Harry announced. The rest of the audience applauded as the scholarship section sang through the chorus, the orchestra finishing before it.

"There's quite a lag, isn't there?" he called. He pointed to his orchestra conductor. "Well, you don't play."

And the scholarship group sang the chorus without orchestral accompaniment.

After two choruses, Harry called: "Women over forty!" There was laughter, but no singing as the orchestra played on. Harry waited. Then he whistled for quiet.

"I know they're out there," he urged. "Let's take another try at it, chaps! Now, women over forty!"

And a small group of voices could be heard through the hall.

Harry came in with another verse. He sang a chorus. He asked for everybody "to seeng ah leetle softer." They did. Then, louder. They did.

The orchestra came in with a loud terminal countermelody. Harry's voice rose to a high crescendo. After almost fifteen minutes, *Matilda* was over. And so was a triumphant concert.

Then the audience sat, stood, whistled, applauded, shouted, roared for more. Harry had to beg off, again and again and again—as one may hear in the entertaining "on the spot" recording that RCA Victor made of the entire concert.

As he walked off-stage, Harry was met by Mrs. Franklin Delano Roosevelt, a trustee of The Wiltwyck School, who embraced and kissed him.

STEREO

FATS WALLER

The frustrations of the Negro musician aspiring in the 20's and 30's to a concert career were never more poignantly portrayed than in the personality, the popularity, and the abortive death of Thomas (Fats) Waller.

An irresistible clown, a fine composer of pop standards like *Ain't Misbehavin'*, *Squeeze Me*, and *Honeysuckle Rose*, a jazz pianist whose mighty left hand made him a leading exponent of stride style, Fats Waller wanted nothing in life so much as to be a fine classical organist. After Lincoln and FDR, Fats' great hero was Johann Sebastian Bach.

Friends tell of how, on a visit to Paris in the early 30's, he climbed to the organ loft of the great Cathedral of Notre Dame with Marcel Dupré, the Cathedral's organist. There, as Fats always proudly told it: "First Mr. Dupré played the God-box and then I played the God-box."

A member of the musical staff of WLW in Cincinnati (also in the 30's), Fats had an extremely popular program known as "Fats Waller's Rhythm Club." Several hours later the station presented a program of organ music to bring the day to a peaceful close. The name of the organist was never announced. And few people knew that the inspired organist was the ebullient clown who played bouncy jazz piano earlier in the evening.

Unreleased up to the present—and perhaps never to be released—is a series of classical organ pieces, including two Bach fugues, which Fats recorded one day in the late 20's in the Camden studios of RCA Victor. What necromancy he used on the record company executives to achieve this afternoon of ecstasy is difficult to know.

"Both Fats Waller and his principal tutor, James P. Johnson," according to jazz critic John S. Wilson, "lived lives of aching frustration. Johnson ached openly because he could find no audience for his serious compositions, but Waller's desire to find acceptance as a serious musician was buried under a heavy coating of pervasive geniality. And while Johnson plodded steadily downhill in puzzled despair, Waller's blithely ironical attitude carried him up and up in the material world—eventually to a level that even his enormous energy could not cope with."

Fats weighed almost three hundred pounds and he could not stay away from the bottle, despite repeated medical warnings, when a conductor on an eastbound train tried to rouse him from what looked like a deep sleep but seemed more like a "feel-no-pain" stupor. Examination by a physician as the train lay outside Kansas City revealed that it was neither. Fats, who had been partying until the last moment in L.A., was dead of pneumonia. He was only thirty-nine.

27. Odds Against Tomorrow

As Harry stepped briskly through the door of the Mayfair Hotel in London—and walked energetically into the second decade of his amazing career—he began whistling a happy tune. On September 20 he was to appear over the BBC in his annual one-man telecast, and later that week, on September 24, he was giving a party in his $150 a day suite to celebrate the second birthday of his son David.

September was not really the calendar beginning of his second decade as a showman. His first professional booking, as a jazz singer at The Royal Roost on Broadway—had begun in January 1949. But jazz singing, like pop singing and even folk singing, had all been second choices, sublimated outlets for an unfulfilled yearning to be an actor. October 1959, however, would bring the world *première* of *Odds Against Tomorrow,* the first of six films in which he was both to star and serve as a fully independent United Artists producer.

An old American friend, Pete Kameron, music publisher and artist manager, was waiting to walk with Harry into the second decade of his career. Pete had been closely associated with Harry in the early days of the *Mark Twain* record album. Their friendship had never attained the intensity of most of Harry's business relationships, nor had it terminated, as most of the intense affairs did, in an overnight, and sometimes bitter, fold.

Yet Harry had a feeling for Pete, which made him, on those comparatively rare moments when their paths crossed, use Pete as a sounding board, if not in a confessional capacity. And they remained friends without being friends. In some strange way, their relationship had started out on a plane where Pete, short and stubby and owl-eyed, had assumed a critical role. Once Harry had introduced Pete to Eddie Fisher and Debbie Reynolds, backstage at a performance of *Three for Tonight,* as "my conscience." That's what Pete had remained. Of all Harry's show-biz friends, he was, perhaps, the only one who needled Harry instead of being needled by him.

"As we walked together through the streets of London," Pete reports, "Harry enjoyed the feeling of being recognized and gawked at. He got a genuine kick out of being part of humanity's main stream, a known and celebrated figure rather than another ripple in the current.

"But he also had not lost the curiosity and animation and the excitement of being alive that were always so much a part of him. At one point, we passed a gathering mob. Harry chased across the street like a kid dashing after fire engines. He had to find out what it was all about. If something interesting was happening, he wanted to know what it was. He still has not lost that youthful urge to be part of everything.

"I was impressed by his youth, but also by his maturity. Once he had been tense—like a crackling wire that could burst into flame without warning. Like a sleeping lion whose hostility could erupt in an instant. Now he seemed relaxed. He spoke of his plans—they were no longer dreams—with clarity and confidence. He was always an impatient, restless man with an almost frantic need for motion. Now he could channel that vitality and nervous energy into specific projects. He seemed to have a million of them going. But he was not vague or dilettante about any of them.

"But he also talked of his responsibilities as a Negro. He's no longer the angry man he once was. But I believe that he's no less conscious of the contribution he should make in the continuing struggle for equal rights. He was very much concerned about the most effective way the medium of the screen could be used in this work.

"Anyone who knew Harry in his early days became immediately aware of the great, overwhelming need he had for love. That's why he tended to convert most of his associations with managers, with conductors, with anybody, into love affairs. But he could not give love.

"I always remember a scene from a play in which a character embraces a badly wounded buddy on a battlefield. Momentarily, he loves and he wants his hurt friend to know that he loves. But in almost the same instant, he pushes the wounded man away. Love carries obligations, responsibilities.

"Harry was that way. He wanted love badly but was afraid to give it. Walking with him through London, I had the feeling that he's met this problem and licked it. In two ways. He's happy in his new marriage; he loves and he feels loved. And he does not want any marriages in his business dealings any more.

"I think he has grown tremendously," Pete Kameron said, "as an artist—yes—but even more as a man. I hadn't seen him for some time and I was impressed."

Chicago was the first stop in Harry's barnstorming tour of the cities premiering *Odds Against Tomorrow*. *The Chicago Daily News* was unstinting in its praise: "Director Robert Wise's recent award-winning *I Want to Live* was romantic fantasy compared with the pain and shock of *Odds* . . . It's incredibly sharp from every point of production and dramatically explosive . . ."

"It's an angry picture," critic Sam Lessner wrote. "Too angry, I feel."

Harry's response was: "It had to be said with crashing force. Cheer up, Sammy. There's a brighter day coming. I hope to play a Cary Grant type of role soon."

Belafonte was reiterating something which he had first said in an AP interview in September, just before sailing for Europe. Then he had told reporters that there had been too many heavy pictures showing the Negro in conflict with the white world.

"I'd like to do something light and frothy," he had said, "a Cary Grant type of picture."

And he had added: "It seems to me audiences would welcome a Negro in an easygoing, delicious, humorous story. I'm not talking about the Amos and Andy kind of thing, but something more sophisticated. About an average guy with an average job in an average situation, but one filled with humor.

"I think it would be just as commercial, and contribute just as much to social advancement for the Negro to be seen in light and pleasant roles for a change. After all, in other countries, the Negro isn't restricted to dramas about racial conflict."

Three days after the Chicago *première*, *Odds* bowed in New York at Broadway's Victoria Theatre. Most reactions were favorable, if not enthusiastic. *The New Yorker*, mainly a minority of one, felt that *The Defiant Ones*, concerned with an analogous situation, had more "bite." *Newsweek*, however, praised the photography as "sharp and stark," the dialogue as "natural and pungent," and the message—that racial hatred leads to disaster—as effectively unobtrusive in relation to the plot. *The Herald Tribune* saluted Robert Wise's direction for its "sensitivity to details of psychology, atmosphere and characterization," but felt that the film lost its momentum, after building unbelievable tension, because it failed to decide whether it was a message movie or a crime melodrama. *Variety's* capsule comment: "Good names, good pic, good b.o."

What no critic apparently bothered to do was to compare the original novel by William P. McGivern with the screenplay by John O. Killens and Nelson Redding. The fact is that both story and characters underwent changes that are quite interesting.

One of the major shifts is the treatment of Earl Slater, the Negro-hater. In the movie he is a static character, who starts out full of malice and is destroyed in an unabating blaze of hate. In the book, however, the author is concerned with Slater's psychological development and regeneration. As the story unfolds in print, Slater find his deep-seated prejudices being dissipated, almost against his will, by sacrifices which his Negro accomplice makes for him. At the end, although he is persuaded by his selfish girl friend to desert the Negro, he ultimately returns to rescue him and thereby loses his life. The Negro is the only one of the three bank desperadoes who is captured alive as the novel ends, with the sheriff admiring and not quite understanding Slater's change of heart and sacrifice.

In the film there is no more change in the Negro than in Slater. Tension develops not only around the holdup that is being planned but as the result of the potentially explosive situation between the two. The Negro is as uncompromising in his hostility as his white taunter. Proudly standing his ground, he is driven finally to shoot it out with Slater. The violent destruction of both underscores the point: We face long odds against tomorrow coming at all unless we develop some understanding and tolerance today.

In contrast with the book, the movie more fully explores the background and motivations of the Negro as played by Harry. It shows us more of his tender relationship to his daughter and his frustrated relationship with his wife, whose "ofay" friends he deeply resents. But in giving up the delineation of Slater's development, the film loses something for which the emphasis on destructive consequences does not compensate. As a crime thriller, the novel comes off better, too, for it builds tension after the robbery as well as before, whereas the film comes to an unsatisfying and abrupt dead end.

What is, perhaps, most interesting is that the alterations in character and plot provide a role for Harry, whose emotional make-up closely resembles that of his own youthful personality. The Negro that bullets from the screen is a young Belafonte—proud, belligerent, defiant, unyielding, and attractively hostile.

"When Harry first began singing folk songs," novelist Bill Attaway has said, "he had this tremendous feeling of protest. It was something an audience sensed the moment he came on-stage. He was the visual embodiment of Poe's dramatic statement: 'Endure? no—no—defy!' I don't know any performer who was so magnificent in his anger."

But among many of Harry's friends of the early days, there is a feeling that he is no longer concerned about the things that once irked him. Old friends of The Vanguard and Blue Angel period who have gone to see Harry at The Waldorf are amazed at his unbelievable, almost magical, control of the chi-chi crowds.

"But the funny thing," they say, "is that Harry isn't angry

any more. It's the strangest thing when you've known Harry as we did to see a Belafonte that's not bristling with anger. People like him now for something else—sex, good looks, charm, personal magnetism, infectious humor, tenderness, and, perhaps, a tease of hostility. But Harry just isn't angry any more. He just isn't."

And somebody in the old crowd quips: "What's Harry got to be angry about now?"

Unquestionably, from a personal standpoint, Harry has little or nothing to be angry about today. But in basic theme, in the presentation of an integrated PTA meeting, and in other more subtle ways, *Odds Against Tomorrow* suggests that Harry is still philosophically and socially angry about the position of the Negro in the world of today.

That he is still very conscious of his Negro heritage and much concerned over the problems of the Negro artist seems clear. Both of his independent movie productions pivotted on Negro-white relationships and presented Negro characters with fresh insight. On his December TV spectacular, he not only provided the first nationwide showcase for Negro folk singer Odetta, but he used wonderful drawings by Negro painter Charles White to shift from scene to scene. Just about the same time, he introduced at The Village Vanguard a new South African jazz singer, Miriam Makeba, whom he had discovered through a film and whose talent he had brought to the notice of Vanguard owner Max Gordon.

As Harry traveled from city to city, he was not happy with the critical reaction to the film. There was praise for many things in it, but no real over-all enthusiasm. Nor were there any signs that *Odds* might turn into a howling box-office success. Yet his barnstorming tour brought a feeling of deep satisfaction, if not elation.

It stemmed from the reaction of the critics to his own work as an actor. "*Odds* would lose some of its richer effects," *The Herald Tribune* wrote, "if the Belafonte sequences were deleted. Not only does he give a good performance, but the scenes with his estranged wife and young daughter are among the film's more touching incidents."

"It's the most sustained acting Belafonte has done," *Variety* said.

"Belafonte has achieved dramatic maturity," wrote *The Chicago Daily News*, "with this bristling role. He is an imaginative and commanding young actor."

It had taken ten years. In 1949 a frustrated and hostile Belafonte, just out of drama school, had wandered the side streets of Broadway, discovering the bitter truth that there was little or no call for the services of a young Negro actor. Now, after ten years of success with a sister art, he was to be able to embark full sail on the journey that had first attracted his creative interest. Now, after serving an apprenticeship in four earlier motion pictures, he had achieved a recognizable maturity as an actor.

While Harry was barnstorming major cities for the première of *Odds,* the first play in which he was participating as a producer opened on Broadway.

His association with *Moonbirds,* starring wraithlike comedian Wally Cox, had been greeted on the drama page of *The New York Times* with a story headed: "Belafonte Turns Dream to Reality." He had become involved in the project while filming *Odds.* A discussion with Leo Kerz, who was art designer for the film, had caused Harry to join Kerz and George Justin in the sponsorship of the well-known Marcel Aymé comedy.

The play, widely admired in France, dealt with a young professor who found himself possessed of the power to turn humans into birds. He did this whenever he found people in pain or trouble. But the exercise of this facility, motivated by humanitarian impulses, involved him in difficulties with the authorities.

In announcing sponsorship of *Moonbirds,* Harry asserted that "prohibitive production costs" were one of the major weaknesses of the Broadway theatre. "Creative abilities have

[318]

been stifled and suppressed," he contended. "Because of the tremendous investment required, producers shun works of artistic merit for the potential commercial success."

Despite its artistic merit, *Moonbirds* unfortunately was not a commercial success. Adverse critical reaction caused its closing after only three nights.

Nor did *Odds* show any signs of being a box-office grosser during its *première* playdates. For Harry, both as an actor and independent producer, a b.o. hit was for the future.

The first Sunday after Harry had breezed through six cities and an unremembered number of press parties for *Odds Against Tomorow*, he headed his new blue Mercedes-Benz toward his old home in East Elmhurst. The car was crammed with gifts—kilts from Scotland were the major item—for Adrienne and Shari.

After the effusive and excited and affectionate greetings were over—"You're a kissing bug, Daddy!" exclaimed Shari; older daughter Adrienne, now ten, shoved a leadsheet into Harry's hands.

"I'm going to record this," she chirped, "and it'll be a big hit."

Harry pretended to examine the leadsheet. Then his pretense gave way to irritation.

"Where'd this come from?" he demanded. The question was addressed, not to Adrienne, but to her mother.

"The postman brought it," Adrienne announced.

Harry took a deep breath and expelled it angrily. "How can you permit the children to be exposed to something like this?" he demanded of Margurite.

The song was a saccharine ditty in which a little girl told Santa to forget about all the gifts she had requested if only he would bring her daddy home for Christmas.

"What makes you think I *permit* things like this?" Margurite asked.

"How else would Adrienne get this?"

"The truth is," Margurite replied, "the postman brought it

[319]

yesterday while I was out shopping. He's an amateur song-writer who's always showing me songs. He seems to think that I have some special connections in the music field. This time he tackled Adrienne while I was out."

Harry shook his head in disbelief.

"He said it would be a big hit," Adrienne exclaimed, "if I recorded it. Don't you think I could record it, Daddy?"

Harry looked nonplused. "I'm afraid, darling," he said, with tenderness, "that it's too late this year. All the record companies have finished recording their Christmas songs."

Adrienne looked crestfallen, and Harry tried to share her suffering.

"There ought to be a way of protecting children—" Harry began.

It was Margurite's turn. "And what makes you think that this is the worst kind of thing they're subjected to? You know about this. But what about all the things that happen that you don't know about? You're not around that often."

"Like what?" Harry asked.

"Like what happened when I brought Shari to school the first day."

Shari, just turned five, had begun pre-school classes.

"Tell me," Harry said with concern.

"A student teacher is in charge of her class. She was calling the roll the first day and after she called Shari's name, she went on to the name of the next kid in the alphabet. Then, she paused, did a double-take, and went back.

" 'You're not Harry Belafonte's daughter?' she exclaimed. 'Or are you?'

"Shari barely nodded.

" 'Really?' she exclaimed. 'It doesn't seem possible! Harry Belafonte's daughter! And does he bring you to school?'

" 'Now, is that necessary?' Shari asked.

"The teacher became flustered at Shari's coolness," Margurite explained.

" 'I'm sorry,' the teacher said. 'It's just that . . . he's one of my favorites . . . I have all his records . . . I just love to listen to him . . . Imagine, being his—'

"Shari just sat there real cool while all her classmates stared at her. 'Here we go again!' she said, as her teacher continued to stammer and stutter."

Harry broke into a soundless chuckle. "My, she's self-possessed," he said. And he grabbed Shari up in his arms and kissed and hugged her until she asked to be put down.

"You're right," Margurite agreed. "She's only five and she's already self-possessed. Both of them, Adrienne, too, have had to learn how to be self-possessed." She paused. "Me, too," she added.

After dinner Harry asked Adrienne and Shari how they would like to have dinner with him during the week. The girls were delighted.

"I'll pick them up after school," he said to Margurite.

"What day?"

"Let's make it Wednesday."

"Okay," Margurite said. "But if it's a date, let's keep it. Yes?"

"Yes," Harry said.

"There's one problem," Margurite said. "You've got to be on time."

"What makes that a problem?" Harry asked.

Margurite began chuckling, and Harry could not avoid joining her.

"There's more than a mile between the two buildings," Margurite explained. "The pre-school division is at Eighty-second while the regular school building is up at Hundred and Tenth Street. Now, if you're late for Shari—"

"Then Adrienne will have to wait."

"And the children are accustomed to find me waiting when they come out. Harry, if you can't make it on time, let's not try it. It's not worth upsetting them."

"I'll make it," Harry said.

"Suppose you take down the details so there won't be a slip-up."

In the Elmhurst house a small desk made of natural blond wood stands in the modest living room, alongside the staircase leading up to the bedroom floor. Harry seated himself at the desk and took up a pencil.

"Yes, teacher," he said.

"Shari's classes let out at ten to three," Margurite said. She gave Harry the address of the building and the name of Shari's teacher.

"Adrienne's classes break at three," Margurite continued. And she spelled the name of Adrienne's teacher and dictated the address of the New Lincoln School at 110th Street.

"You will be on time, Harry, won't you?"

Harry looked up at Margurite from where he sat to where she stood, furrowed his brow, and rounded his lips in mock concentration.

"Uh-huh," he said, as if he were saying "Yes, Mother."

"And don't call up on Wednesday morning," Margurite continued, "to call it off. We won't be stood up at the last minute, will we, girls?"

Adrienne and Shari giggled, enjoying the interplay between their father and mother.

Harry looked up mockingly at Margurite, rounding his lips into a pout.

"Uh-huh," he grunted and nodded.

"But the most important thing," Margurite lessoned, "is to be there on time for Shari so that you'll be on time for Adrienne. There's just ten minutes to make it from one to the other."

"Uh-huh," Harry nodded, looking up at Margurite with the taunting pout on his lips.

There they were again as they had been during the early years of their marriage. Margurite, the schoolteacher, and Harry, the retarded pupil.

At this point Margurite could not help breaking into laughter. Warmed by the dumb-play between their parents, Adrienne and Shari began laughing with Margurite.

"Say," Harry said thoughtfully to Margurite, suddenly reaching back into time, "remember when I went away on my first out-of-town booking—it was '49 or '50—and while I was away, you had some junkmen come up to the apartment and carry away that big chifferobe I liked? You know, without asking me—or even warning me. I just came back from the road to find it gone?"

The chifferobe was a tall, heavy piece of furniture which Harry and Margurite had inherited with the apartment in upper Harlem. Harry kept newspapers, sheet music, and other personal junk crammed into it. Of all the furniture they had been compelled to purchase, this piece was the biggest eyesore to Margurite.

"I guess that I should have discussed it with him," Margurite said recently. And with rare candor she added: "You know, I probably lost Harry that very day—along with the chifferobe." And she laughed heartily, not without a suggestion of self-criticism.

After Harry spent a Sunday at his old home, saying good-by was always a difficult, if not painful, thing. There were times when he would wait till the kids were in bed and asleep and then leave quietly. But Shari and Adrienne were usually keyed up and overtired after a full day of Harry—and it was always hard for them to fall asleep.

This time the prospect of being with their father during the week made Harry's leave-taking a little easier. Still, he came back four or five times to hug and kiss each of the girls. Margurite stood by, watching the display of affection, no less real with Harry than with his daughters. Once his leaving the house had been something she dreaded, not only because of the way the girls reacted but because of the way it left her feeling. All day long—on Harry's Sundays—the house was full of laughter and noise and fun and the sound of affection being exchanged. Then, suddenly, the kids were asleep, he was gone, and all she heard was an occasional car rolling by the house in the quiet of the night, or the roar of a plane taking off in the dark at La Guardia Airport, not too far distant.

This night, as the girls giggled and squealed over Harry's kisses and his leaving and returning, she watched without any emotion. In fact, she noted to herself that the excessive displays of feeling with which he had once showered Adrienne, now seemed to be directed at Shari. And Shari, in some strange

[323]

way, was already responding with a coolness, rare in a five-year-old, to Harry's efforts at charming her.

Finally he was gone. She listened to the soft purr of his Mercedes-Benz as he drove off into the night, pleased that she no longer felt anything.

The kids stood at the windows, watching the tail lights of the car until they were out of sight.

"It gets so quiet when Daddy leaves," Adrienne said.

"But we'll be seeing him on Wednesday," Shari said.

"It's past bedtime," Margurite said, aware that Harry's leaving was still a hard thing for the kids to take.

Thank God, she thought, *it's no longer hard for me.*

Heading into Grand Central Parkway on his way back to Manhattan, Harry thought happily of David, his son, asleep in his crib, and of Julie, who would be waiting for him. He thought of the TV spectacular, which he had begun preparing, and of the one-man show at the Palace he was attempting in December. Only Danny Kaye, Judy Garland, and Jerry Lewis had tried one-man stands at what was once the Valhalla of vaudeville. He would be the first Negro. And unlike the others who appeared only after the intermission—the first half of the bill being a series of variety acts—he would be on stage from the opening to the closing note.

He thought of the Western movie he was planning to make with Sidney Poitier, the TV series he was preparing to produce jointly with Nat "King" Cole as its star, the life of Pushkin he was aiming to shoot in Russia, and of many other projects on which he was at work. "If the Maker were kind enough to give me a hundred years," he sighed to himself, "I couldn't get it all done . . ."

For a moment, his thoughts raced over things that had happened during his first decade. He regretted some. He felt guilty about others. He was proud of many.

But he did not want to think of the past. He had moved. His people had moved. Pressing the gas pedal of his car, he drove at an accelerated speed into his future as the foremost Negro entertainer and entertainment entrepreneur in the American era of integration.

[324]

Index

[326]

[332]

[335]

White, Loray, 156
Wicks, Virginia, 60, 61, 64, 66, 70, 71, 91, 124, 152
Wide, Wide World, 229
Will His Love Be Like His Rum?, 170, 235
Williams, Bert, 5, 53
Williams, Joe, 272
Williams, William B., 65
Wilson, Charles, 244
Wilson, John S., 56, 163, 311
Wilson, Teddy, 90, 110
Wiltwyck School for Boys, The, 305, 310
Winner, The, 294
Winner by Decision, 171
Winsten, Archer, 246
Winterhalter, Hugo, 101
Winters, Shelley, 293
Wise, Robert, 314, 315
Witch Doctor, 13
WLW (Cincinnati), 311
Work, Craig, 66, 78, 93, 95
World, The Flesh and The Devil, The, 75, 288–290, 291, 292, 294
Wouk, Herman, 161
W.P.A., 22
Wright, Melvine Love (See Belafonte, Melvine Love)
Wright, Pearl, 38
Wright, Richard, 155
WSFA (Montgomery, Ala.), 280

Y.M.H.A. (92nd Street, N.Y.), 47
Yordan, Philip, 54
Young Brigade, The, 232
Young, Cecil, 227
Young, Lester, 65, 147
"Youth Wants to Know," 303

Zanuck, Darryl F., 243, 244, 246, 291
Zinsser, William K., 246
Zolotow, Maurice, 131, 175, 177, 296–297, 298, 301

WESTMAR COLLEGE LIBRARY